A CULTURE OF SECRECY

A CULTURE OF SECRECY

THE GOVERNMENT VERSUS THE PEOPLE'S RIGHT TO KNOW

Edited by Athan G. Theoharis

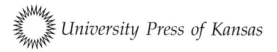 *University Press of Kansas*

1998 by the University Press of Kansas
All rights reserved

Published by the University Press of Kansas (Lawrence, Kansas 66049), which was
organized by the Kansas Board of Regents and is operated and funded by Emporia
State University, Fort Hays State University, Kansas State University, Pittsburg
State University, the University of Kansas, and Wichita State University

Library of Congress Cataloging-in-Publication Data

A culture of secrecy : the government versus the people's right to
  know / edited by Athan G. Theoharis.
     p.   cm.
  Includes index.
  ISBN 0-7006-0880-X (cloth : alk. paper)
  1. Freedom of information—United States—Case studies.
2. Government information—United States—Case studies.   3. Security
classification (Government documents)—United States—Case studies.
I. Theoharis, Athan G.
JK468.S4C85   1998
323.44'5'0973—dc21   98-10670

British Library Cataloguing in Publication Data is available.

Printed in the United States of America

10 9 8 7 6 5 4 3 2 1

The paper used in this publication meets the minimum requirements of the American
National Standard for Permanence of Paper for Printed Library Materials Z39.48-1984.

CONTENTS

ACKNOWLEDGMENTS

The authors of this collective work have accrued numerous debts in furtherance of their research, court cases, lobbying efforts, and administrative responsibilities. It would be impossible to acknowledge all the foundations, public interest and professional associations, historians, journalists, archivists, and attorneys whose invaluable assistance and encouragement advanced our efforts to breach the "wall of secrecy" restricting research into the records of the FBI, CIA, NSA, NSC, White House, and State and Defense Departments.

We do, however, wish to thank Steven Tilley, Kate Martin, Eddie Becker, Michael Tankersley, Alan Morrison, David Vladeck, Kathy Meyer, Diane Tucker, Mark Rosenbaum, Dan Marmalefsky, David Thelen, Tom Blanton, and Steven Aftergood; the American Civil Liberties Union of Southern California; the National Security Archive; the Public Citizen Litigation Group; the staff of the Kennedy Assassination Records Review Board; the representatives to the State Department Advisory Committee of the American Historical Association, Organization of American Historians, Society of American Archivists, and Society for Historians of American Foreign Relations; the J. Roderick MacArthur Foundation; the Field Foundation; the Warsh-Mott Funds; the C. S. Fund; the Fund for Investigative Journalism; and the Institute for Southern Studies. Their support, expertise, and encouragement promoted and sustained our research and litigation challenges. We also acknowledge the commitment and professionalism of the staff of the University Press of Kansas, notably our editor, Michael

Briggs. Lastly, completion of this work of a diverse group of contributors, in a fairly tight time frame, would have been impossible without the support of Marquette University's history department, and in particular Jane Gray. Jane Gray's efficiency and skill proved crucial to meeting the editorial responsibilities inherent in a multiauthored essay collection.

1

Introduction

Athan G. Theoharis

Their experiences as a British colony and during the American Revolution influenced how U.S. leaders of the late eighteenth and early nineteenth centuries defined the national interest and their conceptions of presidential power. Anglo-French imperial rivalries and the decisions of European monarchs had led to the involvement of American colonists in wars with the Indians and French between 1689 and 1763. Then, between 1775 and 1783, American Revolutionary leaders had exploited the Anglo-French rivalry to win their independence from England, obtaining French financial and military assistance. After 1783, American leaders concluded, continued involvement in European affairs could threaten their recently won but fragile independence. They then sought to avoid "entangling alliances" with European states and intervention in Europe's perennial military and diplomatic conflicts. Not disinterested in international developments, they sought instead to capitalize on European conflicts to promote continental expansion, at the same time limiting European influence in the Western Hemisphere. Congress, moreover, insisted on its central role in determining the nation's foreign policy and military commitments.

All this changed during the twentieth century. The United States no longer avoided involvement in foreign conflicts, entering an ongoing European war (World War I) and an ongoing European and Asian war (World War II). More important, during the cold war era the United States intervened in foreign crises and civil wars that earlier policy makers would have avoided. The premise of U.S. policy, outlined in NSC 68 of April 1950, was that "the integrity and vitality of our system is in greater jeopardy than ever before in our history." The principal threat stemmed from the "Kremlin design ... to impose order among nations by means which would destroy our free and democratic system," and the "preferred technique is to subvert by infiltration and intimidation." The ultimate Soviet goal was "the complete subversion or forcible destruction of the machinery of government and structure of society in the countries of the non-Soviet world and their replacement by an apparatus and structure subservient to and controlled from the Kremlin." Containment of this omnipresent Soviet threat accordingly required increased military spending, development and stockpiling of thermonuclear weapons, and a political-military strategy to "defeat local Soviet moves with local action."[1] The Truman administration's response in June 1950 to the North Korean invasion of South Korea reflected this new conception of the nation's security interests: this was not a local civil war between Korean factions but a potentially destabilizing and serious international crisis.

Containing the Soviet threat, in turn, altered the role of the presidency and how decisions were made and implemented. Formerly Congress had played a central role in setting the nation's foreign policy (whether to "declare" war or ratify treaties) and had exercised its powers to limit presidential "conduct" of foreign relations (whether by repudiating U.S. membership in the League of Nations in 1919 or enacting the so-called Neutrality Acts of 1935–37 restricting U.S. financial and commercial relations with belligerent powers). During the cold war era, in contrast, the president's role became determinative. In both the Korean War and the Vietnam War, the United States became involved in military combat without a congressional declaration of war. In November 1950, President Truman unilaterally sent four U.S. divisions to Western Europe, claiming the constitutional right to do so as "commander in chief." During the Cuban missile crisis of 1962, and earlier when authorizing the Central Intelligence Agency (CIA) to fund and train Cuban exiles for the planned Bay of Pigs invasion of April 1961, President Kennedy's unilateral (and, in the case of the Bay of Pigs, secret) decisions brought the nation to the brink of war. In 1973 President Nixon reaffirmed a claimed absolute presidential right of "executive privilege" to deny Congress access to the testimony and the records of all executive branch employees, while presidents since Truman have issued executive orders classifying "national security" information and thereby limiting public and congressional awareness of major policy decisions and programs.

Presidents, moreover, did not publicly reveal the scope, means, or cost of many of their national security initiatives. Both to avert future Koreas and to avoid a divisive debate about planned initiatives, presidents required advance intelligence about Soviet plans and capabilities and the means to undermine unfriendly local movements or assist friendly ones. To achieve these complementary goals, presidents enhanced the powers of the intelligence agencies. They did so through secret executive directives, as in the cases of the CIA's covert operations and the National Security Agency's (NSA) intelligence and counterintelligence activities. Thus, although Congress heatedly debated the Truman Doctrine of 1947, President Truman's 1950 decision to assign four U.S. divisions to Western Europe, the Test Ban Treaty of 1963, and the SALT agreements of the 1970s, presidents unilaterally and secretly authorized the CIA to overthrow the Mosaddeq government of Iran and to sustain the Diem government of South Vietnam, to assassinate Patrice Lumumba and Fidel Castro, to develop and operate U-2 spy planes overflying Soviet territory, and to ensure the NSA's interception of Soviet military and political communications.[2]

Presidents also sought to anticipate and contain the Soviet internal security threat. To do so, they and their attorneys general secretly authorized Federal Bureau of Investigation (FBI) monitoring of American Communists and other radical, conservative, and liberal activists who might unwittingly promote Soviet interests or undermine national unity. In time, FBI operations moved beyond collecting "intelligence" (including by recognizably illegal investigative techniques such as wiretaps and break-ins) to implementing secret programs to contain targeted organizations and their leaders, whether the Communist Party, the Black Panthers, the New Left, or the Ku Klux Klan. These programs and FBI investigations in general were never confined to suspected spies and included "writers, lecturers, newsmen, entertainers, and others in the mass media field" who "might influence others against the national interest or are likely to furnish financial aid to subversive elements." The more prominent were artists and musicians Georgia O'Keeffe, John Lennon, Pete Seeger, and Leonard Bernstein; trade unionists Cesar Chavez and Walter Reuther; reporters, publishers, and columnists Stanley Johnston, Peter Arnett, Eleanor Patterson, Inga Arvad, and Joseph Alsop; and philanthropists Corliss Lamont, Cyrus Eaton, W. H. Ferry, and the J. Roderick MacArthur Foundation. Presidents also requested FBI wiretaps of prominent newsmen (columnist Drew Pearson; reporters Lloyd Norman, Hanson Baldwin, and William Beecher) to identify the sources of leaks.[3]

Presidents succeeded in precluding public and congressional discovery of their most sensitive decisions. An effective national security policy (whether neutralizing Communist efforts to undermine pro-Western governments, stealing Soviet secrets, or counteracting Soviet efforts to steal U.S. secrets) required secrecy. Nonetheless, presidents were equally motivated by domestic political considerations. Disclosures of the secret agreements that President Roosevelt had concluded at the Yalta Conference of 1945, of President Nixon's and his key aides' involvement in the Watergate cover-up of 1972–73, and of President Reagan's and his key National Security Council (NSC) aides' roles in the Iran-contra affair of 1985–86 had caused presidents to lose credibility and public support. Acting in secret, cold war presidents could counteract their adversaries (whether foreign or domestic) without in the process provoking a divisive domestic debate. These twin goals were furthered by expanding the authority of federal intelligence agencies—notably the FBI, CIA, and NSA.

Secrecy also enabled presidents to avoid having to obtain legislative authorization for desired programs and procedures. Thus, FBI wiretapping and bugging were not legalized until 1968 and instead were based on secret executive directives of 1940 and 1954. These directives contravened both the 1934 legislative ban against wiretapping and the Fourth Amendment ban against unreasonable searches and seizures. Although the CIA was created for the purpose of coordinating intelligence information, its evolution into an operational agency was first authorized by secret executive directives NSC 4A and NSC 10/2 of 1947 and 1948 (despite the conclusion of CIA Director Roscoe Hillenkoeter and the agency's legal counsel Lawrence Houston that the National Security Act of 1947 would have to be amended if the CIA were to perform covert operations). A secret (and still classified) presidential directive of November 1952 created the NSA and defined its responsibilities. Congress first learned of the NSA's existence in 1958 and responded in 1959 by enacting Public Law 86-36, which criminalized the disclosure of any information pertaining to the NSA's "function," "activities," and personnel.[4]

This culture of secrecy did not merely foreclose contemporary awareness of the most important presidential decisions and intelligence agency programs of the cold war era. Historical research was thereafter adversely affected. Classification restrictions in effect ensured a distorted understanding of presidential decisions and priorities. The selective release of formerly classified documents and the release of sentences or isolated paragraphs of other documents pose a further research dilemma: how to interpret a knowingly incomplete record? Researchers are thereby denied an understanding of the context, and thus the general purpose, of the disclosed program or decision.

This unknown distortion is illustrated by two examples. In the late

1940s and early 1950s, the Truman administration's internal security and containment policies were bitterly and effectively criticized. Captured in the politics of McCarthyism, conservatives assailed the administration's "softness toward Communism." For reasons of either appeasement or "treason and betrayal," the McCarthyites charged, the administration refused to purge Communists and Communist sympathizers from sensitive government positions, curbed FBI efforts to contain the Communist internal security threat, limited use of American military strength fully in Korea, and rejected policies that would have averted or reversed the communization of Eastern Europe and China.

Owing to the intensification of U.S.-Soviet tensions, and then the outbreak of the Korean War in June 1950, by September 1950 the Truman administration could not repulse demands for more effective internal security measures. Indeed, congressional conservatives exploited this opportunity to enact, over President Truman's veto, the Internal Security Act (or McCarran Act), imposing stringent restrictions on radical political associations and publications and authorizing the preventive detention of Communists and Communist sympathizers. Justifying his veto of this bill, Truman publicly affirmed the need to balance internal security and civil liberties interests.

Dating from August 1948, however, the Truman administration had secretly instituted a preventive detention program, one that restricted civil liberties more than the McCarran Act. Furthermore, following passage of this act, the administration decided not to comply with its congressionally mandated preventive detention standards. Administration officials, nonetheless, recognized that their ongoing Security Index program lacked legal authority. To circumvent this problem, they drafted a presidential proclamation and an authorization resolution that were to be released following the outbreak of war to exploit the crisis atmosphere to pressure Congress to amend the act's preventive detention provisions to comport with the administration's more stringent program. Ironically, the contemporary debate bore little relationship to the reality of the Truman administration's internal security policy. Nor had the administration shackled FBI efforts to monitor and contain suspected "subversives" and Soviet agents; instead, Truman and his attorneys general expanded FBI investigative authority through secret executive directives.[5]

The McCarthyites had similarly challenged the administration's conduct of foreign policy, demanding the replacement of the passive and vacillating policy of containment by a more aggressive and dynamic policy of liberation. These demands to "liberate" Eastern Europe and "unleash" the Chinese Nationalist government exiled on Formosa were incorporated in the 1952 Republican platform and championed by Republican foreign policy spokesman John Foster Dulles and Republican Senate minority leader (and unsuccessful candidate for the Republican presidential nomination) Robert Taft. The Truman administration responded to these criticisms, publicly dismissing calls for "liberation" as reckless and counterproductive.

President Truman had never simply reacted defensively. Dating from 1947, and relying on the CIA, Truman sought to roll back Communist influence and seize the initiative, and to do so endorsed the covert funding of the Italian Christian Democratic Party during the 1948 Italian parliamentary elections, of an anti-Communist trade union in France, and of psychological warfare operations and "political warfare, economic warfare, and paramilitary activities" to undermine Communist governments in Eastern Europe and China. These various covert operations failed, with the exception of Italy and France—the Christian Democratic Party averted a Communist electoral victory, and the CIA-funded anti-Communist trade union neutralized the Communist-led CGT. The reality of these secret "rollback" programs makes the public debate of the 1950s seem surreal.[6]

The FBI's preventive detention program and the origins and scope of CIA covert operations were first disclosed during the 1970s as the result of an unprecedented breach of the secrecy that had heretofore shrouded the actions of presidents and intelligence agencies. Questions about presidential and intelligence agency abuses of power first raised during the Watergate hearings of 1973 and then the intensive inquiry conducted in 1975–76 by special Senate and House intelligence committees (the so-called Church and Pike Committees) were the catalyst to these discoveries. In 1974, moreover, Congress amended the Freedom of Information Act (FOIA) of 1966 to cover FBI and CIA records. The resultant release of formerly secret documents disclosed how presidents had relied on the intelligence agencies to further their policy interests and how they had authorized programs and procedures of questionable legality and morality.

This breakthrough, however, proved to be limited. Since 1975, presidents and intelligence agency officials have successfully limited access to relevant records. They could do so because, with certain exceptions,* Congress was unwilling to challenge executive secrecy

---

*These exceptions include the Presidential Records Act of 1978, defining presidential records as public property and stipulating terms of access; Public Law 102-138 of 1991, mandating the systematic declassification of State Department, CIA, and NSC records over thirty years old to ensure a historically accurate *Foreign Relations* series; and the President John F. Kennedy Assassination Records Collection Act of 1992, empowering a special Records Review Board to order the release of formerly classified and withheld records.

policy. As a result, historians have been unable to build substantially on the revelations of the Church and Pike Committees.

For example, when reviewing the intelligence agencies' activities, the Special Senate Committee on Intelligence Activities (the so-called Church Committee) uncovered and publicized a covert NSA program, code-named Operation MINARET. Under this program, instituted in 1967 and refined in 1969, the NSA intercepted messages of American citizens targeted because of their militant civil rights and anti–Vietnam War activities.* To preclude discovery of the agency's monitoring and dissemination activities, NSA reports based on these interceptions, sent to the CIA and FBI, were neither serialized nor filed with other NSA intercepts. These reports did not identify the NSA as their source, and recipient agencies were to either destroy them or return them to the NSA within two weeks. When Operation MINARET was publicly compromised in 1975, the NSA's involvement in domestic surveillance appeared to have been aberrational, conditioned by the crisis politics of the 1960s. This program had already been terminated in 1973, although NSA officials continued to disseminate "relevant information" to other domestic intelligence agencies (notably the FBI and the Secret Service) acquired through its "collection of foreign intelligence information" but not in "a matter that can only be considered one of domestic intelligence."[7]

Yet, was Operation MINARET exceptional? Did the NSA purposefully intercept the communications of American citizens and disseminate this information to the White House and other intelligence agencies? Did presidents and intelligence agency officials employ the NSA's resources for domestic political and/or policy interests? These questions cannot be answered definitively because relevant NSA records remain classified. Nonetheless, an inadvertent disclosure suggests that MINARET might not necessarily have been aberrational.

In 1978, Harrison Salisbury, a Pulitzer Prize–winning *New York Times* reporter, submitted an FOIA request for his FBI file. Released to him in April 1979, Salisbury's file confirmed that he had become a subject of FBI interest in 1940 and that subsequently FBI officials had disseminated derogatory information about him to senior administration officials. The first known instance occurred in 1954 following Salisbury's temporary return to the United States from Moscow, where he had been stationed as the *Times*'s correspondent. For unknown reasons, the Eisenhower State Department requested an FBI name check on Salisbury. Salisbury was subject to a second name check in

---

*This interception program violated the Communications Act of 1934 and the NSA's charter confining the agency's role to foreign military intelligence and counterintelligence.

1966, apparently triggered by the series of articles he had filed from Hanoi debunking the Johnson administration's claims of its "precision" bombing of military targets in North Vietnam.[8]

Salisbury was not the first or the only reporter subject to FBI and presidential interest. Beginning with Franklin Roosevelt's presidency in 1941, every subsequent president from Truman through Eisenhower, Kennedy, Johnson, and Nixon either requested or welcomed FBI reports on prominent journalists. Those targeted ranged from publishers Eleanor Patterson and Joseph Patterson, syndicated columnists Drew Pearson and Joseph Alsop, and reporters Peter Lisagor and Stanley Johnston. In November 1970, moreover, President Nixon contacted FBI Director J. Edgar Hoover and solicited a report identifying the "known and suspected" homosexuals and "any other stuff" the FBI had compiled on members of the Washington press corps.[9]

Salisbury's FBI file also included reports the FBI had received from the NSA. (Salisbury had concurrently requested his CIA file and learned that that agency had also received reports about him from the NSA.) In both cases, NSA officials refused to release these reports to Salisbury, claiming that doing so would adversely affect national security. Salisbury unsuccessfully sued in federal court to challenge these nondisclosure claims. The courts, however, upheld the NSA's claimed right to withhold this information.[10]

The NSA's success in foreclosing the release of these reports leaves unresolved a series of questions. Had the NSA intercepted Salisbury's communications with his editors in New York (during the time he was stationed as the *Times*'s correspondent in Moscow and Hanoi)? Had the NSA inadvertently intercepted or had it targeted Salisbury's communications? Why did the NSA share this information with the FBI and the CIA—and what information was reported? Were NSA intercepts the catalysts to the Eisenhower and Johnson administration name check requests?*

Salisbury's case raises another research problem for historians. Salisbury could challenge the NSA's withholding claim in court. He could do so because he personally did not have to defray the costs of an expensive court suit, having access to the financial resources of his employer and the journalism community. This option was also available in such high-profile cases as former President Nixon's attempts to destroy and then enjoin the National Archives from releasing the

---

*Understanding the nature, purpose, and results of NSA activities relating to Salisbury would require a broader release of NSA records. The question invariably arises: Had the NSA intercepted and disseminated information about other prominent journalists who were stationed overseas?

Oval Office tapes and the Bush administration's attempts to destroy and then limit access to NSC records in the so-called PROFS case (electronic records pertaining to the Iran-contra affair). Court challenges to these presidential attempts to control public access to sensitive records were funded by public interest law firms. Yet most research projects do not command this attention and most historians cannot afford to litigate. In consequence, the heavily redacted released files lead some researchers to either abandon or modify a planned research project. Furthermore, how are known incomplete records to be interpreted? Would the withheld records rebut, modify, or confirm the conclusions of the recipient researcher?

Salisbury's case, moreover, highlights a further problem: the court's deference toward the executive branch can frustrate even funded court challenges. This is underscored by a federal appeals court ruling in the PROFS case. Overturning a lower court, Judges Douglas Ginsburg and Harry Edwards held that NSC records are not subject to the FOIA's mandatory disclosure requirements. The NSC is merely an advisory body, Judge Ginsburg contended, and "does not exercise independent authority."[11]

Like the CIA, the NSC had been created under provisions of the National Security Act of 1947.* Although originally advisory, it quickly evolved into a policy-making agency. Its directives of 1947 and 1948 (NSA 4A and NSC 10/2) authorized the CIA to conduct covert operations, and that of 1955 (NSC 5412) created a special NSC Planning and Coordinating Group to ensure that all CIA "compatible activities" comported with the president's foreign policy goal to destroy "international communism." Ironically, when ruling on the NSC's advisory status, the court was addressing a request for NSC records on the Iran-contra affair. In this matter, the NSC staff had assumed the operational role that formerly had been the province of the CIA. NSC staff were directly involved in trading arms to Iranian leaders to obtain the release of hostages and diverted the profits from these arms sales to fund the so-called contras in Nicaragua. Furthermore, during 1987 congressional testimony, NSC Director John Poindexter claimed to have made key decisions without briefing the president and seeking his approval.

How, then, can historical researchers uncover and write intelli-

---

Section 101 of the act describes the "function" of the NSC as follows: to "advise the President with respect to the integration of domestic, foreign and military policies relating to the national security so as to enable the military services and other departments and agencies of the Government to operate more effectively in matters involving the national security."

gently about the recent past—the more so given the dominant presidential (and intelligence agency) roles in setting U.S. policy and priorities? Nor is the sole research problem that of overclassification. Past presidential and intelligence agency measures to ensure presidential "deniability" and foreclose public awareness of their potentially controversial activities have created a further research dilemma.

The inevitable by-product of ensuring presidential "deniability" is that created records do not necessarily confirm a president's knowledge of or decisions on important policy matters. As former NSC Executive Secretary James Lay testified in 1975, "If extremely sensitive matters were discussed at an NSC meeting, it was sometimes the practice that the official NSC minutes would record only the general subject discussed without identifying the specially sensitive subject of the discussion. In highly sensitive cases, no reference to the subject would be made in the NSC minutes." NSC officials John Poindexter and Oliver North refined this practice during the 1980s when devising a special "do not log" procedure. "Non Log"–captioned communications were not indexed in the NSC's central records system and could be safely destroyed; when the Iran-contra affair was publicly compromised in November 1986, North proceeded to destroy these records. Because his actions became known and, more important, because he had neglected to destroy the backup memory of the NSC's word processing PROFS system (intended to preclude the inadvertent destruction of electronic records), some of these destroyed records could be reconstructed.[12]

Between 1940 and 1949, moreover, FBI officials devised a series of separate records procedures (informal memoranda, Do Not File memoranda, administrative pages, JUNE Mail) to isolate especially sensitive communications from the FBI's central records system and, when appropriate, ensure their undiscoverable destruction. These procedures involved records of "clearly illegal" activities, information that if reported in the texts of FBI reports would cause "embarrassment to the Bureau, if distributed," and those that revealed sources "illegal in nature," as well as the FBI's "most secretive sources, such as Governors, secretaries to high officials who may be discussing such officials and their attitude, or when referring to highly confidential or unusual investigative techniques."[13]

CIA officials devised similar procedures. In a 1957 report on the agency's drug testing program (the records of which were destroyed in 1973), the CIA's inspector general emphasized the need for "precautions . . . not only to protect operations from exposure to enemy forces but also to conceal these activities from the American public in general. The knowledge that the agency is engaging in unethical and illicit activities would have serious consequences in political and diplomatic circles and would be detrimental to the accomplishment of [the agency's] mission." No written records were kept on the CIA's transfer of toxic agents, a former CIA project director, Sidney Gottlieb, testified in 1975, "because of the sensitivity of the area and the desire to keep any possible use of materials like this recordless." Indeed, a 1963 CIA report described the agency's "present" practice as one of maintaining "no records of the planning and approval of [drug] test programs." Furthermore, in 1962 CIA Director John McCone devised a special "Background Use Only" procedure to "preclude the inclusion of the information in any other document or publication." During the 1960s, moreover, CIA officials destroyed virtually all records of the agency's covert operation to overthrow the Mosaddeq government in Iran, as well as records of other CIA operations involving Indonesia and Guyana. In other cases, CIA agents conveyed information through a back-channel procedure to avoid creating a permanent official record or relied on "soft files," which Acting Director John Blake characterized as "files of convenience or working files" that were not easily retrievable "because they are not official records and they are not indexed as such." More recently, during the Iran-contra affair, CIA officials employed "privacy channel cables." These communications were to be retained "temporarily" and were to be destroyed once the referenced "issue in question is transferred to the command channel or when the temporary circumstances end." The independent counsel uncovered this procedure when attempting to locate a missing cable pertaining to a November 1985 HAWK shipment to Iran. He learned that the CIA station chief in Portugal had destroyed all copies of this cable but that the secretary to CIA official Duane Clarridge (then chief of the CIA's European Division) retained the original cable in an unofficial "shadow" file in her desk—until Clarridge learned, after the Iran-contra affair became public in November 1986, that she had failed to destroy this file.[14]

The following essays discuss the history of FBI, CIA, and NSA officials' efforts to avoid releasing their agency's records; presidential attempts to destroy or to avoid having to release the Nixon Oval Office tapes and the NSC's PROFS records; quasi-successful judicial challenges to Presidents Nixon's and Bush's attempts to preclude release of the Oval Office and PROFS records and to FBI attempts to withhold records relating to the bureau's monitoring of John Lennon, the Supreme Court, and Supreme Court justices; and successful legislative challenges to executive branch attempts either to sanitize the *Foreign Relations* series or to limit the release of CIA and FBI records pertaining to the assassination of President John Kennedy. The most controversial example discussed in these essays involves the Nixon-Sampson agreement of 1974 under which the former president claimed the right to destroy the Oval Office tapes on the grounds that they were his personal property—continuing the practice whereby previous presidents had taken their papers with them upon leaving office and set the terms for when these records would become accessible.

Yet the problem extends beyond a claimed presidential right to destroy or limit access to their papers or the records of the intelligence agencies either because such materials are their personal property or because of the need to safeguard national security interests. Upon leaving office in 1973, CIA Director Richard Helms ordered his secretary to destroy the contents of his office file, including transcripts of office conversations. Former FBI Director Hoover's executive assistant, Helen Gandy, destroyed his "Personal and Confidential File" in the weeks following his death in May 1972 pursuant to his earlier instructions, while in March 1953 Hoover ordered FBI assistant directors to destroy "as promptly as possible but in no case shall they be retained in excess of six months" the various memorandums they retained in their office files separate from the FBI's central records system.[15]

More disturbingly, in 1976 (at the time of the furor over Nixon's proposed destruction of the Oval Office tapes and following the Church and Pike Committees' disclosures of FBI abuses of power), FBI officials responded to the resultant flurry of FOIA requests for FBI records precipitated by the recently amended FOIA by submitting a records disposition plan to the National Archives to destroy all closed FBI field office files—on the premise that their contents were duplicated in FBI headquarters files. National Archives officials approved the plan, without independently verifying the accuracy of this claim. Then, in 1978, FBI officials submitted a follow-up records disposition plan for National Archives approval to purge all closed FBI headquarters files, retaining only "thick" files, and in December 1977 a more limited plan to destroy in its entirety a massive (three-hundred-thousand-page) headquarters file. This latter file consisted of records of the FBI's monitoring of homosexuals since 1937 and of a special FBI Sex Deviates program initiated in June 1951 to purge suspected homosexuals employed in the executive, judicial, and legislative branches of the federal government.

The belated disclosure of these FBI field office and headquarters records disposition plans precipitated a court suit. Ruling on this case, in 1980 Federal Judge Harold Greene enjoined the FBI and the National Archives from implementing these plans, ordering them to devise an alternative plan to ensure the preservation of FBI files of "historical value." By then, however, the Sex Deviates file had already been destroyed, as had most closed field office files.[16]

Classification restrictions and records destruction constitute one legacy of the culture of secrecy that first emerged during and became legitimated by the crisis of the cold war. Yet despite the end of the cold war, this underlying antipathy toward public disclosure and accountability continues to determine federal records practices. Indeed, when commenting on the report of the Commission on Protecting and Reducing Government Secrecy, the commission's chairman Daniel Patrick Moynihan eloquently identified this problem and its solution: "The culture of secrecy in place in the Federal Government will moderate only if there comes about a counterculture of openness which simply assumes that secrecy is not the starting place." Senator Moynihan continued: "The secrecy system has systematically denied American historians access to the records of American history. Of late we find ourselves relying on archives of the former Soviet Union in Moscow to resolve questions of what was going on in Washington in mid-century. This is absurd." To replace this "culture of secrecy" with one of openness and in the process promote historical research, the Moynihan Commission recommended that Congress enact legislation establishing standards for declassification (rather than relying on executive orders) and thereby ensure that information withheld from release will be kept to an "absolute minimum." The commission further recommended that most classified documents should be automatically declassified ten years after their creation and that an independent National Declassification Center should be created to oversee the classification and declassification process.[17]

In effect, the Moynihan Commission's recommendations build upon and refine the experiences related in the following essays by Page Putnam Miller and Anna Nelson pertaining to the *Foreign Relations* series and the Kennedy Assassination Records Review Board—based on legislation enacted in 1991 and 1992. These earlier but limited initiatives have served to curb (but not reverse) the "culture of secrecy." It is time to broaden this approach to encompass all federal records, and to ensure that a bureaucratic and policy interest in secrecy shall not continue to undermine our ability to research and understand the past.

NOTES

1. U.S. Department of State, *Foreign Relations of the United States, 1950,* vol. 1, *National Security Affairs, Foreign Economic Policy* (Washington, D.C.: Government Printing Office, 1977), pp. 262–92.

2. See Thomas Powers, *The Man Who Kept the Secrets: Richard Helms and the CIA* (New York: Knopf, 1979); and James Bamford, *The Puzzle Palace: A Report on America's Most Secret Agency* (New York: Penguin, 1983).

3. Athan Theoharis, *Spying on Americans: Political Surveillance from Hoover to the Huston Plan* (Philadelphia: Temple University Press, 1978), pp. 133–35, 170, 179, 190–92; Athan Theoharis, ed., *From the Secret Files of J. Edgar Hoover* (Chicago: Ivan Dee, 1991), pp. 208–9, 315–16; Athan Theoharis, "The FBI, the Roosevelt Administration, and the 'Subversive' Press," *Journalism History* 19 (Spring 1993): 3–9; U.S. Senate, Select Committee to Study Governmental Operations with Respect to Intelligence Activities, *Supplementary Detailed Staff Reports on Intelligence Activities and the Rights of Americans*, 94th Cong., 2d sess., 1976, book III, p. 447.

4. Theoharis, *Spying on Americans*, pp. 97–99, 106–9; U.S. Senate Select Committee to Study Governmental Operations with Respect to Intelligence Activities, *Supplementary Detailed Staff Reports on Foreign and Military Intelligence*, Book IV, 94th Cong., 2d sess., 1976, pp. 12–40; Bamford, *Puzzle Palace*, pp. 122, 357.

5. Theoharis, *Spying on Americans*, pp. 44–54, 76–80, 99–107, 161–65, 199–209. Section 102, National Security Act of 1947, 61 Statute 495.

6. U.S. Senate, Select Committee to Study Governmental Operations with Respect to Intelligence Activities, *Supplementary Detailed Staff Reports on Foreign and Military Intelligence*, 94th Cong., 2d sess., 1976, book IV, pp. 12–40.

7. Theoharis, *Spying on Americans*, pp. 121–25.

8. Harrison Salisbury, "A Case of 'Security' " (unpublished paper, copy in author's possession).

9. Theoharis, *From the Secret Files of J. Edgar Hoover*, pp. 208–9, 249, 315–16; Theoharis, *Spying on Americans*, pp. 170, 179, 191–93; Theoharis, "The FBI, the Roosevelt Administration, and the 'Subversive' Press," p. 6.

10. Salisbury, "A Case of 'Security.' "

11. *Milwaukee Journal Sentinel*, August 3, 1996, p. 8A. The National Security Council, Ginsburg and Edwards ruled, was a "presidential" (not a "federal") agency, and thus the standards governing access to and preservation of NSC records were governed by the Presidential Records Act of 1978. In May 1997, the Supreme Court denied certiorari, declining to hear an appeal of this ruling.

12. Theoharis, *Spying on Americans*, pp. xii–xiii. *New York Times*, November 28, 1986, p. 1; December 1, 1986, p. 9; February 23, 1987, p. 6; February 24, 1986, p. 4; June 9, 1987, pp. 1, 8, 9; June 10, 1987, p. 9; July 10, 1987, pp. 1, 5, 7. See, for example, *Report of the Congressional Committees Investigating the Iran-Contra Affair*, 100th Cong., 1st sess., 1987, Appendix A, vol. 2, pp. 1321–22.

13. Memo, Sullivan to Tolson, July 19, 1966, "Black Bag" Job folder, Official and Confidential File of FBI Director J. Edgar Hoover; Memo, Hoover to Tolson et al., April 11, 1940, FBI 66-3665-544; Bureau Bulletin No. 34, Series 1949, July 8, 1949, FBI 66-03-996; SAC Letter No. 69, Series 69, June 29, 1949, FBI 66-1372-1; Memo, Wannall to Sullivan, January 17, 1969, FBI 66-1372-49.

14. Athan Theoharis, "In-House Cover-up: Researching FBI Files," in Athan Theoharis, ed., *Beyond the Hiss Case: The FBI, Congress, and the Cold War* (Philadelphia: Temple University Press, 1982), pp. 39–41; *Final Report of the Independent Counsel for Iran/Contra Matters*, vol. 1, *Investigations and Prosecutions* (Washington, D.C.: Reports of the Independent Counsel, 1993), pp. 255–59; *New York Times*, May 29, 1997, p. A11.

15. Theoharis, "In-House Cover-up," pp. 42–43, 46; Memo, Hoover to Tolson et al., March 19, 1953, FBI 66-2095-200.

16. Gerald Haines and David Langbart, *Unlocking the Files of the FBI: A Guide to Its Records and Classification System* (Wilmington, Del.: Scholarly Resources, 1993), esp. pp. x–xi; Susan Steinwall, "The FBI Files Case: Implications for Archivists" (unpublished seminar paper, University of Wisconsin Library School; copy in author's possession); National Archives and FBI, "Appraisal of the Records of the Federal Bureau of Investigation" (report submitted to Judge Harold Greene, 1981–82); Records Disposition Request, James Awe (Records Management Division, FBI) to National Archives, December 1, 1977; Memo, Henry Wolfinger (Records Disposition Director) to Directors National Archives NCP and NNF, December 22, 1977; Memo, FBI Executives Conference to Director, October 14, 1953, FBI 62-93875–Not Recorded; *San Francisco Examiner*, January 13, 1991, pp. A1, A20.

17. *New York Times*, March 25, 1997, p. A11; *Chronicle of Higher Education*, March 14, 1997, p. A28.

2

The Freedom of Information Act Versus the FBI

Athan G. Theoharis

Until quite recently, the role of the Federal Bureau of Investigation (FBI) had not been a major subject of inquiry for historians of twentieth-century America. This seeming disinterest stemmed from the fact that until 1974 research pertaining to the FBI was effectively fore-closed—no FBI record, dating from that agency's creation in 1908, had been deposited at the National Archives. Furthermore, FBI officials succeeded in having otherwise accessible FBI records closed to research upon discovering in the 1950s and 1960s that some FBI documents were accessible either at the National Archives (included among State Department, Justice Department, and Customs Service records) or at presidential libraries.[1]

Passage in 1974 of key amendments to the Freedom of Information Act (FOIA) of 1966 for the first time permitted historians to research a variety of projects: the career of FBI Director J. Edgar Hoover, FBI surveillance policy and practice, major criminal and internal security cases, and the activities of prominent individuals (or organizations) who had been the subject of FBI investigations.* Federal agencies

---

*Released FBI records confirm that the FBI monitored prominent Americans (as well as radical activists), collected derogatory personal and political information (and misinformation) about them, promoted or attempted to subvert their careers and personal interests, or recruited them as informers. The subjects ranged from social reformers (Eleanor Roosevelt, Margaret Sanger), presidential candidates (Adlai Stevenson, Thomas Dewey), businessmen (John D. Rockefeller III, Joseph Kennedy), Supreme Court justices (Potter Stewart,

were required under the FOIA to process requests for and release the contents of specified files, subject, however, to certain conditions. Requesters had to pay processing fees (at ten cents per page); agencies, in addition, could redact information that was classified, that revealed the agency's sources, methods, internal rules, and procedures, or that violated the privacy rights of cited individuals.

Almost immediately, a number of historians employed the FOIA to obtain FBI records. I have contacted a representative sample whose projects have involved right-wing activists and organizations (Gerald L. K. Smith, Elizabeth Dilling, William Dudley Pelley, Laura Ingalls, Hamilton Fish, America First), mainstream activists and organizations (Arthur Schlesinger, Jr., Robert Kennedy, Martin Luther King, Jr., Walter Reuther, Ernest Hemingway, John Lennon, Orson Welles, Huey Long, Supreme Court justices and federal district court judges, Southern Christian Leadership Conference [SCLC], NAACP, CIO), and left-wing activists and organizations (Dorothy Healey, Michael Harrington, Paul Robeson, Malcolm X, W. E. B. Du Bois, Communist Party, Southern Nonviolent Coordinating Committee). I particularly solicited responses from historians whose research projects involved sensitive FBI investigations (e.g., the Owen Lattimore, Julius and Ethel Rosenberg, William Remington, and *Amerasia* cases) or sensitive FBI liaison programs (e.g., with state governors, university officials, the House Committee on Un-American Activities [HUAC], and the Office of Naval Intelligence [ONI], the Military Intelligence Division [MID]).[2]

My respondents in general evaluated the released FBI records as invaluable. Robert Newman described the FBI's Lattimore files as "indispensable," disclosing the results of FBI investigations and identifying Lattimore's accusers and their credibility. The FOIA enabled Sigmund Diamond to obtain "very specific" information about FBI surveillance of labor unions, college faculties, and students, and about the FBI's covert liaison relationship with university officials and cooperative faculty. Ellen Schrecker found the bureau's files "useful" in recounting the day-to-day activities of the subjects of FBI investigations, Justice Department and FBI prosecutive strategies and bureaucratic infighting, and FBI operating procedures and their governing assumptions. The released records, Kenneth O'Reilly and David Garrow concluded, were essential to understanding the FBI's surveillance

Earl Warren, Abe Fortas), reporters and columnists (Harrison Salisbury, Joseph Alsop, Drew Pearson, Don Whitehead, Courtney Ryley Cooper), actors and producers (Walt Disney, Frank Capra, Ronald Reagan, Orson Welles, Frank Sinatra, Rock Hudson), composers (Leonard Bernstein, Aaron Copland), and university officials and professors (James Conant, David Owens, Franz Boaz, Henry Kissinger, Harry Fisher).

of civil rights activists (and, in O'Reilly's case, the FBI's secret liaison relationship with HUAC). His book on the FBI and the Supreme Court "could not have been written" without access to FBI files, Alexander Charns wrote; the files documented "the extent of FBI penetration of the Supreme Court" and the ethics of some of the justices, and were starting points for further research. FBI documents were "extremely important" for Wayne Cole's research on the Roosevelt administration and American isolationists, providing insights into FBI surveillance activities and how the administration sought to "silence" its noninterventionist critics. The FBI's files proved "essential" to Herbert Mitgang's research involving prominent writers; to Glen Jeansonne's involving Huey Long, Gerald L. K. Smith, and Elizabeth Dilling; and to Jon Wiener's involving John Lennon. FBI files, Jeansonne and Wiener commented, also provided insights into their subjects' personal and political activities. In the latter case, Jeansonne and Wiener unexpectedly profited from the FBI's extensive clipping of newspapers—Jeansonne writing that the FBI's press clippings "brought together in one central location a summary of information that otherwise would have required plowing through microfilmed newspapers for long periods," while Wiener discovered "transcripts of some public appearances of Lennon's that were not available elsewhere."[3]

Not all historians commented so favorably, although their negative assessments were the exception and, in some cases, highlighted the limited value of the FOIA as a research tool. Justus Doenecke admitted to not having carefully reviewed the FBI's massive files on the America First Committee and on prominent isolationists. He had become discouraged by the "huge amounts of paper" and, after a "cursory" review, had concluded that the contents were "garbage": "people writing the FBI saying the isolationists are a bunch of Nazis and spies." Because the FBI kept "everything indiscriminately," had he perused "mounds of paper," Doenecke concluded, he would have learned little about the ideology of the anti-interventionists, his specific research interest. Leo Ribuffo was also discouraged from researching FBI records, but for quite different reasons. Having researched the Roosevelt presidential library's extensive collection of FBI summary reports to the White House on right-wing activists of the 1930s and 1940s, Ribuffo filed FOIA requests for the FBI's larger files on three of these activists (Pelley, Smith, and Winrod) with the intention of requesting additional FBI files on the subjects of World War II sedition trials. He abandoned this project, lacking the money to litigate and the emotional energy to pursue the matter, when the FBI official processing his request to open these files and grant him a fee waiver described it as a "loser."* Because his research focused on the "internal dynamics of radical movements," Maurice Isserman did not seek the FBI's massive files on the American Communist Party. He did research the FBI's files on Communist activist Dorothy Healey, which Healey had obtained earlier and had then made available to him. In 1989, however, Isserman filed an FOIA request for Socialist Party activist Michael Harrington's FBI file. Six years later, and despite the intercession of Senator Daniel Moynihan and Congressman Sherwood Boehlert, he had not received a single page of Harrington's FBI file.[4]

For Jeffrey Dorwart and Harvey Klehr, the principal problem was their inability to identify, or fund the processing fees to obtain, relevant FBI records. Having reconstructed the ONI-FBI relationship from ONI records and from FBI summary reports accessible at the Roosevelt Library, Dorwart was unable to file the necessarily specific FOIA request for FBI records owing to the "large gaps of missing letters about intelligence matters that have disappeared" from the library's holdings. As a consequence, FBI files "at the time were all closed" to him.[†] Klehr's problem instead stemmed from the fact that because the FBI's files on the Communist Party were "so vast," "it made no sense" to request them all. Accordingly, he narrowed his request to specific groups and individuals that would "illuminate portions of [Communist] Party history," one such involving the FBI file on the Communist Political Association (the name adopted by the party for the period 1944–45). FBI officials admitted to having this latter file, the processing fees for which would be approximately one hundred thousand dollars; they demanded that Klehr submit a certified check for one-quarter that amount before they would begin processing his request.[5]

Ironically, the FOIA has proved to be of limited value for projects that would benefit most from research into FBI records. The prohibitively expensive processing fees that Klehr was required to pay were the by-product of the priority FBI officials assigned to investigations involving the Communist Party. Ironically, for this very reason, the

---

*In contrast, Cole was able to research the FBI's America First and isolationist files at the FBI Reading Room and paid processing fees only for those pages he wanted photocopied.

†In contrast, Joan Jensen was discouraged from researching FBI records, which were all closed at the time she began her research. She was able to reconstruct the FBI-MID relationship from research into MID records. At the time, she was required to undergo a security clearance and submit any notes she took for review. These notes were withheld for decades, delaying completion of her history of the MID until she threatened to file an FOIA request to obtain them. Letter, Joan Jensen to Athan Theoharis, February 9, 1996.

FBI's history cannot be understood unless historians research FBI files on the party—for the additional reason that the importance assigned to monitoring the Communist threat during the cold war years was the determining factor in the FBI's resultant explosive growth in size and power.

FBI files on the Communist Party are also invaluable for those historians seeking to understand the tactics, strategies, and social composition of the American Communist Party. Isserman was wrong to have concluded that FBI records would not substantially promote research into the "internal dynamics" of radical movements. As both Wiener and Jeansonne discovered, FBI files contain extensive, otherwise not readily accessible information about such movements. For FBI agents not only clipped all newspaper stories about party activists and activities but also collected the party's publications (pamphlets, periodicals, books, and campaign and other literature).* This intense interest also led to the compilation of FBI reports providing background information on rank-and-file members, specifically their community and labor union activities and participation in internal party debates. The resultant permanent written record of the normally inarticulate expands accessible documentation beyond elites. For the social historian, then, FBI records are an unparalleled source—one not replicated even should the Communist Party's records become fully accessible.

FBI records, moreover, document otherwise privileged personal and political activities. As a by-product of the very intrusiveness of FBI investigative techniques (wiretaps, bugs, break-ins, and mail opening), some of the confidential activities of party leaders and members became a subject of record: transcripts of intercepted telephone and room conversations; photocopies of personal and official correspon-

---

*Some of this material is presently accessible at the Library of Congress. Having accumulated a massive collection of radical publications over the years, FBI officials in 1971 and 1978 donated some of these materials to the library. The number of radical publications (individual pamphlets, books, complete serials of periodicals and newspapers, newsletters) that the FBI turned over to the library in 1978 exceeded thirty-two thousand. The FBI's 1971 donation was five and a half times larger: 200 five-drawer cabinets in 1971 and 30 six-drawer cabinets in 1978. For a list of the 1978-donated publications, see Memo, Awe to Bassett, March 27, 1978, and accompanying list, FBI 66-3286-1287. The 66-3286 file, the FBI's Record Destruction file, documents the proposed or actual destruction of specified FBI records. Historians whose research projects involve FBI records about specific individuals or organizations might profitably review this massive file. Two of the more intriguing documented examples of record destruction pertain to Senator Joseph McCarthy and Whittaker Chambers.

dence; photocopies of membership, contributor, and subscription lists, of financial records, of official minutes, and of other secret memorandums.

FBI files on the Communist Party, finally, are essential to resolving questions posed by research into FBI summary reports presently accessible at presidential libraries. The Roosevelt Library, for example, contains a series of letters and reports that FBI Director Hoover sent to the White House during the late 1930s and early 1940s detailing Soviet financing of the U.S. Communist Party.[6] These holdings, however, do not disclose how the FBI obtained this undeniably impressive intelligence nor why FBI officials never exploited this discovery to further prosecutive and anti-Communist political objectives during the cold war era.

More important, despite having discovered the Soviet secret funding of the U.S. Communist Party, the FBI failed in its wartime counterintelligence mission to avert or anticipate attempts by the Communist underground to obtain classified government information. This failure is more striking given other FBI summary reports accessible at the Roosevelt Library, one of which records that as early as November 1939 FBI officials had learned, having bugged a Chicago meeting of the Illinois Communist Party's Executive Committee, that the Illinois party and the party's National Committee had developed plans for a secret apparatus, with Joseph Peters assuming responsibility for this operation for the national party.[7]* Were FBI investigative priorities skewed, focusing on Communist attempts to influence U.S. politics and the labor movement and not Soviet espionage? Quite diferent questions arise over the FBI's awareness of this funding during the cold war era. Why was this documented evidence of a Communist "Trojan horse" never used during the Smith Act trials of the 1940s and 1950s, and why, given the FBI's known covert relationships, was this damaging information on the American Communist Party's subservience to Moscow never leaked to favored reporters and columnists, to HUAC, to the Senate Internal Security Subcommittee, or to Senator Joseph McCarthy?

These questions (and others relating to FBI investigative and dissemination activities) cannot be answered, and not simply because of the prohibitive costs of obtaining FBI records. When interpreting the FOIA's exemptive provisions (national security classified, sources and methods, personal privacy), FBI personnel have so heavily redacted

---

*In the late 1940s, Whittaker Chambers publicly identified Peters as the Communist official to whom he reported concerning his activities in the Communist underground in Washington, D.C.

the released records as to preclude needed research.* The central problem is not the vagueness of the FOIA or legitimate concerns of FBI
officials to safeguard agency operations, national security, and personal privacy interests. Instead, the major reason derives from a bureaucratic culture hostile to the principle of public access to any FBI
records. FBI policy files 62-81830, 62-116273, and 190-3 document this
mind-set. The contents of these files record FBI officials' interpretations of the FOIA's disclosure requirements and of guidelines issued
to govern the processing of FOIA requests. Far more revealingly, they
underscore how FBI officials dating from 1946, and then heightened
following the enactment of the FOIA in 1966 and the more liberalizing
amendments of 1974, sought to preclude the release of any FBI record.

While FBI records had been immune to congressional scrutiny
since 1939, the proposed Administrative Procedure Act of 1946 threatened to subvert this absolute control over whatever information went
outside the bureau. Proponents of this legislation at the time were
concerned not about FBI secrecy but about the expansion of the federal bureaucracy during the New Deal and World War II eras. To
ensure Congress's ability to monitor the sprawling federal bureaucracy, they mandated Congress's right of access to federal agency
records. FBI officials acted quickly to arrest this potential threat by
convincing Assistant Attorney General S. A. Andretta that any rules
governing compliance with this legislation should follow Departmen-
tal Order 3229 of May 2, 1939, which states, "All official records of the
FBI are regarded as confidential and cannot be disclosed except on
the authority of the Attorney General, the Assistant to the Attorney
General, or an Assistant Attorney General acting for him."[8]

Congress revisited this issue in the 1950s, responding then to the
expansion of executive secrecy during the cold war years. The resultant assertion of broad "executive privilege" claims had forestalled

---

*Ironically, historians can learn more about the Communist Party's relation-
ship with the Soviet Union and about some Communist underground activities from recently opened Soviet records. See Harvey Klehr, John Haynes,
and Fridirikh Igorevich, *The Secret World of American Communism* (New Ha-
ven, Conn.: Yale University Press, 1995). Klehr commented, "I found it ironic
that we could get more information about the CPUSA out of Moscow than
from our own government. . . . For the past decade the FBI has been doling
out to me a file on Comintern activities in the United States. . . . It is useless,
with more than 90% of the material blacked out. I have stopped making
FOIA requests because it is a waste of time, energy and money, that can be
utilized more effectively in Russia. This is a shame because I firmly believe
that FBI records throw real light on the issues I study, but the belief that
these fifty to seventy year old files somehow affect national security remains
strong." Letter, Klehr to Theoharis, September 26, 1995.

congressional access to the records of federal agencies. In response, in 1957 members of Congress sought to amend the 1946 act to ensure the public's right to know while recognizing, given prevailing cold war concerns, an undefined national security exemption. FBI officials immediately became concerned that some FBI records would be disclosed. Accordingly, FBI Assistant Director John Mohr recommended that "in the event" Congress amended this act, the FBI's congressional liaison should "take steps to have all the Bureau's records exempted" from its provisions. Instead FBI Director J. Edgar Hoover contacted Deputy Attorney General William Rogers to request that "if it appears that legislation has any chance of enactment" that Justice Department officials ensure that "all of the records and files of this Bureau are confidential and must be protected."[9]

The proposed legislation was not enacted until 1966. Closely monitoring these later congressional deliberations, FBI officials welcomed Congress's willingness to exempt "national security" and "law enforcement" records from disclosure but worried that the proposed legislation lacked "clear exemptions [for all FBI records] and in which we anticipate possible trouble from elements wanting to pry into Bureau affairs." Hoover, indeed, protested to Assistant Attorney General Frank Wozencroft that the proposed exemptions "are by no means so comprehensive and clear as to give this Bureau all the protection which it needs, and that this fact, taken with the philosophy of this Bill that information not clearly protected must be made publicly available, suggests the possibility of problems arising in a number of areas." Sensitive to cold war concerns, Congress did exempt "national security" and "law enforcement" records from the 1966 act's disclosure requirements. FBI officials once again pressured the Justice Department in 1967 and 1968 to rule that all FBI records remained exempt from disclosure. Alert to another potential problem, Hoover reminded National Archives officials that the 1966 act "will or should have" no effect "on the present restrictions in National Archives against *access* to FBI data in other records under [National Archives] control without first clearing with the Bureau."[10]

This success proved temporary. During the 1970s, an increasingly skeptical Congress began to challenge executive restrictions on access to government records. Influenced by the Watergate affair and the Vietnam War experiences, members of Congress were no longer willing to deny access to all records of the federal intelligence agencies.

Acting FBI Director L. Patrick Gray criticized one proposal to limit exemptions to disclosure to "only such [FBI] records as are compiled for a *specific* law enforcement purpose." "These changes," Gray warned, "raise serious questions concerning the protection available to investigative files compiled for general intelligence purposes and we strongly object to such modifications." Instead of broadening the 1966 act "to allow greater access," the Justice Department should seek an amendment "to provide an express exemption for FBI files." In their private deliberations, FBI officials worried that "once in the public domain, [FBI] files can be quoted out of context, inferences can be drawn, and innuendos made that are wholly unrelated to the facts. . . . As a result, the Bureau may suffer irreparable loss of public confidence." Endorsing "a strong stand to preserve the integrity of *all* investigative files regardless of their age or sensitivity," FBI officials concluded that the FBI's "very existence as an investigative agency is based on our ability to instill confidence in the public," and this required preserving the "sanctity of our files." The release of any information, regardless of age, posed an additional problem because it could provoke "a clamor from the public once it was aware there was even a small hole in the dike."[11]

The FBI's absolutist position, however, had come untenable. Justice Department officials could not forestall Congress's approval of legislation to open FBI records. Moreover, Attorney General Elliott Richardson rejected FBI arguments to "protect" all FBI records when issuing, in July 1973, Order 528-73 authorizing the release to "historical researchers" of FBI records more than fifteen years old. Richardson's order did exempt any information that could compromise FBI sources, methods, and sensitive criminal and national security investigations.

FBI officials, nonetheless, remained committed to nondisclosure. They considered classifying all FBI records to exploit Congress's willingness to exempt "national security" information. Concurrently, they pressured the newly appointed attorney general, William Saxbe, to rescind his predecessor's July 1973 order. "Historical researchers," FBI Director Clarence Kelley pointed out, "have an in-depth knowledge of the subject matter of their request." Kelley then cited Professor C. David Heyman's FOIA request for the FBI's files on Ezra Pound. The released records included "reports and other material from which all names and other identifying data of interviewees had been deleted," but Heyman, given his expertise on Pound, successfully "identified a majority of the interviewees whose names had been deleted." Heyman's "will not be a unique situation, and our effectiveness as an investigating agency will be severely damaged" in that current and future FBI sources could not be assured of confidentiality.[12]

Whether Saxbe would have rescinded Richardson's order became moot. The FOIA was amended that year to ensure public (and not solely historical researchers) access to FBI records. Thereupon, FBI officials volunteered their assistance to sustain President Gerald Ford's veto of the amended act, detailing examples of its harmfulness.[13] Ford's veto, however, was overridden, and FBI officials immediately sought to limit the act's effect.

FBI Director Kelley first considered a recommendation of the heads of FBI field offices. These Special Agents in Charge (SACs) had suggested that whenever the FBI processed an individual's FOIA request for his or her FBI file the bureau could release the "same information" to the news media. This concurrent release could act as a "counter," discouraging individuals from requesting their FBI files, "knowing the impact it [public disclosure of the contents of their file] might have on them." The FBI's legal counsel opposed this deterrence strategy as violating the FOIA's privacy requirement and concurrently subverting the FBI's ability to use the privacy exemption to avoid disclosure.[14]

Kelley instead directed SACs to ascertain whether the record custodians of those agencies (local police, banks, credit unions, other federal agencies) from which their offices regularly obtained information take "the position that all records disseminated to the FBI from the agency are to remain confidential." SACs were "not to encourage" such requests but "merely explain to [the record custodian] this procedure is available."[15]

In 1979, moreover, Kelley's successor as FBI director, William Webster, devised a new strategy. Webster directed all SACs to review their office's operations and to report all instances of the FOIA's harmful effect on FBI criminal and internal security investigations. SACs were to report any case where a potential informer refused to cooperate out of fear that his or her identify would be publicly compromised. The resultant nineteen-month inquiry failed to produce the desired evidence.[16]

Having failed to exempt FBI records from the FOIA's disclosure requirements, FBI officials interpreted the act's exemption provisions broadly and capriciously. The resultant release of heavily redacted records has either stymied or discouraged research. Uniformly, historians who have used the FOIA to obtain FBI records have complained, as Klehr commented, that released FBI files are often "so bowdlerized as to be useless." Schrecker added that the released FBI files on the Responsibilities Program, for example, were so heavily redacted as to be "almost useless," while those released on Harry Dexter White made it impossible to ascertain "whether or not White was involved with Soviet espionage." Elaborating, Klehr characterized the information released pursuant to his successful appeals of FBI redactions as "so innocuous" as to raise questions of why this information had been originally withheld. "What was considered too sensitive to reveal" was often "trivial or the [FBI] processor was unaware that the material being blacked out was public information."[17]

Even the successes of some historians in undermining FBI attempts to withhold information pose a broader research problem. The research value of released FBI records oftentimes depends on the caprice of who processes FOIA requests, the context of reported information, when FOIA requests were processed, and whether the individual researcher had access to other sources and relevant documents.

Klehr, O'Reilly, Garrow, and Cole maintain that FBI redactions depend, as Klehr phrased it, "a great deal" on "who processes the material and when it was processed," with Garrow affirming that FBI redactions were oftentimes "the happenstance luckiness of which [FBI] 'team' and analyst different requests ended up being processed by." Thus, whereas the released FBI files on King, the SCLC, and Stanley Levison had few redactions, those on the Student Nonviolent Coordinating Committee were extensively redacted. "Once a young and enthusiastic summer intern appears to have been assigned to my project," Cole commented, "and was eager to press ahead with it. But when the summer ended a permanent staffer informed me that the internee had done things all wrong," resulting in FBI inaction in processing his FOIA requests "despite my periodic inquiries." Only after Cole wrote to his congressman and a member of his staff did they "finally get action from the FBI for me." O'Reilly, Charns, and Garrow also emphasized that FBI redactions, in O'Reilly's words, "became progressively more extensive during the Reagan years" and were "often so thick that the requestor is not left with sufficient information to make any sort of argument."[18]

There is another aspect to the FBI's redactions highlighted by Garrow's striking discovery concerning the FBI's top secret Operation Solo. Under this program, in 1951 the FBI recruited two double agents, Jack and Morris Childs, who commanded the trust of Communist Party officials and became "the crucial link by which Soviet funds approximating one million dollars a year were channeled secretly to the American Communist Party." The brothers were also privy to the "most confidential details of the Soviet CP connection" and advised their FBI contacts that Stanley Levison, one of King's key advisers, had been a secret Communist agent who through his businesses had laundered money for the Communist Party. Garrow's account that the FBI's original interest in King stemmed from the Childses' activities and their disclosures about Levison had not been based on FBI documents released in response to his FOIA requests. All references to

Operation Solo and the Childs brothers in the released FBI records were totally redacted. Garrow's discovery instead derived from "interviews with both CPUSA activists and former Division Five [FBI Intelligence Division] agents."[19]

Garrow's need to breach the FBI's secrecy barrier to further his research is not atypical. And, although the FOIA empowers requesters to challenge agency withholding claims either by appealing to the Justice Department's Office of Information and Privacy (OIP) or by filing suit in federal district court, few historians have exercised either right. Furthermore, should they exercise the right of administrative appeal, historians depend on the good faith of the staff of the OIP, since they generally cannot make a convincing case for why the withheld information should be released. For either the contents of a file or document are withheld in their entirety or the redactions to a portion of a document are so extensive as to preclude an intelligent challenge. One of my successful appeals underscores this problem and also offers insights into the appropriateness of FBI withholding claims and the OIP's appeal rulings.

I have used the FOIA extensively to obtain FBI records, including a 1980 request for the office file of former FBI Director J. Edgar Hoover. This file consists of 164 folders numbering approximately eighteen thousand pages; when it was released to me in 1983, I received approximately six thousand pages, many of which were heavily redacted. The FBI withheld in entirety some of the 164 folders, including one captioned "White House Security Survey." This folder totaled 431 pages and had been withheld on grounds that the information was either national security classified, would reveal FBI sources and methods, would violate personal privacy rights, was exempted from release by statute (not identified), or "would have an inhibitive effect upon the development of policy and administrative direction."

I immediately appealed these withholdings. Given the scope and comprehensiveness of the redactions, at first I could offer only a general challenge to FBI withholding claims. Two years later I was advised that my appeal was partially granted. Nonetheless, the White House Security Survey folder was withheld in its entirety. At this time the codirector of the OIP granted me the right of a second appeal owing to the public interest in the contents of Hoover's office file. Rather than filing a lawsuit, I decided to accept this offer, hoping through this nonadversarial process to alert FBI and Justice Department personnel to the fact that much of the withheld material (in this file, but also in other FBI files) was either otherwise publicly accessible or identifiable by research specialists. For, by 1985, from research in other FBI records (some of which I had obtained through other

FOIA requests and others accessible at the Truman Presidential Library), I had reconstructed the contents of the completely withheld White House Security Survey folder.*[20]

For one, a cover sheet to the White House Security Survey briefly described the contents of this folder. This and other sheets for each of the 164 folders constituting former FBI Director Hoover's Official and Confidential File had been prepared by FBI personnel in 1975 to assist Attorney General Levi during his testimony before a House subcommittee conducting hearings into Hoover's office file. In addition, I had uncovered cross-references (both quoted and paraphrased) to this program in other FBI memoranda included in the Philip Jaffe folder of former FBI Assistant Director Louis Nichol's office file. When processing my request for the Jaffe folder, FBI personnel had not redacted references describing in some detail the White House Security Survey program. The context of the references to this 1945 program seemed innocent and involved memorandums written in 1950 in preparation for possible testimony by FBI officials before a Senate committee. From still other released FBI records, I had learned that under this program the FBI had wiretapped White House aide Edward Prichard and prominent Washington attorney Thomas Corcoran. Hoover had sent the resultant reports to the Truman White House; thus if copies of these reports were withheld when the FBI processed my request for Hoover's office file, the originals were accessible at the Truman Library.

In March 1988, Richard Huff, codirector of the OIP, advised me that my second appeal was partially granted. Were I dissatisfied with the forthcoming release, Huff continued, "you may appeal to this office." Because the White House Security Survey folder was again withheld in its entirety, I submitted a third appeal challenging (among others) the FBI's withholding in entirety of this folder.[†] When submitting this third appeal, I pointed out that this program involved not national security but political loyalty, and that the contents of the claimed classified documents had already been compromised. Then, following a 1993 research trip to the Truman Library, I discovered that the final report that Hoover had sent to the Truman White House in 1945 summarizing the results of the FBI's investigation under the White House Security Survey program was publicly accessible, hav-

---

*This folder's contents pertained to an FBI leak investigation of 1945 conducted at the request of the Truman White House, which focused on Roosevelt appointees suspected of political disloyalty toward President Truman.

†My first and second appeals, however, led to the release of over fifteen thousand pages (in contrast to the original release of six thousand). These releases included memoranda and folders that had also been originally withheld in their entirety but were now released without any redactions.

ing been declassified in October 1976. This accessible 103-page report identified all individuals whom the FBI had interviewed, including those suspected of the leak, described how the FBI's investigation had been conducted and its results, and recommended specified administrative and personnel changes to preclude future leaks. Because my appeal was still pending, I immediately wrote Huff to renew my challenge to the FBI's withholding of this folder. I specifically questioned why information declassified and accessible at the Truman Library since October 1976 had been withheld in 1983 (with the FBI's first release) and then again in 1985 and 1990 (in response to my first and second appeals). Finally, in July 1996, I received the partially redacted White House Security Survey file. I was advised that this folder (and other challenged redactions involving Hoover's office file) had been rereviewed not in response to my appeal but in response to "another requestor's civil action" involving Hoover's Official and Confidential File, *U.S. Department of Justice v. Landano,* and had been based on the guidelines that Attorney General Janet Reno had issued in October 4, 1993. The intent of the guidelines was to ensure "greater openness," institute "foreseeable harm standards," and promote "discretionary releases." The FBI, however, continued to withhold phrases, sentences, and paragraphs from documents in the White House Security Survey folder on national security, sources and methods, and personal privacy grounds. I was further advised that these withholdings were referred to the Department Review Committee "for its review and determination" of whether this material warrants continued classification. Included among the redactions, ironically, were sections (on pp. 48, 49, 50, 53, 56, 58, 61–64, 68, 78–79, 82–84, and 90) declassified in the original copy of the FBI report accessible at the Truman Library. Amazingly, the FBI withheld this information despite acknowledging having processed this folder "in accordance with documents [you] found at the Truman Library [cited in my 1993 appeal letter]."[21]*

This experience underscores the limited value of the FOIA's appeal process. My efforts to ensure the fullest release of Hoover's office file consumed over sixteen years. Even when successfully reconstructing the contents of withheld records, I encountered stony resistance from the staff of the FBI and the OIP.

---

*The FBI advised me in June 1996 that my 1983 and 1985 appeals of redactions to former FBI Assistant Director Louis Nichol's Official and Confidential File, which had been referred to the Justice Department's Review Committee to "determine if the information continues to warrant classification," had "not yet been reviewed" due to a backlog. I was asked if I was still interested in continuing this appeal. Letter, J. Kevin O'Brien to Athan Theoharis, June 3, 1996.

The FBI's resistance to releasing information is further highlighted by the exceptional character of my FOIA request for Hoover's office file. For one, in 1983 the editors of *U.S. News and World Report* had learned that the FBI had recently processed my 1980 request for Hoover's office file and decided to devote their planned "1984" issue to summarizing its content. Their lengthy published summary precipitated extensive national press coverage.* Second, I could convincingly challenge FBI claimed withholdings on "personal privacy" grounds, arguing that when Hoover retained in his office file derogatory personal information about prominent Americans, these individuals' privacy rights had already been violated. Thus, the release of this information was important to understanding why the former FBI director had FBI agents collect the information and what use had been made of it. Finally, I could reconstruct the contents of redacted FBI records owing to the scope of my various FBI requests (and the variance in FBI processing) and my extensive research into the holdings of presidential libraries. My persistence and expertise impressed even FBI officials. Thus, in 1986 the head of the FBI's Records Management Division (now renamed the Information Resources Division) invited me to give a guest lecture to the staff of that division and of the OIP concerning why historians were interested in, and used the FOIA to obtain, FBI records. Nonetheless, while I have been relatively more successful, my successes in appealing FBI redactions have not contributed to more reasonable processing of FOIA requests.

Should, then, historians either individually or collectively file a class action suit in federal district court challenging FBI withholding claims? Such an option is foreclosed to most historians who lack either the financial resources or the high-profile research project that might ensure pro bono legal counsel. Even when attempted, litigation has not furthered the research interests of the historical community.

For example, Newman could file suit because the high-powered Washington, D.C., law firm Arnold and Porter (Lattimore's legal counsel of the 1950s during his congressional testimony and perjury trial) provided pro bono assistance. Newman's attorneys, however, agreed

---

*For a sampling of the news stories, see *U.S. News and World Report*, 95 (December 19, 1983), pp. 45–50; *Chronicle of Higher Education*, February 22, 1984, pp. 5, 8, 9; *Chicago Tribune*, December 13, 1983, section 4, p. 26; *Washington Post*, December 12, 1983, p. A14, and December 13, 1983, p. A3; *New York Times*, December 12, 1983, p. A19; *Philadelphia Inquirer*, December 14, 1983, p. 13A; *Dallas Morning News*, December 18, 1983, pp. 1G, 6G; *Toronto Star*, December 17, 1983; *Milwaukee Journal*, December 20, 1983, pp. 1, 7; *International Herald Tribune*, December 31, 1983; *Parade Magazine*, January 29, 1984, p. 16.

not to go to court if the FBI would "routinely apply favorable court rulings [in concurrent court challenges involving FBI records on the Alger Hiss and Rosenberg cases] on release of classified material." Even then, the FBI withheld an extensive amount of material on claimed national security grounds. In contrast, Diamond, Wiener, and Charns brought court suits. Diamond's son, an attorney, obtained pro bono assistance of lawyer friends associated with two high-powered New York law firms (Skadden and Arps; White and Case); Wiener obtained the pro bono assistance of the American Civil Liberties Union of Southern California; Charns is an attorney practicing in Durham, North Carolina, and was assisted by a lawyer friend, Paul Green.

Diamond's court challenge consumed eleven years. Although he did not need to defray lawyer fees, he personally had to pay the considerable expenses of preparing briefs and photocopying documents (the firms did not assume these costs). His legal challenge ultimately failed, although he won the release of a few additional documents. The time involved in litigating and the FBI's extensive redactions, however, discouraged Diamond from pursuing a second research project involving FBI surveillance of the labor union movement and labor activists. Thirteen years after filing his 1983 lawsuit, and despite a series of favorable rulings, Wiener has not yet exhausted his legal challenge to unresolved FBI withholding claims. He aptly commented, "I have no idea what the costs of thirteen years of litigation might be, but clearly no individual on his own could do what the ACLU has done for me." Charns's lawsuits, filed in 1988 and 1989, are also still pending, although his challenge to FBI withholding claims has been partially successful.[22]

My experience in appealing FBI withholding claims and Wiener's apt comment about the costs of litigation raise the more general issue of whether the FOIA promotes the research interests of the historical community. When initiating a research project, most historians consider the principal obstacle the cost of funding research trips to consult relevant collections at public and private archives. If access to records is denied, we have passively accepted this denial. We have not even thought of acting collectively to ensure that historians as a class have access to government records—diplomatic historians are the notable exception, having recently challenged the classification and reclassification policies governing the State Department's *Foreign Relations* series. That experience was replicated with the creation of the Kennedy Assassination Records Review Board.

Historians had not been the catalyst to the creation of this board. Oliver Stone's controversial movie *JFK*, instead was the impetus. Stone's conspiracy theory, suggesting that government agencies had been involved first in the assassination and then in a resultant cover-up, resonated with a skeptical public. Stone might not have uncovered evidence to document such a conspiracy. Nonetheless, his major themes could not be refuted, in part because of the heavily redacted nature of released CIA and FBI records. Proponents of conspiracy theories often cited these redactions as evidence of a cover-up: why else would FBI and CIA officials claim national security reasons to withhold documents over thirty years old?

Both to address the questions surrounding the Kennedy assassination and to restore public confidence in the intelligence community, members of Congress drafted legislation to ensure "the expeditious disclosure of records relevant to the assassination of President John F. Kennedy." This 1992 law empowered a special Assassination Records Review Board to ensure the centralized collection and "timely disclosure" of all relevant assassination records. Information should be withheld "only in the rarest case," and then only if there were a "legitimate need for continued protection." These exceptions were defined as "an identifiable harm to the military defense, intelligence operations, or conduct of foreign relations" when this harm is "of such gravity that it outweighs the public interest in disclosure." Rejecting the blanket exceptions employed by FBI and CIA officials when processing FOIA requests, proponents of the law would permit withholding information only if it pertained to intelligence agents "whose identity currently requires protection"; intelligence sources or methods "currently utilized, or reasonably expected to be utilized, . . . the disclosure of which would interfere with the conduct of intelligence activities"; information concerning military operations, intelligence matters, or the conduct of foreign relations, "the disclosure of which would demonstrably impair the national security of the United States"; revealing the name or identity of "a living person" providing confidential information to the United States when doing so "would pose a substantial risk of harm to that person"; or compromising the identity of a confidential informer, foreign government, or security or protective procedure "currently" being utilized or "reasonably expected" to be utilized.

FBI and CIA officials, however, would not be allowed to rule on these exceptions. Instead, Congress vested this responsibility in the Assassination Records Review Board, with only the president having the power to override its rulings. To ensure public confidence in the board's independence and professionalism, the law mandated that the president's nominations, which were subject to Senate confirmation, should be made "after considering persons recommended by the American Historical Association, the Organization of American Historians, the Society of American Archivists, and the American Bar Association."[23]*

---

*The four organizations each recommended three individuals. When nominating the five-member board, President Bill Clinton selected four individu-

Although the board did not become operational until 1994, its actions have ensured the centralized collection of relevant assassination records and the release of formerly withheld records. Thus, in 1995–96, the FBI publicly released 26,907 pages involving organized crime leaders (including Sam Giancana and Gus Alex) and 149 pages pertaining to its top secret code-named Operation Solo program. Overruling FBI and CIA claims to withhold information on claimed national security, sources and methods, and personal privacy grounds, as of June 19, 1997, the board authorized the release in full of 764 FBI reports and 481 CIA reports and the release in part of an additional 1,277 FBI reports and 2,286 CIA reports. In addition, the FBI and the CIA on their own released 1,200 other documents based on standards set by the board. The board's disclosure rulings, for example, led to the release of FBI reports on organized crime, Jack Ruby, the U.S. Communist Party, and the Fair Play for Cuba Committee; reports on Lee Harvey Oswald's activities in the Soviet Union in 1961–62 and on a 1963 trip to Mexico City; and information FBI agents had obtained from foreign intelligence agencies, individuals linked to organized crime in Houston and Dallas, and highly placed informers in the U.S. Communist Party.[24]

The laws promoting release of records involving the *Foreign Relations* series and the Kennedy assassination constitute precedents for broader corrective action—and are central to the Moynihan Commission recommendations that Congress legislate classification standards and create an independent National Declassification Center to oversee compliance with these standards.[25] By ending the president's and intelligence agency officials' monopoly in determining secrecy standards, Congress can reverse the cold war "culture of secrecy," which in effect has precluded needed research in FBI records. Exploiting the bureaucratic priorities and "national security" concerns of the cold war era, FBI officials succeeded in withholding information that should properly be in the public domain. The result has been a sanitized record, and a process that effectively delays or discourages research involving important issues, movements, and personalities.

NOTES

1. Athan Theoharis, "The FBI and the Morgenthau Diaries," *OAH Newsletter* 21, no. 4 (November 1993); 3; Athan Theoharis and John Stuart Cox, *The Boss: J. Edgar Hoover and the Great American Inquisition* (Philadel-

---

als from these lists: Anna Nelson (AHA), Kermit Hall (OAH), William Joyce (SAA), and John Tunheim (ABA). Clinton's fifth nominee, Henry Graff, is an emeritus professor of history at Columbia University.

phia: Temple University Press, 1988), pp. 68–69 n, 267–68; Joan Jensen, *The Price of Vigilance* (Chicago: Rand McNally, 1968), p. 314.

2. The following responded to my inquiries: Robert Newman (Owen Lattimore case); Kenneth O'Reilly (House Committee on Un-American Activities, National Committee to Abolish HUAC, Martin Luther King, Jr., SCLC, NAACP, James Baldwin, W. E. B. Du Bois, Medgar Evers, Adam Clayton Powell, Jr., Paul Robeson, Bayard Rustin, Roy Wilkins, Malcolm X, MIBURN case); Glen Jeansonne (Huey Long, Gerald L. K. Smith, Elizabeth Dilling); David Garrow (Martin Luther King, Jr., Stanley Levison, SCLC, SNCC); Leo Ribuffo (William Dudley Pelley, Gerald L. K. Smith, Gerald Winrod); Alexander Charns (Supreme Court Justices Earl Warren, Abe Fortas, and William Douglas, Supreme Court, ELSUR file, Fred Black case, various federal district court judges); Justus Doenecke (America First, Harry Elmer Barnes, Charles Lindbergh); Wayne Cole (America First, Hamilton Fish, Laura Ingalls, Burton Wheeler, Gerald L. K. Smith, FBI liaison relationship with British Security Coordination); Maurice Isserman (Dorothy Healey, Michael Harrington); Jeffrey Dorwart (FBI-ONI liaison relationship and programs); Joan Jensen (FBI-MID liaison relationship and programs); Herbert Mitgang (Ernest Hemingway, Pearl Buck, Robert Sherwood, W. H. Auden, Sinclair Lewis, William Faulkner, Ben Shahn, Georgia O'Keeffe); Sigmund Diamond (Responsibilities Program, FBI surveillance of labor unions, college faculties, and students); Ellen Schrecker (American Veterans Committee, Gerhart Eisler, Clinton Jencks, Louis Budenz, Smith Act cases, United Electrical, Carl Marzani, Responsibilities Program, United Automobile Workers, Harry Dexter White); Arthur Schlesinger, Jr. (Arthur Schlesinger, Jr., Robert Kennedy); Jon Wiener (John Lennon, Orson Welles); and Harvey Klehr (U.S. Communist Party, *Amerasia* case). The following did not respond to my inquiries: Ronald Radosh (Julius and Ethel Rosenberg case, *Amerasia* case); Gary May (William Remington case); Robert Hill (Marcus Garvey, RACON program, FBI surveillance of civil rights organizations and activists); and Clayborne Carson (Malcolm X).

3. Letters, Robert Newman to Athan Theoharis, October 30, 1995; Kenneth O'Reilly to Athan Theoharis, November 28, 1995; David Garrow to Athan Theoharis, December 16, 1995; Alexander Charns to Athan Theoharis, October 27, 1995; Wayne Cole to Athan Theoharis, October 20, 1995; Herbert Mitgang to Athan Theoharis, October 1, 1995; Glen Jeansonne to Athan Theoharis, December 10, 1995; Jon Wiener to Athan Theoharis, September 27, 1995; Ellen Schrecker to Athan Theoharis, March 18, 1996. Telephone interview, Athan Theoharis with Sigmund Diamond, January 27, 1996.

4. Letters, Justus Doenecke to Athan Theoharis, October 7, 1995; Leo Ribuffo to Athan Theoharis, November 1, 1995; Maurice Isserman to Athan Theoharis, October 10, 1995; Cole to Theoharis, October 20, 1995.

5. Jeffrey Dorwart to Athan Theoharis, October 9, 1995; and Harvey Klehr to Athan Theoharis, September 26, 1995.

6. Personal and Confidential Letter, Hoover to McIntyre, December 13, 1938, OF 263; Strictly Confidential Letter, Hoover to Watson, October 25, 1940, and accompanying report, Present Status of Espionage and Counter Espionage of the Federal Bureau of Investigation, October 24, 1940, OF 10-B; Personal and Confidential Letter, Hoover to Morgenthau, November 29, 1940, Morgenthau Diaries, vol. 334, pp. 105–7; Memo, Klaus to Morgenthau, January 13, 1941, Morgenthau Diaries, vol. 347, p. 132; Telephone Conversation,

Harrison and Morgenthau, October 23, 1940, Morgenthau Diaries, vol. 324; pp. 236–38; Letter, Hoover to Watson, January 6, 1940, OF 10-B; all in Franklin Roosevelt Library, Hyde Park, New York. In one report to the White House, Hoover detailed the precise dollar amount of Soviet funding of Steve Nelson's Communist Party activities.

7. Letter, Hoover to Watson, November 16, 1939, and accompanying memo, OF 10-B, FDR Library.

8. Memo, Glavin to Tolson, August 21, 1946; memo, FBI Director to Andretta, August 20, 1946, and undated Attachment; all in FBI 62-81830-2.

9. Memo, Mohr to Tolson, May 7, 1957, FBI 62-81830-4; Memo, Nichols to Tolson, May 13, 1957, FBI 62-81830-6; and Memo, FBI Director to Rogers, June 13, 1957, FBI 62-81830–Not Recorded.

10. Memo, Casper to Mohr, April 25, 1966, FBI 62-81830-47; Memo, Casper to Mohr, April 28, 1966, FBI 62-81830-48; Memo, Hoover to Wozencroft, April 29, 1966, FBI 62-81830-52; Memo, Waikert to Tavel, May 15, 1967, FBI 62-81830-60; Memo, Hoover to Friesen, May 16, 1967, FBI 62-81830-61; Memo, Casper to Mohr, June 20, 1967, FBI 62-81830-65; Memo, Hoover to Yardley, June 21, 1967, FBI 62-81830-68; Memo, Hoover to Christopher, September 11, 1968, FBI 62-81830-97; Memo, Christopher to Hoover, October 2, 1968, FBI 62-81830-98.

11. Memo, Gray to Assistant Attorney General, Office of Legal Counsel, April 20, 1973, FBI 62-81830-183; Memo, Mintz to Ruckelshaus, May 17, 1973, FBI 62-81830-187; Memo, Jenkins to Mintz, May 31, 1973, FBI 62-81830-188.

12. Memo, Cotter to Wannall, January 24, 1974, FBI 62-81830–Not Recorded; Memo, Cotter to Wannall, February 1, 1974, FBI 62-81830–Not Recorded; Memo Franck to Jenkins, February 28, 1974, FBI 62-81830–Not Recorded; Memo, Cotter to Wannall, March 15, 1974, FBI 62-81830-230; Memo, Kelley to Assistant Attorney General, March 20, 1974, FBI 62-81830-232; Memo, Kelley to Assistant Attorney General, Office of Legal Counsel, April 26, 1974, FBI 62-81830-237.

13. Memo, Kelley to Assistant Attorney General, Office of Legislative Affairs, November 1, 1974, FBI 62-81830-288.

14. Memo, Kelley to Callahan, Jenkins, Adams, and Mintz, April 13, 1975, FBI 62-81830-343; Memo, FBI Legal Counsel to Adams, April 25, 1975, FBI 62-81830-343.

15. Memo, Kelley to SAC, Albany, October 5, 1975, FBI 62-116273-89.

16. See FBI file 190-3. This massive file, consisting of ten sections and five enclosures behind the file, contains Webster's original and follow-up directives and the interim and final reports submitted by SACs. In "F.B.I. Informants," *New York Times*, February 10, 1982, p. A31, Carl Stern briefly summarizes this FBI initiative. An NBC correspondent who covered the Justice Department and the Supreme Court, Stern had learned of Webster's inquiry and filed an FOIA request to obtain this file.

17. Letters, Klehr to Theoharis, September 26, 1995; and Schrecker to Theoharis, March 18, 1996.

18. Letters, Klehr to Theoharis, September 26, 1995; O'Reilly to Theoharis, November 28, 1995; Cole to Theoharis, October 20, 1995; Charns to Theoharis, October 27, 1995; and Garrow to Theoharis, December 16, 1995.

19. The Childs episode is recounted in David Garrow, *The FBI and Martin Luther King, Jr.: From "Solo" to Memphis* (New York: Norton, 1981), pp. 11, 14–

15, 35–47, 81–86, 97–98; see, particularly, notes 47, 48, 50, and 52 on pp. 240–41 and note 5 on p. 288. Letter, Garrow to Theoharis, December 16, 1995.

20. Theoharis and Cox, *The Boss,* pp. 244–45; Athan Theoharis, "FBI Wiretapping: A Case Study of Bureaucratic Autonomy," *Political Science Quarterly* 107 (Spring 1992): 112–15.

21. Letters, Richard Huff to Athan Theoharis, March 17, 1988; and Theoharis to Huff, March 13, 1990, and July 28, 1993. Letter, Hoover to Vardaman, August 17, 1945, and accompanying report "intended for President Truman and Naval Aide Vardaman only," PSF FBI, Harry S. Truman Library, Independence, Missouri. Letter, J. Kevin O'Brien to Athan Theoharis, July 23, 1996. In August 1996, Huff advised me that my FOIA appeal was the "subject of litigation by another requestor." Accordingly, the Office of Information and Privacy, in evaluating my appeal, asserted "only the exemptions that we are claiming in litigation." Letter, Huff to Theoharis, August 14, 1996.

22. Letters, Newman to Theoharis, October 30, 1995; Wiener to Theoharis, September 27, 1995; and Charns to Theoharis, October 27, 1995. Telephone interview, Theoharis with Diamond, January 27, 1996.

23. U.S. Senate, Committee on Governmental Affairs, *Hearings on S.J. Res. 282, The Assassination Materials Disclosure Act of 1992,* and *Report on S. 3006, The President John F. Kennedy Assassination Records Collection Act of 1992,* 102d Cong., 2d sess., 1992.

24. Press Releases, Assassination Records Review Board, March 30, 1995; June 21, 1995; July 21, 1995; August 17, 1995; September 13 and 20, 1995; October 5, 19, and 26, 1995; November 21, 1995; December 1, 20, and 28, 1995; January 5 and 25, 1996; February 12 and 14, 1996; April 22 and 23, 1996; May 10 and 15, 1996; June 6, 13, and 14, 1996; July 2, 1996; August 9, 1996; September 4, 1996; October 29, 1996; January 15, 1997; June 19, 1997.

25. *New York Times,* March 25, 1997, p. A11; *Chronicle of Higher Education,* March 14, 1997, p. A28.

3

The CIA and Secrecy

James X. Dempsey

The role of the United States in the world since 1947 cannot be understood fully without researching the conduct of the Central Intelligence Agency (CIA), created in that year. After World War II, as presidents defined U.S. interests globally and perceived a need to respond to Communism wherever it appeared, they came to view the CIA as indispensable. From early in its existence, the agency was expected to know—indeed, to anticipate—everything, everywhere, and not only the superpower flash points but also street riots, coups, and social conditions in countries large and small on every continent. Thus, the records of the CIA merely as an intelligence-gathering agency are of vital importance to understanding how American leaders viewed the world. In addition, presidents and their directors of Central Intelligence were not content to use clandestine methods merely to collect information. They also wished to control political change abroad. Events in Iran (1953), Guatemala (1954), Cuba (1961), Chile (1973), and Nicaragua (1981–86) are among the many covert operations that can be understood only when CIA files are opened.

Nations use intelligence to defend their interests, and some secrecy is necessary to conduct intelligence affairs. But a central lesson of the cold war era is that secrecy can endanger a democratic system by denying the people information about the functioning of their own government. Secrecy has a corrosive effect on the popular trust necessary for democracy to function. Paradoxically, while necessary for intelligence, secrecy can harm the effective conduct of intelligence, by allowing errors, foolhardiness, and criminal conduct to develop and remain uncorrected.

The end of the cold war has not yet produced a coherent realignment of the balance between openness and secrecy. Despite promises of change, many historically important CIA files remain closed. There still persists the mentality of those officials who in 1992 classified and tried to withhold from the public the final report of the CIA "Openness Task Force."

Nonetheless, a growing number of *official* disclosures of CIA records, taken together, challenge the credibility of agency officials' continued claims of absolute secrecy. The Freedom of Information Act (FOIA) itself has produced important disclosures, especially before judicial deference became the norm. In addition, other avenues of disclosure have been opened, as a result of congressional action, public interest pressure, and executive branch reform, including internal CIA reform:

- In 1987, the Iran-contra committees released, with the executive branch's reluctant approval, hundreds of CIA documents.
- The Assassination Records Review Board, an independent federal agency created by a 1992 statute, has prompted the CIA to release thousands of previously classified records on the assassination of President John F. Kennedy.
- In 1996, the president's Intelligence Oversight Board issued a detailed report on CIA operations in Guatemala and released a stack of partially declassified cables confirming that the CIA maintained asset and liaison relationships with Guatemalan military officers involved in human rights abuses.
- Since 1990, under the CIA's historical program, a wide range of intelligence products has been released, including human intelligence reports, satellite photographs, communications intercepts, and national intelligence estimates.

Models of openness have been tried in these and other cases and have proved successful (i.e., records have been disclosed without harm to national security). It now remains to institutionalize the lessons within the CIA. Moreover, the official disavowal of absolute secrecy, however fragmentary, has already gone far enough that the courts should assume their intended role of critically reviewing executive branch decisions intended to withhold national security information from the public.

THE CIA AND SECRECY

The history of the CIA is in part a history of the conflict between secrecy and publicity. The CIA was conceived and operated through much of its first decades in extraordinary secrecy. Congressional hearings on the agency's establishment were held in secret, and both houses of Congress went into executive session to consider the legislation creating the agency. Until the Vietnam era, congressional leaders and newspaper editors alike preferred not to know what the CIA was doing.

Yet, from its earliest days the agency was not always immune to press scrutiny, and the practice of leaks began early. In July 1948, for example, the *New York Times* published a five-part series on intelligence, which included summaries of CIA cables that had been withheld from Congress—perhaps the first, but by no means the last, instance of the press printing CIA information that had been denied to congressional overseers.[1] The series also included candid descriptions of infighting and reshufflings at the CIA that were apparently leaked by a participant in an official survey being conducted by then–private citizen Allen Dulles.

That citizens had to rely on selective leaks to trusted reporters or await fiascoes like the Gary Powers shoot-down in 1960 or the Bay of Pigs invasion in 1961 to learn what their government was doing was not unique to the intelligence field. After all, before 1966 citizens had no enforceable right to demand information from the Agriculture Department either.

THE FREEDOM OF INFORMATION ACT AND THE CIA

Enactment of the Freedom of Information Act in 1966 culminated a ten-year campaign to create an enforceable right of access to government records. The CIA and other intelligence agencies were not exempted from the act. Congress determined that the interests of national security and other governmental interests in secrecy could be satisfied by a scheme of exempting certain records from disclosure, and these exemptions were specified in the statute. Any agency, including the CIA, could rely on any or all of these exemptions, which now total nine. Exemption 1 related to national security and permitted agencies to withhold information "specifically required by Executive order to be kept secret in the interest of the national defense or foreign policy."

The act balanced this authority to withhold specified information, empowering requesters to challenge in federal courts any wrongful withholding of records by agency personnel. The courts were directed to conduct de novo review (i.e., to make a fresh determination) of agency claims. The Senate report accompanying the legislation clearly establishes Congress's intent, stating that de novo review was "essential in order that the ultimate decision as to the propriety of the agency's action is made by the court and [to] prevent [judicial review] from becoming meaningless judicial sanctioning of agency discretion."[2]

Notwithstanding this clear congressional intent, in the years immediately following the FOIA's enactment, the courts interpreted Exemption 1 broadly to permit agencies to withhold all "national security" classified information. An agency needed only to submit an affidavit claiming that the information was classified. The courts were unwilling to test the propriety of executive branch classification.

Following extensive hearings, and against the backdrop of concern over the attempted suppression in 1971 of the Pentagon Papers, Congress amended the FOIA in 1974 and specifically sought to change how national security information was treated. First, Exemption 1 was amended to require that the information must "in fact [be] properly classified pursuant to statute or executive order," imposing on federal agencies the burden of proving that disclosure of the information would cause current harm to the national security. Furthermore, Congress strengthened the de novo review authority by making it clear that the courts could examine the withheld documents in camera (i.e., to ensure a meaningful review, the judge could review the classified documents in their entirety in chambers).

The legislative history expressly addressed the concern that "adverse effects might occur as a result of public disclosure of a particular classified record." Rather than granting a blanket exception for classified information, the House and Senate conferees who finalized the 1974 amendments felt that the national security would be sufficiently protected if the courts "accord[ed] substantial weight to an agency's affidavit concerning the details of the classified status of the disputed record."[3]

At the time, President Gerald Ford recognized that the proposed FOIA amendments curtailed an important executive branch prerogative. He vetoed the amendments in part because the courts were empowered to release information that executive officials had classified. Overriding the veto, Congress in effect granted the courts the authority to review and set aside agency classification decisions.

In 1984, Congress again reaffirmed its intention to subject the CIA to the FOIA. That year, rejecting a Reagan administration proposal to exempt the CIA entirely from the mandatory review and disclosure requirements of the FOIA, Congress instead adopted the CIA Information Act. This act reaffirmed the application of the FOIA to the CIA but exempted from search and review what Congress thought would be only a small category of "operational" files. (The much broader effects of this act are discussed in the following.)

In practice, in no FOIA lawsuit has the CIA been forced to disclose classified information when it adhered through all stages of the case to the claim that disclosure would cause damage to the national security. Rather, the FOIA has worked by compelling the agency, under the scrutiny of the courts, to reexamine its initial, overbroad claims of nondisclosure. Often when litigation results in such a careful review of requested documents, the CIA "voluntarily" releases more information.

The FOIA thus worked to open up substantial quantities of CIA information. In 1980, the Center for National Security Studies made available to interested researchers a list of CIA documents released through the FOIA.[4] These included memorandums on the "Family Jewels" study on CIA domestic spying, as well as documents on CIA mail-opening programs and CIA use of journalists, previously secret congressional testimony on the creation of the CIA, CIA general counsel opinions on the legality of covert operations, and various CIA internal "Studies on Intelligence." Dozens of books and articles were written based entirely or in part on these CIA documents.

"SOURCES AND METHODS"

What Congress Granted, the Courts Renounced

Despite the clear congressional intent in both 1966 and 1974, and the rejection of subsequent legislative proposals to limit the FOIA, from the outset the federal judiciary was reluctant to enforce the act against the CIA. Even though the Congress at several crucial junctures insisted that the FOIA apply to the CIA, the courts increasingly refused to exercise their review powers and eventually created huge exemptions that thwart the intent of the statute.

An important part of this story begins with the CIA's psychological experimentation programs of the 1950s and 1960s, and a subsequent attempted cover-up. Between 1953 and 1966, CIA officials financed a wide-ranging psychological research program, code-named MKULTRA, established to counter suspected Soviet and Chinese advances in psychological techniques. Subprojects were contracted out to universities and research institutions, and some 185 individual researchers participated in this program. Several subprojects involved experiments wherein researchers surreptitiously administered dangerous drugs, such as LSD, to unwitting human subjects. At least two persons died as a result of MKULTRA experiments, and others may have suffered impaired health. Then, in 1973, Director of Central Intelligence Richard Helms ordered the MKULTRA records destroyed. That act of cover-up eventually led to a lawsuit that resulted in the most serious evisceration of the FOIA as it applies to the CIA.

MKULTRA had been mentioned in the Rockefeller Commission Report of 1975 and in the reports and hearings of the Church Committee, but due to CIA Director Helms's record destruction many details concerning this program were thought to be lost forever. In 1977, however, following the completion of the Church Committee's investigation, the CIA located some eight thousand pages of fiscal and financial records related to MKULTRA that had escaped destruction.[5]

The new documents contained only general descriptions of the research subprojects, but they nonetheless identified the institutions and individuals that had contracted to undertake the research. Thus, it became possible by interviewing the identified individual researchers to discover information thought to have been lost owing to Helms's record destruction: the full scope of MKULTRA experiments, the substantive findings of the research, the side effects of various drugs, and possibly even the identities of experimental subjects who remained unaware of their involvement in this project.

The Public Citizen Health Research Group filed an FOIA request for the names of the institutions and individuals that had performed MKULTRA research. The CIA, however, refused to release the names of twenty-one institutions and all the individual researchers. As justification for this denial, CIA officials did not rely on the FOIA's Exemption 1, which permitted only the withholding of information classified on national security grounds. Although the names of the researchers had once been classified, the CIA had subsequently declassified them. As authority to withhold this information, CIA officials instead cited Exemption 3 of the FOIA, which allows the government to withhold information "specifically exempted from disclosure by [another] statute." The exempting statute that CIA officials relied on was section 102(d)(3) of the National Security Act, which states that "the Director of Central Intelligence shall be responsible for protecting intelligence sources and methods from unauthorized disclosure."

Public Citizen filed suit, challenging the CIA's withholding claim in a case, ultimately decided by the Supreme Court. In 1985, the Court held in *CIA v. Sims* that the "sources and methods" language of the National Security Act permitted the withholding of the unclassified names of the MKULTRA researchers.[6] While the facts of the case were narrow, the language of the Court's opinion was sweeping. Through the sources and methods language, the Court held, "Congress vested in the Director of Central Intelligence very broad authority to protect all sources of intelligence information from disclosure." The Court recognized that the CIA collected intelligence from "almost an infinite variety of diverse sources," the vast majority of which were open. The Court nonetheless concluded that when Congress protected "intelligence sources from disclosure, it was not simply protecting sources of secret intelligence information" but also authorizing the CIA to withhold even the identity of nonsecret sources. In a hypothetical example, the Court noted that even the fact that the CIA subscribed to an obscure journal was a "source" to be protected.

While this would have resolved the particular case, the Supreme Court did not stop there. The Court went on to say that the plain meaning of the sources and methods provision "may not be squared with any limiting definition that goes beyond the requirement that the information fall within the Agency's mandate to conduct foreign intelligence." It stated that "the Director must, of course, do more than simply withhold the names of intelligence sources." The very nature of the intelligence apparatus of any country, the Court continued, is to try to find out the concerns of others; bits and pieces of data may aid in piecing together bits of other information "even when the individual piece is not of obvious importance." "Accordingly," the Court concluded, "the Director, in exercising his authority under section 102(d)(3), has power to withhold superficially innocuous information on the ground that it might enable an observer to discover the identity of an intelligence source."

While concurring in the decision, Justice Thurgood Marshall objected to the breadth of the Court's opinion. The interpretation of the sources and methods exemption, Marshall stated, was "neither mandated by the language or the legislative history of any congressional Act, nor by legitimate policy considerations, and it in fact thwarts congressional efforts to balance the public's interest in information and the Government's need for secrecy."[7] The Court's rationale, Justice Marshall objected, allowed the CIA to "avoid making the showing required under the carefully crafted balance embodied in Exemption 1 and thereby thwart[ed] Congress' effort to limit agency discretion. . . . By choosing to litigate under Exemption 3 and by receiving this Court's blessing, the Agency has cleverly evaded all these carefully imposed Congressional requirements." Marshall warned that such an interpretation of the sources and methods language would end up exempting all CIA information because there is virtually nothing the CIA "might have within its many files that might not disclose or enable an observer to discover something about where the agency gathers information."

Marshall's prediction turned out to be prescient. After *Sims*, the sources and methods exemption has become a virtual blanket exemption for all CIA files, even when disclosure of information would not cause harm to the national security. CIA officials have claimed that the FOIA's "sources and methods" exemption covers all CIA "activities," "functions," "targets," "capabilities," "foreign relations sensitivities," "intelligence procedures," "staffing," and "funding." They have even claimed that CIA inspector general reports regarding the involvement of agency officials in the Iran-contra affair constituted, in their entirety, sources and methods. Since *Sims*, the courts have largely accepted these claims, feeling compelled, as one court did, to hold that CIA information was exempt so long as "it is at the very least *'arguable'* that the requested paragraph ... *could* reveal intelligence methods."[8]

The statute's "sources and methods" provision had been tacked on to the 1947 act at the insistence of the military to make sure that the newly created civilian-run intelligence agency would protect the military's secret sources. As a result of the *Sims* case, the phrase "sources and methods" has attained talismanic significance as grounds for withholding from the public information about the CIA. Protecting sources and methods trumps other values. Thus, even when it acknowledged in 1996 that some of its assets were involved in human rights abuses, the CIA continued to protect the identities of those assets, denying the victims and surviving families the opportunity to seek redress and undermining the express U.S. foreign policy goal of supporting human rights and the rule of law.

Congressional Acquiescence

The overbreadth of the CIA's uses of the sources and methods exemption can be remedied by the enactment of legislation making it clear that information regarding intelligence sources and methods, like other national security information, is exempt from FOIA disclosure only when properly classified. Indeed, in 1992, the U.S. Court of Appeals for the Ninth Circuit called on Congress to take notice of the constricting effect that *Sims* had had on the FOIA and to take remedial action.[9] But while congressional intelligence oversight committees have expressed concern about the *Sims* ruling, Congress has failed to take any action to overturn it. In 1992, for example, the intelligence committees undertook a reworking of the National Security Act of 1947, and thus could have reconsidered the sources and methods provision. The intelligence committees, however, passed up this opportunity and reenacted the provision without change.[10] In 1994, Congress again passed up another chance to respond, when it directly addressed the question of classification management and concluded that President Reagan's classification order needed to be updated. Instead of setting its own standards, Congress merely directed the president to issue a new order on classification and declassification of information.[11]

Presidential Inaction

The National Security Act requires the director of Central Intelligence (DCI) to protect "sources and methods," but there is no statutory definition of either the phrase or its constituent elements. Therefore, presidents could direct (or DCIs could adopt) a less restrictive interpretation of the provision, by narrowly defining sources and methods that need to be protected.[12] Furthermore, the act only requires that such information be protected from "unauthorized disclosure," implying that some disclosures even of sources and methods could be authorized. Presidents or DCIs could use this authority to permit (or even specifically require) disclosure of sources and methods when the public interest outweighs the harm to national security. More narrowly, the president or DCI could specify that disclosure of sources and methods is permitted when there would be no harm to national security (i.e., the Exemption 1 standard). No president or DCI has chosen to take any of these steps.

In 1995, President Clinton passed up an important opportunity to address this problem. Clinton issued a new executive order redefining the standards that govern classification and declassification of information. Depending on how it is implemented by federal officials, Clinton's order could ensure disclosures of many historical records of the Pentagon, the State Department, and even the CIA. However, so long as the *Sims* decision stands, Clinton's order may be largely irrelevant to the question of the FOIA's application to the CIA. This is because the order addresses only the standards for classification and declassification of information, which come into play under Exemption 1 of the FOIA. Through their expansive interpretation of the "sources and methods" exemption, which comes into play under Exemption 3 of the FOIA, CIA officials have withheld and will continue to withhold information even if it is not properly classified under the standards of the presidential order. Instead of limiting the CIA's reliance on the sources and methods concept, the Clinton order ratifies this approach, authorizing the DCI to establish special rules for sources and methods but giving no definition of the term.

THE *GLOMAR EXPLORER*

The federal courts have provided the CIA with another extraordinary means to avoid disclosure under the FOIA. Under normal FOIA practice, the government must disclose the existence of any records responsive to a request and must justify the withholding of any of those records on a document-by-document, line-by-line basis. In a series of cases between 1976 and 1981, the U.S. Court of Appeals in the District of Columbia granted the CIA the power to refuse to even confirm or deny whether it had responsive records. The cases that produced these rulings involved requests for records regarding a U.S.-owned vessel known as the *Glomar Explorer;* the exemption, now recognized in other courts, is known as a "Glomar" response.

In 1968, a Soviet submarine carrying nuclear weapons sank somewhere in the Pacific. U.S. officials eagerly sought to recover this submarine, with its missiles, codes, and communications gear. To achieve this, CIA officials turned to billionaire recluse Howard Hughes, who arranged for the construction of an enormous floating platform, the *Glomar Explorer,* and a submersible barge. The recovery operation was finally attempted in 1974 and was partially successful. In February 1975, the *Los Angeles Times* published an incomplete and somewhat garbled account of the episode. CIA officials immediately sought to persuade other newspapers and broadcast media not to pursue this story. This worked for a while, until syndicated columnist Jack Anderson broke the story and other newspapers followed suit.

A number of FOIA requests were immediately filed, including one by the Military Audit Project, which sought the project's contract and budget documents, and one by Harriet Phillippi, who sought information about the CIA's efforts to suppress the story. In both cases, CIA officials responded that they would neither confirm nor deny the existence of relevant records. President Ford's national security adviser, Brent Scowcroft, filed an affidavit in support of the CIA's position, averring that merely acknowledging the involvement of a specific agency in the project "could, in my judgment, severely damage the foreign relations and the national defense of the United States." In its rulings, the appeals court concluded that the FOIA permitted the agency to avoid having to admit or deny the existence of responsive records, in essence allowing the government to treat the mere existence of the records as classified.[13]

In subsequent proceedings, the government changed its position and actually acknowledged the CIA's involvement in the *Glomar Explorer* project. As the case progressed, the CIA released much of the requested information, including transcripts of DCI Colby's conversations with media executives in which they agreed not to publish the story.

The government's changed position when releasing information that officials had previously sworn could not be disclosed without harm to national security should have prompted the courts to be more skeptical of executive national security claims. (The Pentagon Papers case teaches the same lesson.) But the *Glomar* case produced no such epiphany. To the contrary, other courts now accept a "Glomar" response—refusing to confirm or deny the existence of documents on a particular subject—and subsequent rulings have extended this exemption far beyond its original scope.

Indeed, "Glomar" responses have become an agency routine. In cases where an FOIA requester seeks CIA records pertaining to a named foreign national or a specific event abroad, a frequent boilerplate CIA response states that "*in all requests such as yours,* the CIA can neither confirm nor deny the existence or nonexistence of any CIA records responsive to your request" (emphasis added).

At times this is carried to absurd ends. For example, CIA officials have refused to either confirm or deny the existence of records relating to attempted coups in countries of obvious interest to the United States. The agency, in addition, has refused to confirm or deny the existence of any files on the political leaders of major foreign countries. According to CIA officials, merely disclosing that the agency has records on attempted coups overseas or major foreign leaders would harm the national security of the United States.

Such a position makes a mockery of the concept of legitimate secrecy. Part of the CIA's publicly acknowledged mission is to collect and analyze information about major political events and figures in foreign countries.[14] *Glomar* should not apply to requests about a specific incident that is itself public in nature or to requests about noted public figures. Clearly, the CIA is interested in, and therefore creates records on, foreign heads of state, cabinet officials, and other high-level figures. Questions such as whether the agency had access to information from secret sources, and, if so, how much information to withhold to protect those sources can be dealt with adequately after the CIA accepts an FOIA request, conducts a search and review of the documents, and then acknowledges the existence of the documents.

THE CIA INFORMATION ACT

In some cases where the agency possesses responsive records, CIA officials can withhold the records without claiming that disclosure would harm the national security. They do not even have to claim that the records might disclose sources and methods. Instead, they can deny that the agency has any records at all, on the ground that the responsive records are exempt from search and review under the CIA Information Act.

The CIA Information Act was adopted in 1984, in response to the Reagan administration's campaign against the application of the FOIA to the CIA. Rather than agree to a blanket exemption for all CIA records, Congress amended the National Security Act of 1947 to authorize the DCI to exempt only certain CIA "operational files" from the FOIA's search and review requirements.[15] At the time, Congress believed that this restriction was modest. Having to review the agency's operational files was a waste of time, CIA officials argued, since useful information was exempted from release. They further assured Congress that exempting CIA operational files from the FOIA's search and review requirements would result in no noticeable shrinkage in the amount or type of information releasable to the public. Instead, CIA officials argued, resources would be freed up, resulting in swifter responses to other FOIA requests. Congress accepted these claims, believing that the proposed changes would merely relieve the agency of having to search and review files that "almost invariably prove not to be releasable under the FOIA," thereby reducing the processing backlog and delays in responding to FOIA requests, "while preserving undiminished the amount of meaningful information releasable to the public."[16]

The testimony of CIA officials before Congress indicated that the proposed legislation would still subject all intelligence disseminations (including raw intelligence reports from the field) and all matters of policy formulated at agency executive levels (including operational policy) to the search and review requirements.

It is now clear that the CIA Information Act has had broader consequences. CIA officials' attitudes toward the FOIA changed markedly after the act passed. The CIA's FOIA office appears to have implemented the act to exempt all information relating to the Directorate of Operations. Since 1984, it has become much more difficult, if not impossible, for FOIA requesters to obtain anything involving a program that was once in this directorate. Meanwhile, although the agency has been freed of the burden to search for and review operational files, its processing of FOIA requests has not become more efficient; in many cases it is far less responsive to public requests than before.

More significantly, recent CIA disclosures demonstrate that the premise of the CIA Information Act is no longer valid. The CIA's own release of records from some of the very files covered by the act has confirmed that the categorical exemption of operational files is not needed. For example, the initial declassification and release to the public of scores of boxes related to the assassination of President John Kennedy included hundreds of cables from CIA stations in Miami and Mexico City, materials that the act would seem to render wholly unreachable under the FOIA. The CIA has also declassified satellite reconnaissance documents (from the code-named Corona program) under its historical records program, even though it had and has consistently claimed that its photographic intelligence files are exempt under the Information Act for FOIA purposes.

At the very least, releases such as the Corona documents should be accompanied by a new determination that other records in the same category of files are removed from the exemption provided under the CIA Information Act. But the CIA's policy under the act has not been revised to keep up with these developments.

One small incident reveals how CIA officials have failed to treat their obligations under the act seriously. The act requires the DCI at least every ten years to review the exemptions in force and determine "whether such exemptions may be removed from any category of exempted files or any portion thereof." In making this determination, the DCI must consider "the historical value or other public interest in the subject matter of the particular category of files or portions thereof and the potential for declassifying a significant part of the information contained therein." In May 1995, CIA officials advised the Senate Intelligence Committee of the completion of the first of these decennial reviews and indicated that they would therefore process FOIA requests for certain categories of files in the Directorate of Operations. The adopted changes were very narrow, and only covered the administrative files of the now-defunct Office of Policy Coordination and files on the inactive National Committee for a Free Europe and Asia Foundation projects. Moreover, CIA officials made no effort to convey this decision to the public or even to the agency's own advisory review panel of historians.

PROCEDURAL BARRIERS

In addition to excessive delays, CIA officials have employed a variety of obstacles to frustrate FOIA requesters. Under the FOIA, an agency is required to search for all requested records. Agencies, however, need not examine a large quantity of material to ascertain whether records pertain to the requester's interests. CIA officials have taken this concept to preposterous lengths. In one case, CIA personnel replied that they could not search for an October 10, 1992, CIA *press statement* discussing testimony before the Senate Select Committee on Intelligence regarding the Banca Nazionale del Lavoro (BNL) affair. CIA officials did not say that they had searched for the statement and were unable to find it. Instead, they stated that they could not even search for the text of a public statement quoted in the *New York Times,* when the requester gave the subject matter and date of the statement.

Conversely, when requesters ask for records on a general subject, sparing CIA personnel from reviewing agency records for specific items, CIA officials are likely to reject the request on the ground that it would produce "a vast quantity of material," and that "review of the material would impose an excessive and unreasonable burden on the Agency." A sort of triple Catch-22 is at work here. A request might be rejected as burdensome if it is too general, unsearchable if it lacks specificity, or Glomarized if it specifies the name of a foreign national or a foreign event.

At other times, CIA officials claim that they have searched but cannot find any responsive documents. Recently, one requester was advised that agency personnel had searched for but could not locate any analytical papers assessing Soviet military doctrine based on material provided by Colonel Oleg Penkovsky, one of the most important clandestine sources in CIA history. (This claim was made even though the CIA historian had located analyses based on Penkovsky's reporting and published them in a 1992 volume on the Cuban missile crisis, and a major book had been written on Penkovsky's role based on material obtained from the CIA.) Equally incredibly, in May 1996, CIA officials informed a requester that they had searched and could find no after-action reports, schedules, descriptions of routes, or flight folders from any U-2 flights over the Soviet Union between 1956 and 1960.[17]

CIA officials have also contravened the intent of Congress when rejecting fee waiver requests, claiming that release of certain documents would not contribute significantly to public understanding of the operations or activities of the U.S. government. They have done so even when the documents pertain to events central to CIA history or the history of U.S. foreign relations.

EXECUTIVE ORDER

In April 1995, President Clinton issued Executive Order 12958 on classified national security information. The Clinton order, which replaced one issued in 1982 by President Reagan, requires that records more than twenty-five years old should be automatically declassified over a five-year period. As of January 1997, the CIA has 165 million pages of documents more than twenty-five years old, with more maturing every day.[18]

The promise of the Clinton order has yet to be fulfilled. The order allows agencies to exempt certain categories of records from automatic declassification. CIA officials have proposed exempting 64 percent of agency records more than twenty-five years old from this requirement. Moreover, the 36 percent of the records for which the agency requested no exemption include documents pertaining to the Foreign Broadcast Information Service, the great bulk of which were available publicly from the time they were originally broadcast.[19] As of January 1997, the CIA had declassified less than twenty thousand pages, about .0001 of the total covered by the order.[20]

The Clinton order also creates a mechanism called "mandatory classification review," which is separate from the FOIA, and establishes an Interagency Security Classification Appeals Panel (ISCAP) to review denials of requests for declassification. While declassification continues at a snail's pace, the ISCAP in its first year released thousands of pages of documents withheld by federal agencies, including some from the CIA. Nonetheless, without a substantially greater commitment of resources, the automatic declassification process and the panel will be unable to make a significant dent in the backlog of classified information.

RECENT OPENNESS, WHILE SELECTIVE, POINTS THE WAY TO A NEW POLICY

Despite the FOIA's limitations as a tool of openness and accountability concerning CIA records, scholars and the public have been able to obtain information of historical significance and relevance to current policy through a variety of other means. Recently, a few scholars have obtained extraordinary access not available to the ordinary FOIA requester. While the CIA convinced Congress to exempt its operational files from the FOIA search and review requirements, a study on Oleg Penkovsky published in 1992 was based on significant amounts of operational material.[21] Peter Grose's biography of Allen Dulles[22] and Evan Thomas's history of major figures in the clandestine service[23] indicate access to considerable classified information, including information that was at the time and still is being withheld from FOIA requesters.

Leaks are another, increasingly common window into the CIA

and other national security agencies. For example, on May 14, 1996, the *Washington Times* published the entire summary of a 1995 National Intelligence Estimate on ballistic missile defense. As Steven Aftergood of the Federation of American Scientists has pointed out, leaks are a symptom of the overclogged classification system, a "consequence of the failure of intelligence disclosure policy to keep up with current realities and public expectations."[24] Some leaks, Aftergood thoughtfully observes, are really "authorized disclosures on a not-for-attribution basis;" others are genuinely unauthorized disclosures by career officials seeking to discredit official administration policy. In either case, leaks are further evidence that officials directly involved in protecting the national security no longer respect the secrecy system.

The foregoing cases confirm the ad hoc nature of CIA secrecy and disclosure practices, wherein only materials are disclosed that favor one or another point of view. Other, more principled models of disclosure have also been developed, prompted by congressional action, public interest pressure, and executive branch reforms.

The Kennedy Assassination Records Collection Act

As another essay in this book discusses, the JFK act has resulted in the release of important CIA material. This statutory experiment in special standards and procedures, while limited to a defined category of records, offers a test bed for greater openness, confirming the value and feasibility of taking declassification decisions out of the hands of CIA officials.

Congressional Oversight

Congressional inquiries can often be derailed by partisanship and at times can be frustrated by executive branch stonewalling. Nonetheless, they have disclosed historically important information about the CIA's activities. The Church Committee hearings and reports in particular stand out. The history of the CIA published in 1976 by the Church Committee, based on "numerous historical studies and other internal CIA documents that remain classified," remains a "valuable and authoritative account."[25] Through cajoling and negotiation, the Iran-contra committees in 1987 secured the declassification of many CIA records. The joint report of the committees totaled 690 pages. In addition, the committees issued a two-volume appendix of source documents, totaling over three thousand pages, including many CIA documents; twenty-seven volumes of depositions, many also accompanied by previously classified documents; and transcripts of the testimony of thirty-two witnesses, including four CIA officers who had originally testified in executive session.

Intelligence Oversight Board

While the promise of greater openness in the Clinton executive order has not yet been realized, other executive branch mechanisms for declassifying documents give weight to the independent perspectives of officials outside of the agency that had created the information. In March 1995, for example, in the face of intense public interest, President Clinton directed his Intelligence Oversight Board to conduct a government-wide review of certain human rights cases in Guatemala, notably the murder of U.S. citizen Michael De Vine and the disappearance of Guatemalan guerrilla Efrain Bamaca Velasquez. A four-member body composed of persons currently outside the government, the board had extensive access to CIA records. In June 1996, the board issued a report providing significant information about CIA intelligence activities in Guatemala. Moreover, the board prompted the CIA to release portions of a number of field intelligence reports.[26]

Two other increasingly important avenues for release of CIA information are the agency's own historical program and the biographies or memoirs of former CIA officials. These share with leaks a characteristic that limits their usefulness: those who have authorized access to the information in the first place retain control over the disclosure of information. In consequence, information is selectively released by those who have an interest in portraying their actions or opinions in a favorable light. These disclosures nonetheless share another, more profound characteristic: they fundamentally undercut the totalistic approach to information control that the Supreme Court had accepted in *Sims*.

CIA Historical Program

In October 1992, on the thirtieth anniversary of the Cuban missile crisis, an extraordinary event occurred: the CIA held its First Intelligence History Symposium, open to the public, and issued a handsomely printed volume of documents tracing the history of the crisis. This published documentary collection consisted of material that until then had been treated as among the CIA's most sensitive records. These included U-2 flight patterns and analyses, human intelligence reports, intelligence estimates, memoranda of one-on-one meetings between the DCI and the president, so-called Ironbark material provided by one of the CIA's greatest spies ever, Russian officer Oleg

Penkovsky, and minutes of the working group on the covert operation, code-named MONGOOSE. As the CIA claimed in *Sims,* these were precisely the types of records that constituted sources and methods, any disclosure of which would harm the national security.

The symposium and volume were products of the CIA's new program of openness, announced by then-DCI Gates in a speech to the Oklahoma Press Association in February 1992. To carry out the openness program, the CIA's in-house Center for the Study of Intelligence was reorganized to include the CIA History Staff (first formed in 1951) and expanded in size. A new Historical Review Group was created to coordinate the declassification of documents. At the end of 1989, the History Staff began to release the secret and top secret studies the agency had been preparing since 1951. The various authors of these studies had "conducted lengthy contemporaneous interviews with the officials involved and were granted full access to CIA and other government archives, most of which remain classified. . . . For all their limitations, they open an invaluable new resource for serious historians of intelligence."[27]

Other volumes have been released in the succeeding four years. These have included intelligence estimates on the Soviet Union; the Corona Project satellite photographs; and the transcripts of the Venona Project, some twenty-nine hundred Soviet consular messages that had been intercepted by U.S. intelligence during the 1940s, which were then decrypted (by the NSA) and analyzed by the CIA over the course of four decades.[28]

With a few notable exceptions, the disclosures of the Historical Program share one characteristic: all portray the CIA in a positive light. Thus, whereas the CIA has released records of the Cuban missile crisis of 1962, in which intelligence contributed significantly to the successful resolution of a superpower confrontation, it continues to withhold the records of the 1961 Bay of Pigs operation, an intelligence fiasco, despite assurances in 1993 from then-DCI Gates that they would soon be released. Documents on other older programs remain classified, such as those involving the CIA's role in funding and promoting political parties in France and Italy during the 1940s and 1950s, insurgencies in Indonesia and Tibet during the 1950s and 1960s, insurrections in the Congo and the Dominican Republic during the 1960s, secret operations during the Korean and Vietnam Wars, and coups that restored the Shah to power in Iran in 1953. One notable exception is the May 1997 release of the CIA's previously classified history of the 1954 coup that overthrew the Arbenz government in Guatemala. The report described how CIA officials deceived President Eisenhower and was accompanied by the release of a tiny portion of the agency's records on the coup. These included documents showing that the agency had compiled a list of Arbenz government officials targeted for assassination.[29]

In addition, as the panel of outside historians appointed by the DCI has noted, the selective declassification of documents by the CIA does not substitute for the opening of archives that would allow historians not affiliated with the agency to work directly with its records. As of May 1997, no single entire, unredacted collection of CIA records was yet available for research at the National Archives.[30]

CIA officials' interest in secrecy, moreover, continues to infect the preparation of the official documentary record of U.S. foreign policy, the *Foreign Relations of the United States,* discussed in detail in another essay in this volume. Indeed, when the State Department in 1996 issued a volume on Northeast Asia, 1961–63, the Advisory Committee on Historical Diplomatic Documentation noted in the preface that, because of CIA refusal to declassify certain documents, the volume did not constitute a "thorough, accurate, and reliable documentary record" of U.S. policy decisions during this period.

Nonetheless, the significance of the disclosures under the CIA's Historical Program should not be overlooked: they demonstrate that much classified information can be made public without causing any harm to the national security. The selective releases, moreover, hint at the agency's attention to the public interest.

The Political Is Personal

Robert M. Gates served in the CIA from 1966 to 1991, under eight directors of Central Intelligence, ultimately winning confirmation to become DCI. He served on the National Security Council staff of four presidents. When he sat down to write his memoirs, published in 1996, he could claim, "No one had longer uninterrupted continuity in senior or key national security positions during this period."[31] His book unintentionally provides further evidence of the inconsistencies of the CIA's culture of secrecy. Gates writes that his memoir is based largely on classified information and that all of the quoted or summarized documents were officially cleared for use as required under terms of his employment with the CIA. In his acknowledgments, Gates thanks the CIA's reviewers for "their cooperation and promptness, particularly in light of the massive number of classified documents and Agency activities that I describe." He then concedes that "I have revealed in these pages many clandestine CIA activities (both successful and unsuccessful) for the first time."[32]

Gates quotes verbatim from President's Daily Briefs, National Intelligence Estimates, and special intelligence "Alerts," and he summarizes others. (At the very time when the independent scholars at the National Security Archive were being told that the President's Daily Brief could never be disclosed, Gates was allowed to quote verbatim from the President's Daily Brief from August 17, 1991, and September 2, 1983.) He quotes directly, by specific date, CIA memorandums and notes to the president and other senior officials. He describes numerous covert operations (on page 358 alone he lists five). In one scene, he describes a visit to the Kremlin in 1992, in which he carried "the Soviet naval flag that had shrouded the coffins of the half dozen Soviet sailors whose remains the Glomar Explorer had recovered when it raised part of a Soviet ballistic missile submarine from deep in the Pacific Ocean in the mid-1970s."

Again, Gates's disclosures are selective. But the CIA had previously convinced the courts that no selection could be made, that every item, however innocuous, had to be protected lest it disclose something about the intelligence-gathering process. Now, it is clear, selection can be made: some "sources and methods" information can be disclosed, and there is no reason why judges cannot review the process of selection, as Congress originally intended.

CONCLUSION

Against a backdrop of judicial deference, congressional disinterest, and bureaucratic hurdles, there stands a startling development: the CIA has by now discarded the rationale of absolute secrecy. To be sure, the agency's releases have been selective, and therefore are of limited research value. Regardless, in the past, CIA officials had consistently argued that any disclosure would reveal part of the mosaic and thereby had to be opposed. Now the CIA has inadvertently demonstrated that no category of records is off-limits. Choices can be made, based on a determination of what will cause current harm to the national security. And the Assassination Records Review Board, the Interagency Securitiy Classification Appeals Panel, and the Intelligence Oversight Board experiences confirm that authorities outside the agency can participate in decisions to declassify sensitive records.

In the end, a former CIA insider, William Colby, offered the best argument for openness when concluding that "intelligence substance can be disseminated to the public while its sources are kept secret." In his book *Honorable Men,* Colby wrote:

In a political debate where knowledge can be power, intelligence judgments must be supplied impartially to all factions, to help the best solution to emerge, rather than the favored one. Photographs must be declassified, backgrounders attributed, publications edited to protect the sources but allow the substance of the reports and assessments to circulate to Congress and the public. The estimates will then be debated and the sage unanimity of the cloistered world of intelligence will be challenged by those close to the struggle and fearful of irrational and foolhardy, but real, surprises. Out of the process will come a better understanding of the role and value of modern intelligence, as well as better intelligence itself.[33]

NOTES

1. "It was learned, however, that the messages produced for Congress and published were not, by any means, the only indications gleaned of the Colombian situation. Other messages—at least one of them forecasting the participation of some of the Bogota police—... were received." Hanson W. Baldwin, "Intelligence—II," *New York Times,* July 22, 1948, p. 2.

2. "Clarifying and Protecting the Right of the Public to Information," S. Rep. No. 813, 89th Cong., 1st sess. 8 (1965), reprinted in "FOIA Source Book: Legislative Materials, Cases, Articles," Senate Committee on the Judiciary, 93d Cong., 2d sess. (1974) at p. 43.

3. "Conference Report on the Freedom of Information Act Amendments," S. Rep. No. 93–1200, 93d Cong., 2d sess. (1974), reprinted in Allan Adler, ed., *Litigation Under the Federal Open Government Laws* (New York: ACLU Foundation, 1995) at A-21.

4. Reprinted in "The Freedom of Information Act: Central Intelligence Agency Exemptions," Hearings before a subcommittee of the House Committee on Government Operations, February 20 and May 29, 1980, 96th Cong., 2d sess. (1981) at pp. 124–27. Overall, the testimony of CNSS Director Morton Halperin provides an excellent overview—and defense—of the application of the FOIA to the CIA from 1974 to 1980.

5. John Marks obtained portions of these records under the FOIA and used them in his book *The Search for the "Manchurian Candidate": The CIA and Mind Control* (New York: Times Books, 1979). In 1995, the presidential Advisory Committee on Human Radiation Experiments was able to secure the declassification of more records on MKULTRA and related CIA human behavior projects, including most of the 1963 CIA inspector general report on MKULTRA, which had been declassified in heavily redacted form in 1975. The Advisory Committee recommended that the remaining CIA documents be reviewed, concluding that "most if not all of the records could be declassified without harming the national security." Advisory Committee on Human Radiation Experiments, Final Report (October 1995) at 839.

6. *CIA v. Sims,* 471 U.S. 159 (1985).

7. 471 U.S. at 182.

8. *Maynard v. CIA,* 986 F. 2d 547 (1st Cir. 1993)(emphasis added).

9. *Hunt v. CIA,* 981 F. 2d 1116, 1120 (9th Cir. 1992).

10. Conference Report on Intelligence Authorization Act for Fiscal Year 1993, Rep. No. 102-963 at 88; 1992 U.S. Code Cong. & Admin. News 2614.

11. Conference Report on Intelligence Authorization Act for Fiscal Year 1995, H.R. Rep. No. 103-753 (1994).

12. The Moynihan Commission recommended in March 1997 that the clarification be accomplished by issuance of a DCI directive. Clarifying the scope of and reasons for sources and methods protection would not put at risk information that is truly sensitive. Report of the Commission on Protecting and Reducing Government Secrecy, S. Doc. 105-2, at p. 70. (The report can be found at <http://www.access.gpo.gov/int>.)

13. *Military Audit Project v. Casey*, 656 F. 2d 724 (D.C. Cir. 1981); *Phillippi v. CIA*, 546 F. 2d 1009 (D.C. Cir. 1976).

14. In April 1995, then-acting DCI William Studeman testified in open session before the Senate Intelligence Committee that the CIA regularly provides information on such issues as "civil wars, terrorism, narcotics, weapons proliferation, organized crime and other forms of conflict around the globe."

15. Public Law 98-477, 50 U.S.C. 431.

16. Report of the House Permanent Select Committee on Intelligence, H.R. Rep. No. 726, Part I, 98th Cong., 2d Sess. (1984) at 4.

17. FOIA requesters are not the only ones unable to locate CIA records. The Justice Department officials appointed by Attorney General Janet Reno to investigate the Banca Nazionale del Lavoro case found that "the CIA's ability to retrieve information is limited. Records are 'compartmentalized' to prevent unauthorized disclosure; only some of those records are retrievable through computer databases; no database encompasses all records; and not all information is recorded. In the course of our work, we learned of 'sensitive' components of information not normally retrievable and of specialized offices that previously were unknown to the CIA personnel assisting us."

18. Moynihan Commission report, p. 74.

19. See Page Putnam Miller, "Capitol Commentary," *OAH Newsletter*, November 1996.

20. Evan Thomas, "Taming Uncle Sam's Classification Compulsion," *Washington Post*, March 9, 1997, p. C2.

21. J. Schecter and P. Deriabin, *The Spy Who Saved the World* (New York: Scribner's, 1992). Schecter explains how he and Deriabin came to write the book. Deriabin had been a KGB officer. He defected, went to work for the CIA, and had translated Penkovsky's briefing papers. In 1987, twenty-five years after Penkovsky's arrest, the two "wrote a letter to the CIA information and privacy coordinator requesting permission to be afforded access to historical documents in search of relevant materials for a biography," subject to a review of their manuscript by the agency to determine that no classified information was contained therein. They wrote their letter on June 7 and received permission on September 26.

22. P. Grose, *Gentleman Spy: The Life of Allen Dulles* (Boston: Houghton Mifflin, 1994), p. 588.

23. E. Thomas, *The Very Best Men* (New York: Simon and Schuster, 1995). Thomas first approached the CIA in 1992. After two years of negotiation, he was granted access to classified files and signed a secrecy agreement allowing the agency to review his manuscript. According to Thomas, the CIA

"objected only to the use of classified cryptonyms and information that would reveal 'sources and methods' in a way that could genuinely harm national security" (p. 342).

24. S. Aftergood, "Secrecy and Accountability in U.S. Intelligence" (paper presented at the Center for International Policy's Seminar on Intelligence Reform, October 9, 1996). Aftergood's informative and insightful "Secrecy & Government Bulletin" and a wealth of other information on secrecy policy are available at <http://www.fas.org/sgp/>.

25. Grose, *Gentleman Spy*, p. 588.

26. Another example of a special body prompting release of CIA material is the Advisory Committee on Human Radiation Experiments, created by President Clinton by executive order on January 15, 1994, to investigate and report on the use of human beings as subjects of federally funded research using radiation. The committee had access to classified CIA documents and successfully urged the CIA to release a number of documents with only minimal redactions.

27. Grose, *Gentleman Spy*, p. 587.

28. Central Intelligence Agency, *Venona: Soviet Espionage and the American Response, 1939–1957* (Washington, D.C.: Center for Study of Intelligence, 1996). The National Security Agency even posted the transcripts on the Internet. Also in the category of official historical releases is the eleven-hundred-page compilation issued in the *Foreign Relations of the United States* series, entitled "Emergence of the Intelligence Establishment." The preface to the FRUS volume offers a good overview of CIA records, as do the footnotes in Grose's book.

29. In 1993, then-DCI R. James Woolsey testified that he had directed that many of these records undergo declassification review. They still have not been released. See "Increasing Accessibility to CIA Documents," Hearing before the House Permanent Select Committee on Intelligence, 103d Cong., 1st sess. (1993) at 4.

30. Report from the DCI Historical Review Panel, September 1996, available at the FAS Web site.

31. Robert M. Gates, *From the Shadows: The Ultimate Insider's Story of Five Presidents and How They Won the Cold War* (New York: Simon and Schuster, 1996), p. 19.

32. Ibid., pp. 3–4.

33. William Colby and Peter Forbath, *Honorable Men: My Life in the CIA* (New York: Simon and Schuster, 1978), pp. 465–66.

4

"Not So Anonymous": Parting the Veil of Secrecy About the National Security Agency

Matthew M. Aid

In 1995, the Canadian historian John Ferris wrote, "We know very little about American signals intelligence. Because its product was not circulated widely or referred to explicitly in intelligence summaries, its significance will be unusually hard to trace." Nonetheless, Ferris added, "The government may well be able to keep most of the evidence from the public record if it wishes to do so."[1]

There is no question that the National Security Agency (NSA), the most publicity-shy component of the American intelligence community, prefers that its work remain perpetually shrouded in secrecy. *Baltimore Sun* reporters Tom Bowman and Scott Shane aptly described NSA as "an American institution that for four decades has been immensely important and virtually invisible."[2]

Located on a 447–acre tract of land on the grounds of Fort George G. Meade, Maryland, halfway between Baltimore and Washington, D.C., in 1996 NSA directly employed approximately thirty-eight thousand military and civilian personnel and had an annual budget of $3.7 billion, although neither of these figures includes tactical military Signals Intelligence (SIGINT) units and support personnel indirectly controlled by NSA. This makes NSA by far the largest intelligence agency within the U.S. intelligence community, dwarfing the Central Intelligence Agency's seventeen thousand personnel and $3.1 billion budget. Only the National Reconnaissance Office (NRO), which develops, launches, and controls all American spy satellites, has a larger annual budget ($6.2 billion in fiscal year 1996)—although with a staff of only one thousand government personnel plus several thousand contract employees.[3]

The NSA currently performs three national missions pursuant to Executive Order 12333, *United States Intelligence Activities,* and National Security Council Intelligence Directive (NSCID) No. 6, *Signals Intelligence.* It manages and directs all U.S. SIGINT collection and processing activities around the world; is responsible for overseeing the security of the U.S. government's communications and data processing systems (referred to within the NSA as Information Security, or INFOSEC), including ensuring the security of all government computer systems; and manages the U.S. government's Operations Security (OPSEC) program. Approximately 65 to 70 percent of NSA's manpower and budgetary resources are devoted to SIGINT collection, processing, analysis, and reporting, although the INFOSEC mission has increased in importance and size over the last fifteen years as the NSA has poured more manpower and budgetary resources into the increasingly important field of computer security.[4]

To perform its SIGINT mission, the director of the NSA (DIRNSA) manages and exercises direct operational control over the U.S. Signals Intelligence System (USSS), the unified organization comprising the NSA and those components of the three military services and the CIA engaged in SIGINT collection. At the core of the USSS are the three so-called Service Cryptologic Elements (SCEs), comprising the cryptologic elements of the U.S. Army Intelligence and Security Command (INSCOM) at Fort Belvoir, Virginia; the Naval Security Group Command (NAVSECGRU) at Fort George G. Meade, Maryland; and the U.S. Air Force's Air Intelligence Agency (AIA) at Kelly Air Force Base, Texas. Of the three agencies, only the Naval Security Group Command is a pure SIGINT-INFOSEC organization. In contrast, INSCOM and AIA are all-source intelligence collection agencies, with sizable measurement and signature intelligence (MASINT), imagery intelligence (IMINT), human intelligence (HUMINT), scientific and technical intelligence (S&T), and counterintelligence (CI) components working together (but not necessarily harmoniously) with their SIGINT brethren within the same organization. The NSA also exercises operational control over the joint CIA-NSA SIGINT organization called the Special Collection Service (SCS). Based in suburban Maryland, the SCS manages covert listening posts located in several dozen American diplomatic establishments around the world.[5]

The NSA operates some twenty large listening posts in the United States and abroad, the largest and most important of which are five Regional SIGINT Operations Centers (RSOCs). Three of the RSOCs are in the United States at Kunia in Hawaii, which covers Asia; the

Medina Annex outside San Antonio, Texas, which covers Latin America; and Fort Gordon, Georgia, which covers Southwest Asia and Africa. The RSOCs at Bad Aibling Station, Germany, and Menwith Hill Station in England share coverage of Europe, the western half of the former Soviet Union, the Middle East, and North Africa. In addition, the NSA maintains varying degrees of operational and tasking control over several constellations of SIGINT spy satellites currently in orbit over the earth, dozens of covert listening posts in American diplomatic establishments around the world, almost fifty navy and air force SIGINT collection aircraft, over forty navy warships with SIGINT equipment, and teams of SIGINT personnel on virtually every U.S. Navy attack submarine operating at sea. The NSA also receives materials from dozens of tactical SIGINT units controlled by army, navy, and air force theater commanders, as well as through collaborative arrangements with the SIGINT agencies of Great Britain, Canada, Australia, New Zealand, and a number of other countries.[6]

These facts, however, describe only the NSA's "external" operations and do not portray the totality of the agency's activities, information about which is difficult to obtain. It is far more difficult to move beyond these externals to the heart of the NSA—to describe the foreign code and cipher systems that the agency has been able to read over the last fifty years and the role SIGINT has played in the formulation and implementation of U.S. defense and foreign policy since the end of World War II. This is because of the secrecy surrounding the NSA and its work. Only in the last couple of years has this curtain of secrecy around the NSA's work been parted, but only ever so slightly.

Some analysts believe that, despite the NSA's huge workforce and budget, it produces on a dollar-for-dollar basis more "bang for the buck" than any other intelligence source, with perhaps the exception of the NRO's spy satellites.[7] For example, the NSA played a vital role during Operations Desert Storm/Shield in 1990–91, collecting much of the intelligence information that allowed Allied warplanes to destroy the Iraqi national command and control and air defense systems early in the war. SIGINT's role was crucial to Allied forces' victory in the Battle of Khafji in January 1991.[8] The NSA was also a primary source of intelligence information during the war in Bosnia from 1991 to 1996.[9]

Since the breakup of the Soviet Union in the early 1990s, the NSA's attention has shifted to other targets. One of the most important of its new priorities is expanded SIGINT coverage of international economic matters, including international trade negotiations and economic summits, bribery attempts by foreign governments and companies competing with American companies for international business, and money transfers by international banks. The NSA has moved in a significant way into the war against drugs, with the agency expanding its cooperation with the CIA and the Drug Enforcement Agency (DEA) in ongoing intelligence-gathering operations aimed at rooting out and destroying international drug rings, particularly in Latin America. And the NSA's intelligence coverage of international terrorism and the sources of its financing has been expanded and refined, especially since the 1993 bombing of the World Trade Center in New York City.[10]

But this constitutes only the tip of the iceberg of the NSA's activities; the vast majority of its activities (whether accomplishments or failures) remain classified, and if NSA officials have their way, will remain so for the foreseeable future.

Few branches of the U.S. government have invested as much time and energy ensuring the secrecy of their operations as have the NSA and its predecessor organizations. The degree to which the NSA has protected its secrets is the stuff of legend. British historian Ronald Clark aptly described the agency's obsession with secrecy as a "near-pathological passion for security."[11] Voicing the view of the SIGINT professional, William F. Friedman, the "father of Army cryptology," told his colleagues in 1947: "It has always been the lot of the men and women in our work to remain behind the scenes, away from the view of the public and even of their co-workers. This isolation from the outside world is part of the very nature of the work and is necessary to its success."[12] In a March 1979 speech at NSA headquarters at Fort Meade, Maryland, former NSA Director Bobby Ray Inman told the assembled NSA staff members:

NSA's ability to provide such intelligence information has rested—and will continue to rest—on maintaining a high degree of secrecy about all aspects of its intelligence mission. The conduct of that mission is based on intelligence sources and methods of the utmost fragility and sensitivity. Disclosure of information about such sources and methods poses unacceptable risks that they will be irretrievably damaged.

Consequently, the Agency has traditionally engaged in secrecy to an extraordinary extent. Our employees have accepted the sacrifice of not telling their spouses and their families what they do, and frequently the no less sacrifice of not knowing much about what goes on elsewhere in the Agency or even in the same office. Until recently, the Agency enjoyed the luxury of relative obscurity. Generally unknown to the public and largely uncontroversial, it was able to perform its vital functions without reason for public scrutiny or public dialogue.[13]

In an unpublished 1976 report, the House Government Affairs Committee concluded that "much of the secrecy surrounding [the NSA's] operations is obsessive and unfounded," adding that "much of the basis for this secrecy is historical habit, in which intelligence agencies traditionally attempt to keep *everything,* even, when possible, their very existence—hidden."[14] Indeed, the hypersecretive nature of the agency's work has led some within the U.S. intelligence community to facetiously tell their colleagues that NSA stood for "No Such Agency" or "Never Say Anything."[15]

Times have changed. Today the NSA is the subject of feature stories in daily newspapers and is mentioned on television and radio news reports; it is the topic of conversations at trendy dinner parties in Washington, D.C., and is mentioned prominently in the novels of popular writers such as John Le Carré and Tom Clancy. The NSA personifies the sinister American intelligence agency on popular television shows such as *The X-Files,* a role formerly the monopoly of the CIA.[16] More important, senior U.S. government officials are increasingly willing to publicize SIGINT information to justify national security policy decisions during crisis situations, and the amount of SIGINT information leaked by high-level government informants has also increased dramatically in the last twenty years.[17]

A June 1987 *NSA Security Awareness Bulletin* summarizes NSA officials' unhappiness with this changing environment, reporting to the agency's workforce, "You have no doubt heard that NSA stands for 'No Such Agency' or 'Never Say Anything'—references to the extremely low profile this Agency once enjoyed. Unfortunately, because of people like James Bamford, Seymour Hersh, and Ronald Pelton, NSA has received a great deal of unwanted media exposure in recent years."[18] The resultant avalanche of disclosures concerning the NSA and its activities, coupled with the increasing public awareness of its role and functions, has led a new generation of Washington pundits to describe the agency's initials as standing for "Not So Anonymous."[19]

It was inevitable that this curtain of secrecy would be parted; as the age-old dictum reminds us, "the only secret is that there are no secrets." Officials at the NSA have long known that the NSA would have to part with some of its secrets, albeit reluctantly. In a 1946 top secret memorandum, one of the founding fathers of the NSA, Solomon Kullback, wrote, "It is obvious that we cannot hope to keep the cryptologic achievements of the United States and Great Britain completely secret for an indefinite or large number of years."[20]

Despite Kullback's admonition, the NSA has zealously tried for more than fifty years to keep its work a secret, even from the White House, other members of the U.S. intelligence community, and Congress. For example, the NSA attempted to hide its involvement in the Iran-contra scandal of the mid-1980s. In 1986, NSA officials refused to comply with a request by Secretary of Defense Caspar Weinberger (the agency's boss) for information about the NSA's involvement in the Iran-contra affair. Secretary Weinberger was told that neither he nor the State Department was cleared for access to SIGINT regarding Lieutenant Colonel Oliver North's arms for hostages operations. When NSA Director William E. Odom fired the number three man in the NSA's Communications Security Organization in 1988 for assisting North's covert efforts in Central America, a number of senior NSA civilian officials resigned in protest, privately telling anyone who would listen that the fired official was being made a scapegoat, since Odom had been fully cognizant of the NSA's involvement with North's covert efforts. Finally, the NSA's insistence on secrecy surrounding the important role of SIGINT in the Iran-contra affair severely hindered Special Prosecutor Lawrence Walsh's attempts to prosecute North and the other Iran-contra defendants.[21]

Many high-ranking American intelligence officials were particularly upset that the climate of secrecy at the NSA not only kept cryptologic information out of the hands of the public but also prevented the flow of SIGINT to intelligence consumers at the CIA and to others within the intelligence community who needed it the most. For example, a classified 1960 study of the U.S. intelligence community found that the classification levels for access to SIGINT were so high and the handling criteria so rigid that key personnel were "at times deprived" of information "vital to the discharge of their responsibilities." This penchant for excessive secrecy came to be known within the American intelligence community as the "Green Door" syndrome, whereby the vast majority of U.S. government officials and members of the intelligence community were effectively denied access to SIGINT, preventing the effective integration of SIGINT with other forms of intelligence information. Not until the 1980s did NSA officials ensure the wider distribution of the agency's SIGINT product among intelligence consumers.[22]

In striking contrast to the plethora of material published about the CIA, precious little has been written about either SIGINT or NSA operations in general. Ferris correctly observes that "we know more about the CIA than the NSA, even though the latter probably had more influence on American diplomacy and strategy."[23]

How little has been written about the NSA is documented by the small number of SIGINT citations in the few bibliographic books on intelligence matters. There are surprisingly few detailed studies of the role played by SIGINT even for the World War II period.[24] The NSA's Center for Cryptologic History has compiled a twenty-four-page list of books and articles written about SIGINT called *Sources on Cryptology*, which also lists the Special Research Histories released by the NSA to the National Archives, since 1977. Not surprisingly, the list of books and articles concerning post–World War II SIGINT is even shorter.[25]

The number of serious book-length works about the NSA and its predecessor organizations is less than ten. Written in 1967 and issued in a revised edition in 1996, David Kahn's book *The Codebreakers* remains one of the most important and comprehensive histories of codes and ciphers ever written. James Bamford's *The Puzzle Palace*, published in the United States in 1982, was the first detailed examination of NSA and its role in the American intelligence community. Currently being revised and updated, *The Puzzle Palace* remains the best single work on the subject, a testament to Bamford's superb work. Jeffrey T. Richelson's numerous books and articles on the organization and functions of the U.S. intelligence community are by far the best works on the subject, particularly in the field of spy satellites and imagery intelligence. His book *The Ties That Bind*, coauthored with the noted Australian writer on intelligence matters, Desmond Ball, remains the best work to date about the intelligence collaboration between the United States, Great Britain, Canada, Australia, and New Zealand. Pulitzer Prize–winning investigative reporter Seymour M. Hersh's book *The Target Is Destroyed* best describes the NSA's inner workings and how its intelligence product has been used and abused by American policy makers. Finally, in 1996 New Zealand researcher Jeffrey Nicky Hager published *Secret Power*, a detailed examination of New Zealand's role in the U.S.-British SIGINT network led by the NSA, including the first comprehensive examination of the current importance of economic SIGINT.[26]

Press coverage of the NSA's activities has increased dramatically in the years since the initial publication of James Bamford's groundbreaking book *The Puzzle Palace*. These news stories are available on any of the rapidly proliferating number of computer databases, such as NEXIS and DOW JONES. NSA officials continue to object to the publication of news stories about the agency, but their efforts to prevent publication have become increasingly halfhearted, perhaps because of the realization that the publicity is necessary if the NSA is to compete for scarce budgetary resources with the other better-known members of the U.S. intelligence community.

This quantitative increase in reporting has not necessarily ensured a commensurate improvement in quality. Few feature pieces have been written in the last fifteen years about the NSA, and the quality of the press coverage of the agency has varied dramatically. Much of the reported information is wrong or distorted, demonstrating either ignorance of the subject matter or the willingness of harried reporters to accept at face value information from their sources without the benefit of confirmation.[27]

Moreover, since the early 1980s only a few useful academic studies have been published about SIGINT. By far the best are published in the specialist journals *Intelligence and National Security, Cryptologia,* and *International Journal of Intelligence and Counterintelligence.* To date, most of the writing on SIGINT in these journals has focused on code breaking during World War II, with virtually nothing written about the postwar activities of the NSA or its foreign collaborators.

Why has academia shied away from SIGINT or other forms of technical intelligence given the proliferation of interest on campuses throughout the United States in the general subject of intelligence? Historians and political scientists suffer from the same hurdle faced by journalists: excessive secrecy surrounding the subject makes it extremely difficult to understand SIGINT, much less gauge its relative importance. Moreover, the subject's technical nature is so complex that even veteran SIGINT practitioners sometimes find this difficult to explain. Many academics interested in intelligence are further discouraged because of the prevailing assumption that virtually nothing has been declassified about the subject, precluding any original research.

Given the dearth of published studies, researching the history of the NSA and its antecedents requires great patience and perseverance. The logical starting place for researching primary source material concerning the NSA is the National Archives. In the course of ten years of research into the history of the NSA, I found useful information concerning American cryptologic activities from 1917 to the present day in no less than twenty-one different document record groups (RGs) at the National Archives.

The most important of these is RG-457, the records of the NSA and its predecessor organizations. At the heart of RG-457 are more than four hundred special research histories (SRHs), a disparate collection of partially declassified documents relating principally to American cryptologic operations during World War II. These SRHs, however, contain little documentation about post–World War II cryptology. This record group also contains thousands of pages of declassified German, Japanese, Italian, and Vichy French military and diplomatic decrypts from World War II, as well as several dozen historical documents released by the cryptologic agencies of the U.S. Army, Navy, and Air Force. These documents vary greatly in value, although their overall research value is disappointing, in large part because deletions in many of the most important documents far exceed the pages of declassified text.[28]

Much useful information relating to SIGINT is accessible in the Harry S. Truman and Dwight D. Eisenhower Presidential Libraries, less at the John F. Kennedy and Lyndon B. Johnson Libraries. The accessible records of subsequent American presidents contain virtually no declassified documents concerning the NSA. The U.S. Army Center for Military History, the Naval Historical Center, and the U.S. Marine Corps Historical Center, all located in Washington, D.C., contain much useful documentation, as do the U.S. Army Military History Institute at Carlisle Barracks, Pennsylvania, and the Air Force Historical Research Agency at Maxwell Air Force Base outside Montgomery, Alabama. Finally, some post–World War II SIGINT documents are accessible at a number of private research libraries, particularly at the MacArthur Library in Norfolk, Virginia, and the Marshall Library in Lexington, Virginia, which holds the personal papers of Marshall Carter, director of NSA from 1965 to 1969, and William F. Friedman, who served with the NSA and its antecedents from 1929 to 1955.

All of these records, however, have been heavily culled by the NSA, with thousands of document withdrawal cards inserted in lieu of the referenced documents. In exceptional cases, documents withdrawn from some files were later found intact in other record groups at the National Archives. It will take years for the NSA and other government agencies to review these records for possible declassification pursuant to President Clinton's April 1995 Executive Order 12958. The cryptologic exemption of this order makes it highly unlikely that the NSA will have the inclination to review these files and declassify the documents in question. In consequence, little can be expected from the NSA in the near future, leaving it to individual researchers to use the Freedom of Information Act (FOIA) to get these documents declassified.

Trying to crowbar information out of the NSA through the use of the FOIA is both time-consuming and frustrating. Prior to 1990, NSA officials made it clear that they had no intention of declassifying any documents relating to post–World War II SIGINT before the year 2001. Virtually every document in the NSA's archives is marked "Exempt from the General Declassification Schedule," ensuring their continued classification as long as NSA officials deem this necessary. Some documents I obtained were marked such that they were to be kept classified in perpetuity, with no mandatory declassification review dates indicated on the documents.[29]

When I began researching a history of the NSA ten years ago, submitting an FOIA request to the NSA almost guaranteed an immediate rejection of the request in its entirety. An appeal to the agency's FOIA Appeal Authority guaranteed a similar rejection. The grounds for rejection were predictably uniform, with two legal provisions repeatedly cited: Title 18 U.S.C. Section 798 and Public Law 86-36.

The genesis of these laws dates from World War II. During the war, American intelligence officials became infuriated over a number of newspaper articles discussing various aspects of American cryptologic activities. The worst incident occurred in the summer of 1942, when a number of press reports trumpeted American code-breaking successes against the Japanese navy during the Battle of Midway. Cooler heads barely managed to persuade the Roosevelt administration not to prosecute the worst of the offending newspapers, the *Chicago Tribune*, for fear that doing so would alert the Japanese to the American code breakers' success. Cryptanalysts at the U.S. Navy's code-breaking organization, OP-20-G, were enraged when the Japanese navy changed its principal operational code, JN-25, following the newspaper revelations. Thus, while the OP-20-G struggled to solve the new cipher used with JN-25, in the three months following the *Chicago Tribune* revelations the U.S. Navy in the South Pacific suffered punishing losses in naval battles at Cape Esperance, Santa Cruz, and Guadalcanal, losses that may have been unnecessary had navy cryptanalysts been able to read the Japanese operational code.[30]

With the end of World War II, army and navy intelligence officers began pressing for legislation to prevent a recurrence of these events, to include harsh punitive measures should similar violations occur. In the fall of 1945, Representative Francis E. Walter (D-PA) introduced a bill to "safeguard military information." Such legislation was needed, Walter argued, emphasizing "that their [military and intelligence personnel] lips should be sealed when it comes to the discussion of some of the things that made possible the winning of the war." Walter was referring to American code-breaking successes during the war. Walter's bill was killed, however, with its critics successfully arguing that its "gag" provisions clearly infringed on First Amendment constitutional rights.[31]

The bill's failure only inspired army and navy officials to redouble their efforts to safeguard cryptologic information. After considerable lobbying from the Department of Defense and the Armed Forces Security Agency, the predecessor organization to the NSA, on

May 1, 1950, Congress passed a criminal statute (Title 18 U.S.C. Section 798), commonly referred to as the "COMINT Law," which made it a criminal offense for anyone to communicate to any "unauthorized person" any "classified" information regarding: (1) the nature, preparation, or use of any code, cipher, or cryptographic system of the United States or any foreign government; (2) the design, construction, use, maintenance, or repair of any device, apparatus, or appliance used or prepared or planned for use by the United States or any foreign government for cryptographic or communication intelligence purposes; (3) the communication intelligence activities of the United States or any foreign government; (4) information obtained by the process of communications intelligence from the communications of any foreign government knowing the same to have been obtained by such processes.[32]

Approved by Congress, the bill was signed into law by President Truman on October 31, 1951. Under its provisions, violation of any section was punishable by a ten-thousand-dollar fine, ten years in prison, or both.

This harsh and uncompromising statute has been wielded with considerable effect on a number of occasions. Federal prosecutors used the COMINT Law during the espionage trials of Joseph S. Petersen, Jr., in 1954, Christopher Boyce in 1977, and Ronald W. Pelton in 1986. In 1986, CIA Director William Casey threatened to prosecute any newspaper reporter who published details concerning the NSA's intelligence operations during the Pelton trial.[33]

Title 18 U.S.C. 798 is one of only two federal statutes providing special protection for a specific kind of government information. The other statute, the Atomic Energy Act of 1954, designates as "restricted data" all information regarding the development, testing, construction, and maintenance of America's nuclear weapons stockpile and grants classification protection equal to that given three years earlier to cryptographic information. U.S. government officials subsequently asserted that all information concerning nuclear weapons was "born secret," a legal doctrine that NSA officials have wholeheartedly embraced for cryptologic information.[34]

NSA officials, however, were not content with the protection afforded by the COMINT Law. On May 29, 1959, Congress passed Public Law 86-36, more generally referred to as the National Security Agency Act of 1959. Section 6 of this act stipulates that "no law shall be construed to require the disclosure of any information concerning the organization, functions or activities of the National Security Agency, or of any information regarding the names, titles, salaries, or number of persons employed by NSA." NSA officials have subsequently interpreted this phrase to mean that the agency has the legal authority to protect from public disclosure any *unclassified* information about the NSA or its operations that they deemed to be "sensitive." For all intents and purposes this interpretation exempts NSA records from the mandatory disclosure provisions of the FOIA.[35]

For years NSA officials have effectively used the COMINT Law and Public Law 86-36 to deny access to any information requested through the FOIA relating specifically to SIGINT, even if the information is unclassified. Legal suits challenging either the applicability or the validity of these statutes to the FOIA have invariably failed. In general, federal district and appellate courts have found for the NSA, ruling that the release of requested documents to the plaintiffs pursuant to the FOIA either would disclose a function of the NSA (since signals intelligence is one of the agency's primary functions) or would disclose information about the agency's activities (since any information about an intercepted communication concerns an NSA activity), thus falling within the rubric of Public Law 86-36.[36]

Furthermore, the small and overworked NSA FOIA staff cannot keep up with the ever-increasing number of FOIA requests involving agency records, resulting in a growing backlog of unprocessed FOIA requests. Recent budget cuts of 1995 have also forced the NSA to fire its staff of retirees who had heretofore processed many of these FOIA requests on a part-time basis and to trim the number of full-time NSA employees handling FOIA requests. Consequently, there has been an appreciable slowdown in the NSA's processing of FOIA requests.[37]

NSA officials, moreover, frequently utilize the FOIA "fee waiver denial" to discourage FOIA requests for NSA documents, demanding that requesters agree to pay, in some cases hundreds of dollars, to process their FOIA requests even when there is no likelihood that the requester will get any substantive response. Not surprisingly, a significant number of those submitting FOIA requests for NSA records have given up. Ironically, foreign intelligence operatives would likely pay any amount to obtain NSA secrets through the FOIA and would therefore not be deterred by an NSA fee waiver denial.

As a matter of standard operating procedure, the NSA processes the easiest FOIA requests first, such as requests for copies of the *NSA Newsletter,* but delays processing more difficult requests for classified documents that would require extensive time and effort. It is not unusual, then, for requesters to wait upwards of five years before receiving any NSA reply, substantive or otherwise. The reply often produces disappointment and frustration, without much in the way of tangible results.

Some of this denied information, obtained through other channels, is innocuous. In some cases the NSA's deletions border on the silly. For example, until recently NSA officials and subordinate military components deleted from the documents they released any mention of SIGINT, COMINT, ELINT, or intercepts, despite the fact that the context confirmed what had been excised. NSA officials are also not above "reclassifying" information. For example, portions of a document concerning the 1964 Gulf of Tonkin incidents were deleted. When carefully examined, the deleted material involved verbatim quotations from the Gravel edition of *The Pentagon Papers,* which mentioned COMINT. Rejecting an FOIA appeal that brought up this matter, NSA officials simply declared that "the information had been improperly declassified."

Appeals of the NSA's FOIA denials invariably fail, no matter how well crafted or well justified. In fact, lower court rulings are invariably the final word on the subject. Faced with this seemingly insurmountable wall, most researchers choose not to challenge the NSA's FOIA denials in court.

In recent years, a few hardy souls have taken the NSA to court and have experienced limited success. In November 1992, NSA officials declassified two fifty-year-old texts on cryptanalysis requested by California computer scientist John Gilmore following a short but intense legal battle. They did so only after Gilmore revealed that since 1977 the documents had been accessible at a number of public libraries. Before settling the case, the NSA tried to reclassify the documents, and the U.S. Justice Department threatened to prosecute Gilmore for violating the COMINT Law if he distributed copies of the two texts he had obtained from a public library, stressing that the NSA held that the documents were still classified.[38] After the NSA rejected his initial FOIA request, historian Gar Alperovitz of the Institute for Policy Studies in Washington, D.C., filed suit to declassify World War II diplomatic decrypts. After years of stonewalling, in August 1993 the NSA quietly walked away from the lawsuit and released eight hundred pages of the formerly top secret decrypts to Alperovitz.[39] NSA officials dropped the Alperovitz and Gilmore suits in part because attorneys for both men had filed legal briefs questioning the constitutionality of the COMINT Law and Public Law 86-36, something the NSA desperately wishes to avoid being adjudicated in a court of law.[40]

NSA officials have secretly tried for over fifteen years to exempt agency records from the FOIA for fear that one day the courts may strike down the tenuous protection offered by Public Law 86-36. These fears were heightened by the government's abortive 1979 lawsuit to prevent publication of an article by freelance writer Howard Moreland in *The Progressive* magazine. Moreland's article, which purported to show how a hydrogen bomb was constructed, had been based entirely on declassified documents and open source materials. NSA lawyers recognized the danger posed by this case to their Public Law 86-36 protection from the FOIA because the lawyers for *The Progressive* directly challenged the underlying tenets of the Atomic Energy Act, which in effect stated that all matters involving nuclear weapons were "born secret." Had the federal court in Wisconsin or any appellate courts hearing the case ruled that the provisions of the Atomic Energy Act were unconstitutional, the same argument could have been applied to Section 6 of Public Law 86-36. The constitutional issues posed by *The Progressive* case, however, were never litigated. After leaked copies of Moreland's article began appearing in various publications in the United States and overseas, the government suspended its attempts to block the article's publication.[41]

But *The Progressive* case frightened NSA officials into taking what some in the intelligence community thought was a series of rash and inappropriate actions. In late 1980, NSA Director Bobby R. Inman, Jr., tried unsuccessfully to convince the newly elected Reagan administration to endorse amendments to the FOIA to exempt NSA records from many of the act's provisions. Although the NSA's cryptologic secrets had some statutory protection under Public Law 86-36, Inman advised the Reagan administration that not every court in the land accepted the NSA's interpretation that Public Law 86-36 exempted the agency from the FOIA, and that the exemption was "under continuous and systematic attack by groups seeking access to NSA's records." "This protection," Inman added, "has been eroded by judicial action."[42]

The NSA's proposed total exemption was opposed by many even within the U.S. intelligence community. Inman then proposed amending the act to include a broad exemption for all intelligence information and records, as well as revising the b(3) exemption to make cryptologic records specifically less subject to judicial action. Inman further recommended that President Reagan amend Executive Order 12065 (which set classification standards) to ensure greater protection for cryptologic information and to restore, for cryptologic information, the "concept" that individual items of unclassified information might reveal sensitive information in the aggregate and, as such, deserved classification protection. The Department of Defense and the director of the CIA opposed Inman's recommendations, knowing full well that Congress, which was then controlled by the Democrats, would never agree to this proposal and that, if challenged in court, these modifications to existing law would more than likely be found to be unconstitutional.[43]

Fortunately, there are other avenues for getting some information about SIGINT without having to go through the NSA. Researchers can learn more about the NSA's SIGINT operations by submitting FOIA requests to the three military cryptologic agencies (called SCEs) that are subordinate to the NSA. These SCEs are the U.S. Army Intelligence and Security Command (INSCOM) at Fort Belvoir, Virginia; the Naval Security Group Command (NAVSECGRU) at Fort George G. Meade; and the Air Intelligence Agency (AIA) at Kelly Air Force Base outside San Antonio, Texas. INSCOM's Freedom of Information/Privacy Act Office at Fort Meade is by far the most helpful and professional of the three services, and over the last ten years has proved to be unfailingly helpful and conscientious, following both the letter and the spirit of the FOIA. The AIA's FOIA office does its job well, although I have experienced multiyear delays in obtaining information, in large part because the AIA refuses to declassify any cryptologic information without the NSA's line-by-line approval. Strangely, INSCOM does exactly the same thing but manages to release information to FOIA requesters much faster than the AIA, suggesting that INSCOM does a better job of riding herd on the underfunded and -staffed NSA FOIA unit. In the past, I experienced numerous problems with the Naval Security Group Command's FOIA unit when it was run out of the command's Security Office. But the FOIA function is now managed by the command's Staff Judge Advocate, which has taken steps to revamp and improve the command's FOIA program.

In 1995 a version of glasnost finally descended on the nation's capital. On April 17, 1995, President Clinton issued Executive Order 12958, entitled *Classified National Security Information.* At the time many in the academic and journalistic communities hailed the order because it mandated the declassification within a period of five years of all documents generated by all U.S. government agencies prior to April 1970. Recently, however, academicians have become increasingly frustrated with the snail's pace exhibited by the CIA and other agencies of the intelligence community in declassifying documents pursuant to this order. There is little likelihood that the order will ensure the bulk declassification of any significant records relating to the NSA or post–World War II SIGINT. Section 3.4 of this order exempts from automatic declassification any documents that "reveal information which would impair U.S. cryptologic systems or activities." Not surprisingly, NSA officials have interpreted this provision to mean that NSA records are generally exempt from its provisions, and thus documents relating to post–World War II SIGINT can continue to be withheld from public release. The order's only concession relating to access to cryptologic information is buried in a sentence: "After consultation with affected agencies [meaning NSA], the Secretary of Defense *may* [emphasis added] establish special procedures for systematic review for declassification of classified cryptologic information."[44]

Given the extreme reluctance of NSA officials to release any of the agency's documents, the release of any NSA documents relating to postwar SIGINT is unlikely until after the turn of the century. The NSA currently holds in its cryptologic archives at Fort Meade approximately 129.3 million pages of documents twenty-five years old or older that are subject to Executive Order 12958, almost three times as much paper as held by the State Department. However, the NSA will review only 53.3 million pages of these documents by the year 2000, meaning that the NSA has exempted the remaining 76 million pages from the mandatory review, most of which presumably are from the post–World War II era.[45]

At the urging of former NSA Director John M. "Mike" McConnell, some steps have been taken to open up NSA records. These have included the declassification and release to the public of monographs written by the NSA's Center for Cryptologic History about World War II SIGINT and related topics, allowing NSA and military personnel to publish carefully edited articles about SIGINT in professional journals, and permitting the NSA's small corps of historians to present papers at historical symposia on the accomplishments of the NSA and its predecessor agencies. The NSA has even opened a museum near its Fort Meade headquarters, which contains declassified documents and displays of cryptologic memorabilia.[46]

Despite this new mood of openness, most Washington-based intelligence researchers attribute the spirit of "Glasnost at the Fort" to a two-year public relations campaign by the CIA and the rest of the intelligence community to salvage as much as possible of their budgets in the wake of the end of the cold war and calls for greater fiscal austerity in the American intelligence community. An interesting example of this is the NSA's recent release of several thousand pages of Russian intelligence messages that the NSA had successfully decrypted between 1946 and 1980. Under pressure from Senator Daniel Patrick Moynihan, in July 1995 the NSA and the CIA released the first batch of documents relating to this so-called Venona Program, the joint NSA-FBI operation that began after World War II. Under this program, the NSA sucessfully decrypted Soviet KGB and GRU message traffic (transmitted through Soviet consulates in New York and Washington) and worked with the FBI to identify Soviet agents who had operated in the United States during the war. By October 1996, the NSA had released twenty-nine hundred translations of partially decrypted

Venona traffic and, in conjunction with the CIA, issued a 450–page book containing a selection of the translated documents.[47]

The twenty-nine hundred pages of Venona decrypts and the Venona book mark an excellent beginning toward greater openness at the NSA. At the same time, the Venona releases reveal some basic truths about secrets that have long outlived their usefulness, and they raise the question of why they had been kept secret until the mid-1990s. For example, the Venona materials raise serious questions about the FBI's counterintelligence failures in curbing Soviet espionage activities in the United States throughout World War II, and thus why no public official ever challenged FBI Director J. Edgar Hoover for this failure. The same holds true in England, where British counterintelligence failed to detect the sizable Soviet espionage apparatus operating during the war.

The released Venona documents also raise other questions. Why did the Venona Program continue for thirty years and yet show only modest results following the arrest and conviction of the Rosenberg spy ring in 1950? The released Venona decrypts do not answer the controversy about whether Alger Hiss has been a Soviet spy; they add relatively little to the historical record about why the FBI and MI-5 took three years to identify British Foreign Office official Donald D. MacLean as a Russian spy and yet were unable to keep him and fellow spy Guy Burgess from escaping arrest; and the documents do not explain why the U.S. Justice Department failed to prosecute the dozens of Soviet spies whom NSA and FBI agents did manage to identify through the Venona decrypts—notably Nathan Gregory Silvermaster, William Ludwig Ullman, George Silverman, Lauchlin Currie, Theodore Alvin Hall, and Maurice Halperin.

More important, the NSA, the CIA, and the FBI have still not released a significant number of documents in their possession about the Venona Program, such as NSA's seven-hundred-page internal history of the program and supporting documentation contained in the NSA's Venona Collection at Fort Meade. For reasons that defy easy explanation, the names of a number of American and British individuals identified in the released Venona decrypts as Soviet agents have been deleted. The NSA and the CIA released virtually no information concerning the cooperation between American, British, Canadian, and Australian SIGINT and counterintelligence agencies during the course of the Venona Program, nor have any documents been released about how the FBI identified specific individuals as Soviet spies based on the paltry information contained in the Venona decrypts.[48]

The time has come for NSA officials at minimum to adopt the same constructive approach to selectively declassifying documents of historical importance as their counterparts in the CIA and NRO. In the last five years, the CIA's Center for the Study of Intelligence has released several thousand pages of documents and several book-length publications regarding the history of the CIA from 1946 to the present day, including on the Cuban missile crisis and the Corona spy satellite system, with more releases forthcoming. None of these declassified documents have in any way harmed U.S. national security, but they have advanced our knowledge of the important role the U.S. intelligence community played in formulating policy during some of the most important events in our nation's history. The NSA's equally important contribution to American intelligence history remains unknown, still hidden behind a curtain of secrecy that only becomes more transparent as time goes by.

At a minimum, the remaining documents concerning SIGINT prior to 1946 should be declassified, including all oral histories and the classified historical reports concerning SIGINT written by the staff of the Center for Cryptologic History and its predecessor organizations during the period from World War I to the end of World War II. Then, working in conjunction with the CIA's Center for the Study of Intelligence, the NSA should immediately begin declassifying documents relating to post–World War II SIGINT.

For example, my research has determined that the NSA played a vital intelligence collection role before and during the Cuban missile crisis of 1962. Given the high level of historical interest in this crisis, and the fact that the CIA has already declassified hundreds of pages of documents on the subject, the NSA should join its colleagues in the rest of the intelligence community and reveal its important role in one of the seminal events in twentieth-century American history. As the CIA releases new documents in the years to come on topics such as the role of the intelligence community in the Korean and Vietnam Wars, it is hoped that the NSA will fully participate in these declassification efforts so that a more balanced and complete view of the American intelligence community's role in these events can become publicly accessible.

NOTES

1. John Ferris, "Coming in from the Cold War: The Historiography of American Intelligence, 1945–1990," *Diplomatic History* 19, no. 1 (Winter 1995): 102.

2. Tom Bowman and Scott Shane, "Busy Signals at NSA," *Baltimore Sun*, December 24, 1995, p. 1L.

3. Commission on the Roles and Capabilities of the United States In-

telligence Community, *Preparing for the 21st Century: An Appraisal of U.S. Intelligence* (Washington, D.C.: Government Printing Office, 1996), pp. 96, 132; Memorandum for the NSA/CSS Representative Defense, *NSA Transition Book for the Department of Defense,* December 9, 1992, Top Secret Edition, p. 22 (a copy of this document was provided to the author by Jeffrey T. Richelson); Tom Bowman and Scott Shane, "Battling High-Tech Warriors," *Baltimore Sun,* December 15, 1995, p. 22A; R. Jeffrey Smith, "Making Connections with Dots to Decipher U.S. Spy Spending," *Washington Post,* March 12, 1996, p. A11; Rear Admiral Donald Harvey, USN (Ret.), "Intelligence Notes," *American Intelligence Journal,* Autumn/Winter 1994, p. 94.

4. Executive Order No. 12333, *United States Intelligence Activities,* December 4, 1981, in U.S. House of Representatives, Permanent Select Committee on Intelligence, *Compilation of Intelligence Laws and Related Laws and Executive Orders of Interest to the National Intelligence Community,* 101st Cong., 2d sess., 1990, pp. 528–29; United States Signals Intelligence Directive (USSID) 1, *SIGINT Operating Policy,* June 29, 1987, p. 1, NSA FOIA; Department of Justice, *Report on Inquiry into CIA-Related Electronic Surveillance Activities,* June 30, 1976, pp. 77–79; Memorandum for the NSA/CSS Representative Defense, *NSA Transition Book for the Department of Defense,* pp. 1–2.

5. USSID 1, *SIGINT Operating Policy,* p. 1, NSA FOIA; USSID 4, *SIGINT Support to Military Commanders,* July 1, 1974, pp. 1–2, NSA FOIA; USSID 18, *Limitations and Procedures in Signals Intelligence Operations of the USSS,* October 20, 1968, p. 7, NSA FOIA; Memorandum for the Special Assistant, Office of the Secretary of Defense, *NSA Transition Briefing Book,* December 9, 1980, p. 1, via Jeffrey T. Richelson; NSGTP 69304-B, *Naval Cryptology in National Security,* 1985, p. 59, Naval Security Group Command FOIA; "NSA/CSS Future Day: The Services Perspective," *National Security Agency Newsletter,* October 1996, p. 2, NSA FOIA; Tom Bowman and Scott Shane, "Espionage from the Frontlines," *Baltimore Sun,* December 8, 1995, pp. 1A, 20A.

6. Desmond Ball, *Signals Intelligence in the Post–Cold War Era* (Singapore: Institute of Southeast Asian Studies, 1995); Jeffrey Nicky Hager, *Secret Power: New Zealand's Role in the International Spy Network* (Nelson, New Zealand: Craig Potton Publishing, 1996); Jeffrey T. Richelson, *The U.S. Intelligence Community,* 3d ed. (Boulder, Colo.: Westview Press, 1995), pp. 24–29, 171–96; Mark Urban, *UK Eyes Alpha* (London: Faber and Faber, 1996), pp. 56–69; Neil Munro, "The Puzzle Palace in Post–Cold War Pieces," *Washington Technology,* August 11, 1994, p. 14; Jeffrey Richelson, "Cold War's Wake Transforms Signals Intelligence," *Defense Week,* July 24, 1995, pp. 6–7; Jeffrey Richelson, "Despite Management/Budget Woes, NRO Launches Continue," *Defense Week,* August 12, 1996, p. 16.

7. David A. Fulghum, "Sigint Aircraft May Face Obsolescence in Five Years," *Aviation Week and Space Technology,* October 21, 1996, p. 54.

8. Vice Admiral Michael McConnell, letter to Senator Sam Nunn, April 28, 1992, p. 6, via Jeffrey T. Richelson; Urban, *UK Eyes Alpha,* pp. 159, 169–70; Brigadier General Robert H. Scales, USA, *Certain Victory: The U.S. Army in the Gulf War* (Washington, D.C.: Brassey's, 1994), pp. 189–90; Michael R. Gordon and Bernard E. Trainor, *The General's War* (Boston: Little, Brown, 1995), pp. 285–87.

9. Rick Atkinson, "GIs Signal Bosnians: Yes, We're Listening," *Washington Post,* March 18, 1996, p. A14; Walter Pincus, "U.S. Sought Other Bosnia Arms Sources," *Washington Post,* April 26, 1996, p. A15; Charles Lane and

Thom Shanker, "Bosnia: What the CIA Didn't Tell Us," *New York Review of Books*, May 9, 1996, p. 11; Urban, *UK Eyes Alpha*, p. 217.

10. William M. Carley, "As Cold War Fades, Some Nations' Spies Seek Industrial Secrets," *Wall Street Journal*, June 17, 1991, pp. A1, A5; David E. Sanger and Tim Weiner, "Emerging Role for the CIA: Economic Spy," *New York Times*, October 15, 1995, pp. A1, A12; Paul Blustein and Mary Jordan, "U.S. Eavesdropped on Talks, Sources Say," *Washington Post*, October 17, 1995, p. B1; Scott Shane and Tom Bowman, "America's Fortress of Spies," *Baltimore Sun*, December 3, 1995, p. 12A; Bowman and Shane, "Battling High-Tech Warriors," p. 22A.

11. Ronald Clark, *The Man Who Broke Purple* (Boston: Little, Brown, 1977), p. 249.

12. *ASA Review*, May–June 1947, p. 15, INSCOM FOIA.

13. Vice Admiral B. R. Inman, Jr., "The NSA Perspective on Telecommunications Protection in the Nongovernmental Sector," *Cryptologic Spectrum*, Summer 1979, p. 5.

14. U.S. House of Representatives, Committee on Government Operations, Draft Report, *Interception of International Telecommunications by the National Security Agency* (also known as the "Fink Report"), 1976, p. 23, a copy of which is in the author's files.

15. James Bamford, *The Puzzle Palace* (London: Sidgwick and Jackson, 1983), p. 281.

16. James Burridge, "SIGINT in the Novels of John Le Carré," *Studies in Intelligence*, no. 37 (May 1994): 125–32.

17. The U.S. government has publicly used SIGINT in a number of instances, such as the Tonkin Gulf incidents in August 1964, the North Korean seizure of the USS *Pueblo* in 1968, and the C-130 (1958), EC-121 (1969), KAL 007 (1983), and Brothers to the Rescue shootdown incidents (1996). President Ronald Reagan publicly justified the 1986 air strikes on Libya with NSA intercepts linking Libya to the La Belle Disco bombing in Berlin.

18. NSA, Office of Security, Security Awareness Division, *Security Awareness Bulletin: Protecting Your NSA Affiliation*, June 1987. I am indebted to James Bamford for providing a copy of this document.

19. Mark Tapscott and Myron Struck, "U.S. Intelligence Agencies at an Historic Crossroads," *Defense Electronics*, November 1991, p. 25.

20. Memorandum, *The Necessity for Continuance of Research and Development in the Cryptologic Field*, undated, p. 2, in *Army Security Agency Summary Annual Report, Fiscal Year 1946*, Tab 5, INSCOM FOIA.

21. Lawrence E. Walsh, *Iran-Contra: The Final Report* (New York:: Times Books, 1994), pp. 13, 207; Stephen Engelberg, "Three Agencies Said to Have Received Data About Iran Money Transfers," *New York Times*, November 27, 1986, p. A1; Stephen Engelberg, "A Career in Ruins in Wake of Iran-Contra Affair," *New York Times*, June 3, 1988, p. A18; George Lardner, Jr., "Uncompromising NSA Frustrated North Prosecutors," *Washington Post*, March 19, 1990, pp. A1, A4.

22. *The Joint Study Group Report on Foreign Intelligence Activities of the United States Government*, December 15, 1960, pp. 48, 75. The author thanks Jeffrey T. Richelson for making a copy of this document available.

23. Ferris, "Coming in from the Cold War" p. 92.

24. See, for example, Donal J. Sexton, *Signals Intelligence in World War II: A Research Guide* (Westport, Conn.: Greenwood Press, 1996); Neal H. Pe-

tersen, *American Intelligence, 1775–1990: A Bibliographic Guide* (Claremont, Calif.: Regina Books, 1992); Jonathan M. House, *Military Intelligence, 1870–1991: A Research Guide* (New York: Greenwood Press, 1993); Ferris, "Coming in from the Cold War," pp. 102–5; Hayden B. Peake, "SIGINT Literature, World War I to Present," *American Intelligence Journal,* Spring/Summer 1994, pp. 88–92.

25. A copy of this document can be obtained from the Center for Cryptologic History, National Security Agency, Fort George G. Meade, MD 20755-6000.

26. David Kahn, *The Codebreakers* (New York: Macmillan, 1967); Bamford, *The Puzzle Palace;* Jeffrey T. Richelson and Desmond Ball, *The Ties That Bind* (Boston: Allen and Unwin, 1985); Richelson, *The U.S. Intelligence Community;* Jeffrey T. Richelson, *American Espionage and the Soviet Target* (New York: William Morrow, 1987); Seymour M. Hersh, *The Target Is Destroyed* (New York: Random House, 1986); Hager, *Secret Power.*

27. The best recent feature articles about the NSA are a two-part series written in March 1990 by George Lardner, Jr. ("National Security Agency: Turning On and Tuning In," *Washington Post,* March 18, 1990, p. A1; and "Uncompromising NSA Frustrated North Prosecutors," *Washington Post,* March 19, 1990, p. A1); a two-part series by technology writer Neil Munro that appeared in 1994 ("The Puzzle Palace in Post–Cold War Pieces," *Washington Technology,* August 11, 1994, pp. 1, 14; and "Fear and Loathing, Myths and Mythmakers," *Washington Technology,* August 25, 1994, pp. 18–20); and a six-part series written by reporters Scott Shane and Tom Bowman in the *Baltimore Sun* that appeared between December 3 and December 15, 1995.

28. Other important records regarding American cryptology are contained in the papers of the Joint Chiefs of Staff (RG-218); Records of the Office of the Chief of Naval Operations (RG-38); Records of the Department of State (RG-59); Records of the Secretary of the Navy/CNO (RG-80); Records of the Secretary of War (RG-107); Records of the Office of the Chief Signal Officer (RG-111); Records of the War Department, General Staff (RG-165); Records of the Central Intelligence Agency (RG-263); Records of the National Security Council (RG-273); Records of the Department of the Army (RG-319); Records of the Secretary of Defense (RG-330); and Records of Headquarters, U.S. Air Force (RG-341).

29. For the NSA's refusal to declassify documents relating to the Korean War until after the year 2000, see Eliot A. Cohen, "Only Half the Battle: American Intelligence and the Chinese Intervention in Korea, 1950," *Intelligence and National Security,* January 1990, pp. 131–32; and Eliot A. Cohen and John Gooch, *Military Misfortunes: The Anatomy of Failure in War* (New York: Free Press, 1990), pp. 181–82.

30. See Rear Admiral Edwin T. Layton, USN (Ret.), with Roger Pineau and John Costello, *"And I Was There": Pearl Harbor and Midway—Breaking the Secrets* (New York: William Morrow, 1985), pp. 454–56; Ralph Macpherson, "The Compromise of U.S. Navy Cryptanalysis After the Battle of Midway," *Intelligence and National Security,* April 1987, pp. 320–23; Report for U.S. Army-Navy Communication Intelligence Coordinating Committee, *The Need for New Legislation Against Unauthorized Disclosures of Communication Intelligence Activities,* June 9, 1944, RG-457, Historical Cryptologic Collection, Box 1374, National Archives, College Park, Maryland.

31. George Lardner, Jr., "Curtain Around Cryptography," *Washington Post*, May 18, 1986, p. A1.

32. U.S. House of Representatives Report No. 1895, *Enhancing Further the Security of the United States by Preventing Disclosures of Information Concerning the Cryptographic Systems and the Communications Intelligence Activities of the United States*, 81st Congress, 2d sess. (Washington, D.C.: Government Printing Office, 1950); U.S. House of Representatives, Permanent Select Committee on Intelligence, *Compilation of Intelligence Laws and Related Laws and Executive Orders of Interest to the National Intelligence Community*, 101st Cong., 2d sess. (Washington, D.C.: Government Printing Office, September 1990), pp. 285–86; "The Law on COMINT," *Law and National Security Intelligence Report* 8, no. 6 (June 1986): 1.

33. Lardner, "Curtain Around Cryptography," p. A1.

34. U.S. House of Representatives, Permanent Select Committee on Intelligence, *Compilation of Intelligence Laws*, pp. 297–314.

35. See National Security Agency Act of 1959, Public Law No. 86–36, 73 Stat. 63 (codified as amended at 50 U.S.C. 402), 1988; Senate Report No. 284, 86th Cong., 1st sess., 1959; House of Representatives Report No. 231, 86th Cong., 1st sess., 1959; U.S. House of Representatives, Permanent Select Committee on Intelligence, *Compilation of Intelligence Laws*, pp. 93–102; "Provision of Cryptologic Information to the Congress," *Cryptologic Spectrum*, Summer 1981, pp. 12–13, NSA FOIA.

36. See *Founding Church of Scientology v. National Security Agency*, 197 U.S. App. D.C. 305, 610 F. 2d 824 (D.C. Cir. 1979); *Thomas E. Hayden and Jane S. Fonda v. National Security Agency*, 608 F. 2d 1381; 5 Media L. Rep. 1897; 197 U.S. App. D.C. 224 (D.C. Cir. 1979).

37. Thus, at the time this article was written, I had seventeen FOIA requests still outstanding with the NSA, the oldest of which was more than five and a half years old. The latest reply from the NSA responsive to an FOIA request (June 1996) indicated at the time that the NSA had a backlog of 445 FOIA requests, compared with a backlog of 372 cases in January 1996. Over the last ten years, the average time between submission of an FOIA request and the receipt of documents responsive to that request has been approximately two years!

38. "Cryptography Texts Are Declassified," *Washington Post*, November 27, 1992, p. A20; John Markoff, "In Shift, U.S. Shrugs at Found 'Spy' Data," *New York Times*, November 28, 1992, p. A8.

39. Tim Weiner, "U.S. Spied on Its World War II Allies," *New York Times*, August 11, 1993, p. A9; "Papers Detail U.S. Spying on Its Allies Late in WWII," *Washington Times*, August 17, 1993, p. A6.

40. *John C. Gilmore v. National Security Agency*, 1993 U.S. Dist. LEXIS 7694 (U.S.D.C. Northern District of California, 1993).

41. Vice Admiral B. R. Inman, Jr., "The NSA Perspective on Telecommunications Protection in the Nongovernmental Sector," *Cryptologic Spectrum*, Winter 1979, p. 10, NSA FOIA.

42. The following discussion is based on Memorandum, Inman to Special Assistant, Office of the Secretary of Defense, *Transition Coordination*, December 9, 1980, Chapter VIII, C.2. I thank Jeffrey T. Richelson for making a copy of this document available.

43. Confidential interviews.

44. Executive Order 12958, *Classified National Security Information*, April

17, 1995, contained in *Federal Register* 60, no. 76 (April 20, 1995): 19825–43; Ann Devroy, "Clinton Eases Government's Secrecy Rules," *Washington Post,* April 18, 1995, p. A1.

45. *Report of the Commission on Protecting and Reducing Government Secrecy* (Washington, D.C.: Government Printing Office, 1997), p. 74.

46. Ken Ringle, "Only Sleuths Can Find This Museum," *Washington Post,* January 24, 1994, p. A1.

47. The twenty-nine hundred Venona translations can be found on NSA's Internet homepage at http://www.nsa.gov:8080\. The joint CIA-NSA book is Robert Louis Benson and Michael Warner, eds., *VENONA: Soviet Espionage and the American Response, 1939–1957* (Washington, D.C.: Center for the Study of Intelligence, 1996), which can be obtained from the CIA Center for the Study of Intelligence's Homepage at http://www.odci.gov/csi.

48. The still-classified "Special Analysis Reports" written by NSA cryptanalyst Meredith Knox Gardner (on September 18, 1947; April 16, 1948; April 20, 1948; April 27, 1948; May 11, 1948; June 4, 1948; and July 8, 1948) detail the progress of ASA's cryptanalysts in solving one of the KGB codebooks used during World War II. Without these reports and related FBI memorandums on the counterintelligence investigations undertaken based on the Venona decrypts, it is impossible to deduce how and when certain individuals were identified as Soviet spies during World War II.

5

"National Security" and Freedom of Information: The John Lennon FBI Files

Jon Wiener

"The concept of the 'official secret' is the specific invention of bureaucracy," Max Weber wrote, "and nothing is so fanatically defended by the bureaucracy." This interest in secrecy contravenes a democratic politics dependent on a public informed about government decisions, policies, and actions. Typically, government officials everywhere "keep their knowledge and intentions secret" and thereby avoid criticism, hinder opposition, and maintain power over citizens and their elected representatives.[1] Classified files and official secrets lie at the heart of the modern governmental bureaucracy, and permit the undemocratic use of power to go unrecognized and unchallenged by citizens.

Democracy, however, is not powerless before this practice. In the fight against government secrecy, America has led the world. The Freedom of Information Act (FOIA) was passed by Congress in 1966, requiring officials to make public the information in their files to "any person" who requests it—unless that information falls into a small number of exempted categories, including "national security." The act was substantially expanded in 1974, in the wake of the Watergate revelations of White House abuse of power. The FOIA in effect created a notable challenge to the practice whereby executive officials sought to restrict access to government information and established a different set of priorities dedicated not to the collection and maintenance of secrets but rather to their release to the public. Journalists, scholars, and activists have used the FOIA to scrutinize the operations of government agencies and to expose official misconduct and lying, including the FBI's illegal efforts to harass, intimidate, disrupt, and otherwise interfere with lawful political actions. The FBI files on John Lennon provide an example.

The FBI began its file on Lennon in 1971, when the "clever Beatle" was living in New York and singing "Give Peace a Chance" at anti-war rallies. The Nixon administration learned that he and some friends were talking about organizing a national concert tour to coincide with the 1972 election campaign, a tour that would combine rock music and radical politics, during which Lennon would urge young people to register to vote, and to vote against the war. Early in 1972, Senator Strom Thurmond wrote to Attorney General John Mitchell reporting on Lennon's plans and suggesting that "deportation would be a strategic counter-measure." The Nixon administration promptly began deportation proceedings against Lennon.[2] (Watergate interrupted, and the Ford administration later granted Lennon a green card.)

In 1981 I filed an FOIA request for the John Lennon FBI files. In response, the FBI released approximately two hundred pages, but withheld parts of another one hundred pages, many under the "national security" exemption, claiming among other things that their release "can reasonably be expected" to lead to "foreign . . . military retaliation against the United States."[3] The FOIA permits requesters to appeal such decisions to withhold material by going to federal court. In 1983 the American Civil Liberties Union (ACLU) of Southern California filed suit on my behalf, challenging the FBI's national security claims (and others). The story of that litigation is also the story of how presidents from Reagan to Clinton have responded to the FOIA.*

Before considering that history, it is important to acknowledge that in many respects the FOIA has been a spectacular success, as Americans have demonstrated an impressive appetite for government information. In 1990 federal agencies received 491,000 FOIA requests and spent $83 million responding to them. The Defense Department

---

*Editor's Note: In September 1997, after the manuscript of *A Culture of Secrecy* had gone to press, a settlement was reached in Wiener's suit challenging the FBI's withholding of portions of FBI documents in the FBI's John Lennon files. Under this settlement, the government agreed to pay $204,000 in legal fees and released all withheld information excepting ten documents (withheld on claimed "national security" grounds). The released information added little new information about the FBI's surveillance of Lennon—included in the withheld information were descriptions of an antiwar activist training a parrot to speak profanities and other apparently trivial information about antiwar activists. Wiener and his attorneys at the American Civil Liberties Union of Southern California intend to continue their suit for the release of the withheld ten pages. (See *New York Times*, September 25, 1997, p. B1.)

received 118,000 requests; the Justice Department, 62,000; the INS, 45,000; the EPA, 39,000; the FBI, 11,000; and the CIA, 4,000. The FOIA further requires that agencies report the extent of their denials of such requests: the agency with the highest denial rate in 1990, strangely enough, was the Office of Ethics, which refused to release 75 percent of requested documents. In contrast, the Department of Health and Human Services denied only 2 percent of the requests it received. The staff at the FBI's Freedom of Information section processing FOIA requests consists of eight agents and 245 support employees, 65 of whom work on national security declassification. In 1990, 421,000 previously classified pages were released; requesters filed 993 administrative appeals of decisions to withhold documents; 263 requests that had been denied were in litigation.[4]

The most fundamental justification for governmental secrecy is "national security," and the FOIA exempts from disclosure any material "which reasonably could be expected to cause damage to the national security."[5] Because of the long-standing belief in the legitimacy of keeping secret diplomatic and military information, the claim that releasing particular documents would damage "national security" has been difficult to refute, and thus has been open to abuse by officials with something to hide. How federal officials have interpreted the FOIA's national security exemption provides the most important test of government practice, and lies at the heart of the John Lennon FBI files litigation.

The original FOIA of 1966 had no provision for judicial review of claimed national security information. Material could be exempted "specifically required by Executive Order to be kept secret in the interest of national defense or foreign policy." The law, however, contained no provisions authorizing how courts should consider government decisions to withhold documents under the national security claim. In a 1973 Supreme Court ruling, Justice Potter Stewart pointed out this flaw: the FOIA provided "no means to question any Executive decision to stamp a document 'secret,' however cynical, myopic, or even corrupt that decision might have been."[6] The Court went on to note that Congress could establish procedures to permit courts to review such decisions.

This use of the "national security" exemption to conceal government misconduct came to the fore in 1974, in the wake of the Watergate revelations of the Nixon White House abuses of power. At that time the issue was framed in an apolitical way as a problem of "overclassification of national security information." Congress held extensive hearings documenting this problem, and it accepted the Supreme Court's suggestion, passing a series of amendments that significantly strengthened the FOIA, especially in relation to national security claims. The 1974 amendments instructed courts to determine de novo whether the national security exemption was being properly applied in particular cases. Courts were authorized to conduct in camera reviews of documents for which the government claimed the national security exemption. Most important, courts were empowered to overrule executive officials' decisions classifying documents under this national security claim. For the first time, courts could order the release of improperly classified documents. President Ford vetoed the legislation, objecting specifically to the provision empowering the courts to overrule executive branch classification decisions. This provision, he declared, was an unconstitutional infringement on executive power. Congress overrode Ford's veto, and the amendments became part of the FOIA.

The FOIA assigns the task of determining what constitutes "damage to the national security" to the president, who issues executive orders on classification of documents. During the Carter administration, an executive order permitted the release even of classified national security information—if the public interest outweighed the possible damage to national security.[7] This policy constituted a significant departure from past practices and a major contribution to the democratic process.

The Reagan administration eliminated this balancing act; starting in 1983, the FBI could withhold all documents "the unauthorized disclosure of which reasonably could be expected to cause damage to the national security." Under this policy, the FBI was permitted to withhold any information that might possibly result in damage to the national security, no matter how great the public interest that would be served by its release, and no matter how insignificant or unlikely the damage.

Litigation over the FOIA's national security exemption provides a dramatic record of the fight against government abuse of power, as well as case studies of reason and unreason in the battle between democracy and bureaucratic secrecy. Executive orders governing national security classification recognize the potential for abuse and provide a strong basis for challenging such claims: "In no case shall information be classified in order to conceal violations of law . . . or to prevent embarrassment to a person, organization or agency." The withholding of the Lennon FBI files, which document Nixon's campaign to silence a critic, constitute such a case.

In response to my Lennon FBI files case, the Bush administration argued in court that the assignment of a "national security" classification to any FBI document is "absolute." The judicial review process provided for in the FOIA, it argued, was "limited to a determination that the procedures set forth by the applicable Executive Order have been followed and that the classification decision was made in good faith"; in other words, the Bush administration argued, "the court may not review or second-guess the substantive decision to classify."[8]

The argument that FBI national security claims are inherently legitimate is a statement that FBI misconduct does not exist. It can be an invitation to a police state. This claim of absolute discretion in national security classification has been accepted by some federal courts. The District of Columbia (D.C.) Circuit was one. In another case, the court ruled that judges "lack the expertise necessary to second guess such agency opinions in the typical national security FOIA case," and "any affidavit or other agency statement of threatened harm to national security will always be speculative to some extent."[9] In this view, the job of intelligence agency officials is to determine what constitutes a threat to the national security; it is not the job of the courts.

Since the FOIA in fact permits the federal courts to review agency decisions to classify material, much of the battle against government secrecy has focused on the arcane procedures governing judicial review. The act gives the courts the power to make an independent determination—"de novo" review, including in camera examination of documents the FBI claims concern national security. According to the act, "The burden is on the agency to sustain its action."[10] On the face of it, this section provides a strong check on illegitimate classification and a powerful weapon in the hands of those seeking to expose government wrongdoing.

In practice, however, the federal courts have not been eager to serve as a check on FBI abuse of this process. The courts are not required to conduct such reviews; the law only permits them to do so. Under the standard for judicial review of claimed national security deletions under the FOIA, the court must accord "substantial weight" to an agency's statements about why it seeks to withhold a disputed record. Before the court can conduct an in camera inspection of the withheld documents, it must give the government an opportunity to persuade it not to. The decision to examine disputed documents in any particular case "rests in the sound discretion of the court."[11] Who could object to "sound discretion"? With that guidance, most appeals panels have held that a court need not conduct its own in camera inspection of contested documents if three conditions are satisfied: (1) the FBI has claimed a "reasonable" basis for finding potential harm in the release of documents, (2) the information logically falls under "national security," and (3) no evidence can be found that contradicts the government's claim or that suggests bad faith.

But a finding of bad faith is not a prerequisite for in camera review: a judge may order in camera inspection on the basis of "an uneasiness, or a doubt he wants satisfied." The D.C. Circuit adopted the position of Max Weber when it declared in 1978 that illegitimate claims of secrecy are a characteristic of bureaucracy: "Government officials who would not stoop to misrepresentation may reflect an inherent tendency to resist disclosure, and judges may take this natural inclination into account." The appropriate response, the court declared, is in camera review. Public interest counts: cases in which the public has a strong interest in disclosure would necessitate in camera inspection.[12]

Judicial examination of secret documents provides one check on government abuse of power, but one having an inherently undemocratic aspect: the judicial examinations themselves are secret. The discussion in camera takes place between the judge and the government; the plaintiff seeking release of information is not permitted to participate in such proceedings. The judge hears only the FBI's side of the story, without benefit of arguments from the plaintiff. The adversary nature of legal proceedings is thus lost. Courts have attempted to mitigate this problem by requiring that the public record of a case be as detailed as possible. Communications between the government agency and the judge that are kept secret from the plaintiff and the public—"ex parte submissions"—are permitted "only where absolutely necessary."[13]

When Congress passed the 1974 amendments to the FOIA, bringing the FBI under its authority, lawmakers encouraged participation by plaintiff's counsel in in camera proceedings "whenever possible." Conservative judges, however, have systematically refused to do this in cases involving a claimed national security exemption: "It is not possible without grave risk to allow access to classified defense-related material to counsel who lack security clearance," the D.C. Circuit declared in 1980; another court declared in 1982, "The risk presented by participation of counsel . . . outweighs the utility of counsel, or adversary process" during consideration in camera of national security documents.[14]

Another court of appeals panel went beyond the "reasonable basis" standard for withholding documents and proclaimed a standard of "utmost deference" to U.S. Army decisions regarding the classification of national security documents. "In view of the knowledge, experience and positions held by the three affiants regarding military secrets, military planning and national security, their affidavits were entitled to the 'utmost deference.' "[15] If "utmost deference" were to become the prevailing standard, the judicial review provisions of the FOIA would become virtually useless. Were this to become the standard, the Lennon files would never be released. The pope is supposed to receive utmost deference from Catholics, but nobody in a democracy should be required to treat any government agency with such reverence.

Whenever forced by litigation to defend its refusal to release material on national security grounds, the FBI employs a "codebook approach" to index, itemize, and justify deletions. This approach has been a battleground for those seeking to expose government abuse of power. Under the codebook procedure, the bureau provides the court with an affidavit known as a "Vaughn index," identifying each document withheld, the legal basis claimed for withholding it, and an explanation justifying the withholding.[16] The purpose of the index is to provide the FOIA requester with a meaningful opportunity to contest the FBI's arguments in court. But instead of providing specific written arguments justifying each deletion from an FBI file, the bureau marks deleted passages with code numbers that refer to a master list of justifications for withholding material. Obviously the codebook arguments are generic—boilerplate. The FBI submits the same master list of justifications in all FOIA litigation. Despite the vagueness and generality of the codebook, the courts have been sympathetic to the FBI's claims that its boilerplate procedures are necessary. The codebook played a key role in the John Lennon FBI files litigation.

Executive classification orders have defined "national security" to include foreign government information. That seemingly reasonable definition has provided for some remarkable arguments by the FBI when refusing to disclose particular documents in the Lennon files. The FBI's position was explained in a court declaration on the Lennon files by Special Agent Robert F. Peterson, supervisor of the National Security Affidavits Unit at FBI headquarters, who reported that he has been "designated by the Attorney General of the United States as an original Top Secret classification authority." Peterson informed the court that "intelligence information gathered by the United States . . . from a foreign country" must be withheld from release under the FOIA "due to the delicate nature of international diplomacy." Release of the Lennon information could "jeopardize the fragile relationships that exist among the United States and certain foreign governments." The information in the Lennon file, "if disclosed, could lead to political or economic instability, or to civil disorder or unrest" in the foreign country that supplied the information, or could "jeopardize the lives, liberty or property of United States citizens residing in or visiting such a country or could endanger United States Government personnel or installations there . . . resulting in damage to the national security."[17]

What could the John Lennon FBI file contain that, if released, might have these dramatic consequences? Lennon's file shows that the Nixon administration began deportation proceedings against Lennon in 1972, after learning of his antiwar and anti-Nixon activities in an election year. This is the point at which "information gathered by the United States . . . from a foreign country" enters the story. The Nixon administration claimed as the legal basis for its effort to deport Lennon his 1969 conviction on misdemeanor charges of marijuana possession in Britain. Presumably the FBI's Lennon file contains information from the British government regarding that event, as well perhaps as other information about his political activities there. Canada is another country that almost certainly provided the FBI with information about Lennon; when Lennon was temporarily banned from entering the United States in 1968, he went to Canada to do a series of antiwar broadcasts and interviews aimed at the American media.

Thus, when processing my FOIA request for the FBI's Lennon file, the FBI classification officer deleted material that probably originated with the British and Canadian governments; he marked the blacked-out passage with the code referring to "information concerning the foreign relations on foreign activities of the U.S."; the appropriate codebook section then describes "damage to the national security reasonably expected to result from unauthorized disclosure," and among the boilerplate list of possible damages the FBI includes "foreign military retaliation against the U.S." The codebook was submitted to the court along with Special Agent Peterson's boilerplate claim that in the FBI declarations "every effort was made to devise language of reasonable and sufficient detail to demonstrate the appropriateness of the exemption claims and to provide the Court with a 'suitably informed basis' upon which it can rationally determine that those portions of the documents withheld . . . are in fact properly withheld."[18] The FBI's court documents defending its withholding of the Lennon FBI files refer only to generic damage to the national security; they never refer specifically to Lennon.

What, then, was the court to make of the FBI's claim that release of portions of its Lennon file "can reasonably be expected . . . to lead to foreign military retaliation" against the United States, apparently by Britain and Canada? The Department of Justice brief in the Lennon files litigation defended the FBI's claim that release of portions of the Lennon file could lead to foreign military retaliation against the United States, although toning it down a bit: "At the very least, breach of a confidential relationship with a foreign government could cause a chilling effect on the free flow of vital information of U.S. intelligence and law enforcement agencies."[19]

Despite the vagueness of the FBI's claim that release of particular documents could lead to foreign military retaliation, courts had accepted similar claims in other cases. A 1982 decision of the D.C. Circuit, affirmed by the Supreme Court in 1983, held that "even speculative or ambiguous prediction of harm to foreign relations through release of information provided by foreign governments is sufficiently reasonable and plausible to warrant deference to opinion of agency experts." In another case, a federal district court in Washington, D.C., ruled that requiring an agency to release information obtained from a foreign government in confidence "would undermine future attempts of the United States to gain information from a foreign government source pursuant to a promise of confidentiality."[20]

After the federal district court in Los Angeles accepted the government's arguments regarding withholding the Lennon files, the ACLU appealed to the Ninth Circuit. Ten years after my initial FOIA request for the Lennon files, in July 1991, the Ninth Circuit Court of Appeals called the FBI's claim of foreign military retaliation "far-fetched"—it's hard to disagree with that—and ruled that the bureau had failed to justify withholding documents in the Lennon file.

The Ninth Circuit decision was significant because it held not just that the FBI had failed to process the Lennon files correctly but that the codebook approach was itself unacceptable. The codebook approach, the Ninth Circuit declared, provided the requester with "little or no opportunity to argue for release of particular documents," because "the index provided no information about particular documents." The court ruled that an adequate *Vaughn* index must "not merely inform the requester of the agency's conclusion that a particular document is exempt from disclosure . . . , but afford the requester an opportunity to intelligently advocate release of the withheld documents." The FBI cannot give "broad explanations of alternative harms that might result from the release of withheld information"; instead, the FBI must tie its "general concern about disclosure" with "the facts of this case" by describing the specific injury to national security that would result from each particular disclosure.[21]

The FBI's boilerplate national security claims were not adequate, the Ninth Circuit voted unanimously, because the codebook procedure lacked specificity; the FBI had failed to provide a description of the injury to national security arising from the disclosure of each document. The court instructed the FBI to present a detailed analysis of how it determined in each instance that release of information would harm national security.

Instead of complying with the Ninth Circuit ruling, the FBI appealed to the Supreme Court to review the case. In its brief, the Bush Justice Department declared that the Ninth Circuit decision "poses a serious risk of unlawful disclosures" and "places an intolerable burden on the government." Unconvinced by this argument, the Supreme Court denied the FBI's request to hear the case; all the Nixon, Reagan, and Bush appointees to the Court sided with the ACLU, while the lone vote supporting the Bush Justice Department was Kennedy holdover Byron "Whizzer" White.[22] The case was thereupon remanded to U.S. District Court in Los Angeles, where it had been argued originally.

When Clinton became president, his administration initially took some promising steps toward reversing twelve years of official hostility to the FOIA, stimulating hopes for a resolution of the Lennon FBI files case. Early in Clinton's first term, Attorney General Janet Reno declared a policy she called "maximum responsible disclosure"; Clinton's FOIA policy, she announced, will be based on "a presumption of disclosure." The question remained how the new administration would respond to litigation: when a government agency refuses to release information, and the requester sues to force its release, what kinds of information would the Clinton administration ask the courts to keep secret? In 1993 President Clinton took a significant step when he rescinded the 1981 Reagan policy requiring that the Department of Justice defend in court federal agencies' withholding of information whenever there was a "substantial legal basis" for doing so.

Under the new policy, the federal government will go to court to prevent material from being released "only when an agency reasonably foresees that disclosure would be harmful." In cases where the requested information "might technically or arguably fall within an exemption," Reno declared, "it ought not to be withheld from an FOIA requester unless it need be." This won't radically transform government practice, but it ought to change it. And she concluded with a ringing endorsement of freedom of information: the Clinton administration will administer the FOIA to "make government throughout the executive branch more open, more responsive, and more accountable."[23]

She also promised "a complete review and revision of our regulations implementing the FOIA." Here the task was simple and clear: restore the "balancing act" instituted by former President Carter regarding the national security exemption, a policy that was rescinded in 1983 by the Reagan administration; balance the public interest in release of particular information against the significance and likelihood of damage to the national security caused by its release. This standard could have special significance in the John Lennon FBI files case, where public interest was high and the possible damage resulting from release of the information low.

But the committee that Clinton appointed to consider restoration of the public interest balancing act standard—along with other changes in FOIA policy—consisted exclusively of representatives from the agencies that classified information. Clinton failed to appoint any members representing consumers of information such as journalists, scholars, or public interest groups. Given the presumption among government officials in favor of withholding information, it was not surprising that, when Clinton finally issued his own executive order on classification in 1995, the national security exemption included an extremely weak version of the public interest balancing act. Clinton's order stipulates that, in "exceptional cases," the need to protect national security information "may be outweighed by the public interest in disclosure of the information, and in these cases the information should be declassified."

But who decides? And on what basis? These are obviously the key issues. The Clinton policy assigned this responsibility in all cases to the head of the agency that classified the information, who is to determine, "as an exercise of *discretion,* whether the public interest in disclosure outweighs the damage to national security that might reasonably be expected from disclosure." The term "discretion" means that the agency head is not required to consider the public interest. And the executive order further states that this provision does not "create any substantive or procedural rights subject to judicial review."[24] In a devastating blow to the hopes for expanded freedom of information, in cases like the John Lennon FBI files, Clinton made the public interest balancing act optional.

As of this writing (March 1997), the John Lennon FBI files case remains in U.S. District Court in Los Angeles, where the Clinton Justice Department continues to defend the denial of release of information under the national security exemption.

Even had Clinton and Reno been determined to revive the FOIA, their task would not have been easy. Enemies of the FOIA within the government have developed their own strategy: prevent the creation of documents subject to release under the act. A memo circulated within the space agency (NASA) in 1989 was titled "Suggestions for

Anticipating Requests Under Freedom of Information Act." It pointed out several techniques that could prevent the public from obtaining agency documents. The memo recommended that officials either destroy notes of meetings or rewrite them "in such a way as to minimize any adverse impact should they be publicly disclosed." Officials were instructed to destroy drafts of documents, since "each draft constitutes a separate document potentially subject to disclosure."

The memo further recommended that officials not make annotations directly on their copies of documents, since under the FOIA an annotated copy is regarded as a separate document potentially subject to release. Instead, officials were advised to use "stick-on" notes for annotations; the notes would be subject to release, but "since there is no obligation under FOIA to provide documents in any particular order or relationship to one another, furnishing out-of-context copies of stick-ons can render the information significantly less meaningful." The memo recommended that documents should "avoid references to other documents," since cross-references "can lend context to a document and thereby enhance its informational value should it ultimately be disclosed."[25]

The FOIA exempts from disclosure correspondence and memorandums that are "pre-decisional and deliberative in nature"—an effort to "protect full and frank discussion within the government." This provision, officials were advised, could be employed to prevent disclosure: documents could not be released if they were clearly identified as recommendations rather than decisions. The memo continued, "If you must document a decision"—apparently an action to be avoided if possible— "do not cross-reference any pre-decisional documents or prior recommendations unless you intend to specifically adopt them as part of your decision."[26] There is no reason to think that NASA is the only government agency taking such steps to subvert the FOIA.

Alongside these new initiatives to undermine freedom of information, old patterns of secrecy remain entrenched. CIA Director Robert Gates declared in 1991 that, with the end of the cold war, the agency would reduce secrecy and "make CIA and the intelligence process more visible and understandable" to the public. To accomplish this worthy goal, Gates established a CIA Openness Task Force. The Center for National Security Studies in Washington, D.C., an organization affiliated with the ACLU, filed an FOIA request for documents relating to this task force. Max Weber, the theorist of official secrecy, would not have been surprised by the CIA's reply:

We recently completed a thorough search for material pertaining to your request for records regarding the "recommendations of the Openness Task Force set up by Director Gates" and located one document, a report dated 20 December 1991, which we have determined must be withheld in its entirety.

You have a right to appeal this determination. Address your appeal to the CIA Information Review Committee. Should you decide to do this, please explain the basis of your appeal.[27]

NOTES

1. Hans Gerth and C. Wright Mills, eds., *From Max Weber: Essays in Sociology* (New York: Oxford University Press, 1958), pp. 233, 235. Weber found evidence in a characteristically wide range of examples: "The treasury officials of the Persian shah have made a secret doctrine of their budgetary art and even use secret script. The official statistics of Prussia, in general, make public only what cannot do any harm to the intentions of the power-wielding bureaucracy" (p. 233). The only exception he found in the world history of bureaucracy was in imperial China, where "the official Gazette published the personal files and all the reports, petitions and memorials" of the prebendary officials, which meant that the entire work of officials "took place before the broadest public" (p. 437).

2. The story is told in Jon Wiener, *Come Together: John Lennon in his Time* (New York: Random House, 1984).

3. *Jonathan M. Wiener v. FBI* [hereafter *Wiener v. FBI*], Peterson Declaration, 32–33.

4. *Access Reports* 17 (Oct. 30, 1991), 5; author's interview with Marvin Lewis, assistant chief, FOIA/PA Section, FBI.

5. 5 U.S.C. 552 (b)(1). Weber recognized the ubiquity of the "national security" claim: Gerth and Mills, *From Max Weber*, 233.

6. *EPA v. Mink*, 410 U.S. 73, p. 95.

7. Executive Order No. 12065, 3 C.F.R. 190 (1979).

8. "*Wiener v. FBI*," "Defendants' Memorandum of Points and Authorities in Support of Motion for Summary Judgment," n. 5, 13–14.

9. *Halperin v. CIA*, 144, 148.

10. 5 U.S.C. 552(a)(4)(B).

11. *Ray v. Turner*, 587 F. 2d (D.C. Cir. 1978), 1187.

12. *Hoch v. CIA*, 593 F. Supp. 675 (D.D.C. 1984), 680–84; *Ray v. Turner*, 587 F. 2d 1187 (D.C.Cir. 1978), 1195; *Allen v. CIA*, 636 F. 2d 1287 (D.C. Cir, 1980).

13. *Allen v. CIA*, 1298.

14. Ibid., 1386; *Weberman v. NSA*, 668 F. 2d 676 (2d Cir. 1982).

15. *Taylor v. Department of the Army*, 684 F. 2d 99 (D.C. Cir. 1982).

16. The term "*Vaughn* index" comes from *Vaughn v. Rosen*, 484 F. 2d 820 (D.C. Cir. 1973), cert. denied, 415 U.S. 977 (1974), which established the system of itemizing and indexing the government's justifications for refusing to disclose a document.

17. *Wiener v. FBI*, Peterson Declaration, 1–2, 26, 32–33.

18. *Wiener v. FBI*, Peterson Declaration, 9.

19. *Wiener v. FBI* on appeal, Brief for the Defendants, 19.

20. *American Jewish Congress v. Department of the Treasury,* 549 F. Supp. 1270; aff'd mem, 713 F. 2d 864; cert. denied, 464 U.S. 895; *Republic of New Afrika v. FBI,* 656 F. Supp. 117 (D.C. Cir. 1986).

21. *Wiener v. FBI,* 943 F. 2d, No. 88–5867 (9th Cir. July 12, 1991), 8747, 8748.

22. *Wiener v. FBI,* on appeal, Defendant's Petition for Rehearing, 13; *FBI v. Wiener,* Petition for Cert., April 1992, 19, 21.

23. "Clinton Memorandum on Administration of Freedom of Information Act," October 4, 1993.

24. Executive Order 12958 on Classified National Security Information, issued April 18, 1995. See also John Wicklein, "Foiled FOIA," *American Journalism Review,* April 1996, p. 36; "The Struggle Against Secrecy," *New York Times* editorial, January 3, 1996, p. A14.

25. The memo was published under the title "Instructions: Lost in Space," *Harper's,* June 1992, pp. 25–26.

26. The document was discovered in 1992 by investigators for the House Subcommittee on Investigations and Oversight; the subcommittee's chairman, Howard Wolpe, called it "a very serious and deliberate attempt by [NASA] to subvert not only the Freedom of Information Act but the rights of Congress and the public to review agency decision-making processes" (quoted in ibid., p. 25).

27. "Gates's Glasnost," *Harper's,* June 1992, p. 25.

6

Playing the Information Game: How It Took Thirteen Years and Two Lawsuits to Get J. Edgar Hoover's Secret Supreme Court Sex Files

Alexander Charns and Paul M. Green

Imagine the Freedom of Information Act as a television game show. Say, "WHEEL—OF—FORTUNE!" And picture Vanna White, the silent, smiling model who launched a thousand vowels, in charge of information management at the Federal Bureau of Investigation. To play, address your request to Vanna at the J. Edgar Hoover Building in Washington, D.C. There are 10,500 other requests queued up for a chance to look at 3.3 million pages of documents. How will this affect the book you're writing about how the FBI corrupted the Supreme Court?

Six years go by. WHEEL OF FORTUNE is popular. It's finally your turn. Rows of squares filled with thousands of blackened letters appear on a giant board. You must guess which squares hide the records you requested. Stand right there, next to game show host and director of the FBI, Pat Sajak. Speak into the microphone. If you guess correctly, Vanna will turn the card over and reveal the records—if they exist and are not subject to one of the nine statutory game show exemptions.

The rules of the game are complex, and your request must be precise. It's really best if you have a lawyer standing by. Vanna's helpful up to a point, and you get boxes of documents no one else has ever seen. Some are heavily censored. Then Pat Sajak orders Vanna not to turn the card.

You have to sue Vanna in federal court. It takes your lawsuit eight and a half years from start to a partial settlement. You publish your book four years before the litigation is even close to ending. The book has some juicy revelations of official misconduct, but you still don't know what's behind the many rows of

WHEEL OF FORTUNE squares. Vanna smiles her information Mona Lisa smile. You are still curious.

Your lawsuit is ongoing. You've played through three information Dark Ages overseen by Republicans. The Democratic president and his attorney general announce an information perestroika with a presumption in favor of disclosing information. The new openness allows you to settle large portions of your legal claims. Perky Vanna is gone, along with her Republican overseers, and the new document hostess gives you a memo that the bad old FBI claimed you didn't even request.

The memo is from Hoover's supersecret stash of files he kept in his own office. It's a bombshell like something out of a John Grisham novel. One of the justices, an FBI informer himself, might have been blackmailed by allegations of homosexuality by J. Edgar, who himself had been hounded by questions about his sexual proclivities. That would have made an explosive addition to your book. It has been thirteen years since you requested this information.

Trying to obtain FBI records using the Freedom of Information Act (FOIA) is not supposed to be like a TV game show. After thirteen years seeking the FBI's documentation of its relationship with the Supreme Court and various of its justices—eight of those years spent in litigation—we have found that while the process can be just as much *fun* as a game show, it might yield less reliable results.[1]

REAL "X-FILES": THE TRUTH IS OUT THERE
(MAYBE)

The FBI, with television agents Fox Mulder and Dana Scully in pursuit, really does maintain "X-Files," records containing secrets of historical significance that it holds dear and prefers not to release.[2] Some of these secrets are neither exempt from the FOIA nor properly classifiable. This essay will recount our series of FOIA requests, through the morass of FBI bureaucracy, onto the shoals of federal litigation, and finally to the receipt of thirty-year-old memos about the alleged sexual escapades of a Supreme Court justice.

Somewhere, Over the Rainbow . . .

If the Freedom of Information Act[3] could be taken at face value, an FOIA request would seem to be a straightforward and efficient tool for historical research. One need only request all FBI records about a particular justice or the Supreme Court, and twenty days later a package would be sent containing all the FBI documents necessary to write the desired history.

Unfortunately, it never worked that way. To begin with, the FOIA exempts nine categories of information from mandatory disclosure. These exemptions are subject to interpretation and are quite nettlesome to apply. As a practical matter, an agency might not be able to review documents and separate out the nonexempt information within a time frame remotely close to the time period mandated by the FOIA.

For another thing, it is simply not in the perceived self-interest of a secretive agency, such as the FBI, to release sensitive information that may subject it, or persons with whom it has had dealings, to controversy or criticism. There is certainly some degree of internal bridling against the FOIA, and some degree of covert resistance against its requirements by the very officials responsible for its implementation.

I first began research about the FBI and the Supreme Court in 1983 when submitting an FOIA request for all FBI records on Chief Justice Earl Warren, Associate Justice William O. Douglas, and the FBI's surveillance of the U.S. Supreme Court. In response to my repeated follow-up letters, FBI officials finally informed me in May 1984 that my request about the Supreme Court was not specific enough. So, I tried again: "I am requesting a complete search of all filing systems and locations for records . . . pertaining to the United States Supreme Court as a body."[4] Since this broad request about the high court seemed to be difficult for the FBI to process, I also asked for all FBI records on Justices Abe Fortas, Felix Frankfurter, and Hugo Black and on other specified federal judges and court personnel.

In response, the head of the FBI's Records Management Division wrote me on September 4, 1984: "A search of the indices to our central records system files at FBI Headquarters did not reveal any pertinent information on the United States Supreme Court as a body."[5] What I did not know at the time was that on August 6, 1984, an FBI employee (probably the same one who prepared the September 4 letter) had checked the FBI's general indices[6] and had located three main files and five cross-references to the "United States Supreme Court," including a document called "United States Supreme Court Law Clerks"—the latter pertaining to an alleged "left-wing ring" of clerks, which was itself just one serial in a two-thousand-page file containing a variety of information on the Supreme Court.[7] The FBI's general indices listed this file under the heading "Supreme Court."

I found out about this two-thousand-page trove of records about the high court only because bureau officials had sent me, apparently by mistake, part of an internal memorandum that described who I was, what I was doing, and the type of information I was being provided.[8] Thus prompted, I requested my own FBI file, which I received in 1987 after a three-year delay. This file totaled some nine hundred pages of correspondence, search slips (which revealed the search prompts used and the files located as a result of the search), and internal memorandums, which showed that FBI personnel had indeed located as early as 1984 both main files and "see references" on the Supreme Court at the very time I was being told that the FBI maintained no such records.[9] This discovery, in turn, prompted me to request previously "overlooked" files.[10]

My new requests prompted a phone call, on August 11, 1987, from Helen Near, an employee of the FBI Freedom of Information–Privacy Acts (FOIPA) Section. When processing one of my requests, she informed me, an entire file on the Supreme Court had been located. The file totaled twelve hundred pages (later expanded to some two thousand pages when a newspaper clippings appendix was added). Did I want it? It ultimately proved to be headquarters file 62-27585, consisting of reams of documents, including the memo on left-wing law clerks, identified on the August 6, 1984, search slip as the seventy-fourth serial in this file.[11]

By this time, the FBI had released enough information to enable me to write several articles on individual justices and the bureau.[12] However, I had yet to receive the FBI's largest file on the Supreme Court, and it appeared that FBI officials were determined to ignore my other requests for a search of the bureau's electronic surveillance indices, as well as "special file rooms," "do not file" files, and "official and confidential" files. With the J. Roderick MacArthur Foundation and the Institute for Southern Studies now providing financial support, I found myself an attorney, and in March 1980 we filed a complaint in the federal court in Greensboro, North Carolina.[13]

In response to our initial flurry of motions, Justice Department lawyers filed an answer that basically said I should be sent packing. My lawyer, Paul Green, was advised that if I would withdraw all my pending motions, I would be invited to FBI headquarters in Washington, D.C., for a special tour of the FBI FOIA Section. I could then talk with an FBI representative about how I might better frame my FOIA requests. Their view seemed to be that I was trying to "make a career" out of requesting FBI records but had been "shooting [my]self in the foot" by misframing my FOIA requests.

We declined the offer. However, our aggressive litigation strategy seemed to be having all the effect of shooting spitballs at the hindquarters of a brontosaurus. We were particularly disappointed that the court wouldn't allow pretrial discovery into the FBI's policies and procedures for complying with the FOIA itself. Nonetheless, Paul Green discovered that such information was required to be kept publicly available under another subsection of the FOIA, whether or not it was formally requested. Because the FBI was not complying with this other subsection, Paul and I exchanged hats, and I, acting as his lawyer, filed suit in the U.S. District Court for the Eastern District of North Carolina in Raleigh, where Paul maintained his law office.[14] During the ensuing two years in court, we obtained thousands of pages of internal FBI memorandums dating back to the FOIA's inception,[15] plus an injunction requiring the FBI to maintain and make available to the general public a current edition of its *Freedom of Information/Privacy Acts Manual* at the reading room at FBI headquarters in Washington, D.C., as well as a court order for attorney fees. Even though the judge denied our motion for frivolous litigation sanctions against the government attorneys (the FBI had taken the ridiculous position that it was not an "agency" within the meaning of FOIA subsection (a)(2), despite a federal regulation explicitly requiring the FBI to place its policy materials in the J. Edgar Hoover Building Reading Room), the idea of making a career out of suing the FBI was beginning to have a certain charm.

The *FOIPA Manual* shed little light on Hoover's "Official and Confidential" (O&C) files, which had been a bone of contention from the outset. We had argued that this eighteen-thousand-page collection of Hoover's most private records must be searched page by page for references to the Supreme Court and its justices. In response, the FBI had steadfastly maintained that Hoover's O&C file was fully integrated within the FBI's general indices, and thus no special search was required.

On March 28, 1989, Judge N. Carlton Tilley held a hearing to inquire into this and other matters. Three FBI agents, including Chris Flynn and Angus Llewellyn, attended from Washington. Flynn addressed the court about my requests concerning Hoover's O&C files, conceding for argument's sake that "there may be a mother lode of information that Mr. Charns is interested in." The problem was accessing these files. The only index, Flynn said, was the FBI's general indices and the electronic surveillance (ELSUR) index, which were set up for the convenience of the FBI, not FOIA requesters.

We later found out that this wasn't exactly true. Hoover's O&C file contains an index to the 164 folders contained therein; the index lists the names of four Supreme Court justices, all of whom were the subjects of my FOIA requests then under litigation.

Even without this knowledge, we convinced Judge Tilley that the FBI had not proved that its search for records was adequate. Tilley accordingly ruled that the FBI's exemption claims would have to be reviewed in camera, in the judge's chambers, without our presence. He then appointed U.S. Magistrate Russell Eliason to serve as Special Master. Eliason set a relaxed timetable, allowing more than eighteen months for the FBI to process records and file declarations establishing that it had complied with the FOIA.

As one result, the FBI finally released its file entitled "Supreme Court," which showed, among other revelations, that three highly placed court employees served as FBI sources of information during the 1950s.[16] Then, out of the blue, in December 1989, the FBI released to me memorandums detailing the FBI's 1966 approach of Justice Abe Fortas regarding a criminal case then pending before the Supreme Court.[17] These memos were the first indications that Justice Fortas had served as an FBI informer while on the high court. Subsequent research indicated that the FBI's contact with Fortas may have influenced the high court's deliberations in cases involving illegal FBI electronic surveillance.[18] Although the memos had clearly come from Hoover's O&C files and were responsive to my FOIA requests, the FBI steadfastly continued to maintain that it had no *obligation* to find the memo and give it to me. These memos were being provided "as a courtesy."

In addition to the "courtesy" copies of memorandums long kept secret at FBI headquarters, bureau officials produced many pages of records under a court-supervised scheduling order. In 1991, Eliason issued his recommendation: some of the FBI's exemption claims would be upheld, some would be overruled, and the FBI would have to provide better evidence that Hoover's O&C files had been properly indexed and the index adequately searched.

There the case sat for five years. Except for occasional correspondence, we all went on to other things. (I did finish my book, published by the University of Illinois Press under the title *Cloak and Gavel: FBI Wiretaps, Bugs, Informers and the Supreme Court*.) Pending lawsuits, however, have many annoying qualities, one of which is that they very seldom go away all by themselves. Eventually, Judge Tilley reviewed Eliason's recommendation, upheld most of it, and set a date by which the FBI had to comply.

As a July 26, 1996, hearing date approached, Paul reviewed everything the FBI had ever submitted about Hoover's O&C file and prepared a memorandum to the court relying almost entirely on the FBI's own statements. These included admissions such as the FOIPA section chief's 1989 letter to me stating that information in Hoover's O&C files was "not separately retrievable through our indices,"[19] and a declaration on file with the court in which Agent Llewellyn stated under oath that "[a] page-by-page review of the voluminous [Hoover

O&C] file would have been necessary to locate the specific references to Abe Fortas."[20]

We also studied the actual index to the Hoover O&C files, which had been sent to me by another FOIA requester.[21] Only a few folder titles were blacked out. By now, all but perhaps a thousand pages of Hoover's O&C file had been made public at least in part—including files entitled "Frankfurter, Felix," "Jackson, Robert H.," and "Murphy, Attorney General Frank."

WHEEL OF FORTUNE!

But the index held an important clue. Paul noticed that one of the blacked-out titles, folder 71, happened to fall right between folder 70 ("Foreign Influence in the Black Extremist Movement") and folder 72 ("Foxworth, P. E."). In addition, the black censor's mark for folder 71 was exactly eleven letters long—the exact number of letters in F-O-R-T-A-S, A-B-E, including the comma and the space. Elated, we pointed out our discovery in a memorandum to the court, hopeful that this would clinch our motion for a page-by-page search of the O&C files.

Days before the hearing, the government's lawyer admitted that, indeed, folder 71 was entitled "Fortas, Abe." When we arrived at the courthouse in Greensboro, Julia Eichhorst,[22] an FBI FOIA analyst, handed me the folder documenting a sexual allegation against a sitting Supreme Court justice. There was no claim that the material was being provided merely as a courtesy.[23]

Do You Want to Know a Secret? Will You Promise Not to Tell?

Liberal Justice Fortas had served many masters while he was on our nation's highest court from 1965 until 1969, at which time he resigned in disgrace following allegations of financial improprieties. Fortas served variously as presidential adviser, associate justice, and confidential informer for the FBI. During 1966, Fortas revealed the secret Supreme Court conference discussions of his brethren involving an electronic surveillance case of special importance to FBI Director Hoover. Fortas did this in an effort to help President Lyndon Johnson politically against his rival Robert Kennedy.[24] At Hoover's behest, Fortas had also convinced Justice William Brennan to fire his law clerk Michael Tigar because of his perceived radical politics.[25] By the summer of 1967, with the city of Detroit in flames, Abe Fortas, presidential adviser and justice, became the one informed upon.

The newly released records showed that on July 20, 1967, Joseph

Purvis, the head of the FBI's Washington Field Office, sent Cartha DeLoach, the number three man at FBI headquarters, a three-page memo reflecting "possible homosexual activities on the part of Justice Abe Fortas." This must have been very troublesome for DeLoach. Fortas and DeLoach were very close to President Lyndon Johnson. Fortas was married to high-powered Washington, D.C., tax lawyer Carolyn E. Agger, a partner in the prestigious firm of Arnold and Porter. DeLoach considered Fortas a brilliant lawyer and a friend with whom he occasionally socialized.[26] And Fortas had been "friendly with the FBI."[27]

DeLoach took the memo to Clyde Tolson, second in command and longtime companion of FBI Director Hoover.[28] Tolson and De-Loach recommended to Hoover that "a memorandum be prepared forwarding this information to the Attorney General [Ramsey Clark]," the liberal son of conservative Supreme Court Justice Tom Clark.

Why report such an allegation to the head of the Justice Department? FBI procedures in place at the time required such reports. As early as the 1920s, moreover, Hoover had created a so-called obscene file to maintain, separate from the FBI's main files, examples of pornography that agents had collected throughout the country. In the 1950s, a separate index was created listing the names of alleged homosexuals. Congress had come to view gays as a security threat because of their perceived susceptibility to blackmail. In response, in 1951 the FBI director started a formal "sexual deviates" program to identify, document, and remove homosexuals working for the federal government. A person was even "designated to receive information concerning sex deviates among employees of the Judicial Branch of the Government."[29]

Hoover, however, decided not to report the homosexuality allegation against Fortas to Attorney General Clark, whom he despised. Beneath the Tolson and DeLoach recommendation, Hoover scrawled his response: "No. DeLoach should see Fortas." DeLoach met Fortas and reported back on this meeting:

> Pursuant to the Director's instructions, I saw Justice Fortas at his home at 5:10 P.M. on 7/24/67. I told him we received an allegation from a source of information reflecting participation in homosexual activities on his part. I stated that the Director wanted this matter discreetly and informally brought to his attention so that he would be aware of such an allegation. I mentioned that the FBI was taking no further action in connection with this matter and that the fact that the Director was making this available to him was strictly for his own personal protection and knowledge.

Justice Fortas was handed the attached memorandum[30] so he could read it personally.*

After reading this memorandum, [Fortas] told me that the charges were ridiculous and absolutely false. He stated he had never committed a homosexual act in his life and while he might be properly accused of normal sexual relations while a young man and during his married life, he most certainly had never committed homosexual acts at any time.

With respect to the arrest records of one XXXXXXX XXXXXXXXXXXXXXX who had been arrested on three different occasions by the Metropolitan Police for homosexual activity, Justice Fortas told me he wasn't surprised to learn of this as he and XXXXXXXXXXXXXXXXXXX always felt a little suspicious toward XXXXXXXXXXXXXXXXXXXXX and has served in this capacity for the past five years. XXXXXXXXXXX stated that he and XXXXXXXXXXXXXXXXXXXXXXXXXX in the past, have noted that XXXXXXXXX seems to be somewhat effeminate and that he never tried to date the girls XXXXXXXXXXXXXXXX While not making any commitment, Justice Fortas stated that XXXXXXXXXXXX arrest record could certainly prove most embarrassing to XXXXXXXXXXXX and that something would have to be done about the situation.

Justice Fortas expressed great appreciation for having been provided with the above facts. He asked that his thanks be extended to the Director for having handled the matter in this manner. There followed a brief discussion concerning the racial situation in Detroit inasmuch as Justice Fortas has been at the White House all day at the President's request,[31] working on this matter.[32]

---

*The attached memo, dated July 20, 1967, follows:
XXXXXXXXXXXX is an active and aggressive homosexual who has been an informant of the Washington Field Office since XXXXXXXXXXX He is XXX and over the years has provided a great deal of reliable information. . . . On XXXXXXXXXXXXXXXX advised a Washington Field Office agent that XXXXXXXXXXXXXXXXXXXXXXXXXX he had "balled" with Abe Fortas on several occasions prior to Mr. Fortas' becoming a Justice of the United States Supreme Court. Informant stated that to "ball" is to have a homosexual relationship with another male. Informant quoted XXXXXXXX as stating XXXXXXXXXXXXXXXXXXXXXXXXXXXX Informant stated XXXXXXXX said he had met Fortas through XXXXXXXXXXXXXXXXXXXXXXXXXXXXXXXXXXXXXX Informant stated he knew XXXXXXXX personally as a homosexual who had in fact been arrested in the past at a "gay" party. Metropolitan Police Department records reflect additional arrests of XXXXXXXXXXX for Disorderly Conduct. He elected to forfeit $10. fine on each occasion. These records show his occupation as XXXXXXXXXX

Was Hoover blackmailing a sitting Supreme Court justice or protecting a political ally and friend to the president? He might have been doing both. While DeLoach liked and respected Fortas, Hoover "didn't like Fortas"[33] and referred to him as a "screwball."[34] DeLoach claims that Fortas was given the memo as a "gratuity" or a "tip-off" for having helped the FBI in the past.[35]

Hoover and his subordinates were no strangers to the game of sex, sleaze, and slime. In an infamous example, bureau officials had attempted earlier to brand the Reverend Martin Luther King, Jr., as a sexual degenerate. After an anonymous FBI threat did not silence King, surveillance transcripts were leaked to the press, but nobody in the media would publish them.[36] Washington insiders were not immune to a slightly more genteel version of this game. Other researchers have noted that "when the Bureau did hold compromising information about a congressman, it was standard procedure to confront him with that knowledge and then promise to be discreet."[37] Unlike King, however, Fortas had done nothing to offend the powerful FBI director. On the contrary, he had proved to be a useful ally, or at least a serviceable tool. As Justice William Brennan commented years later, LBJ and Hoover "used Fortas for a lot of things."[38]

Hoover treated this homosexuality allegation against Fortas differently from a damaging sexual allegation against LBJ three years earlier. In 1964, DeLoach and Fortas had themselves worked together to ward off a charge that LBJ had sex with a Washington, D.C., prostitute. Fortas, as "a close friend of President Johnson," was given a tape-recorded interview with a "20 year old prostitute" that recounted "her numerous alleged sexual relationships with a number of prominent Government officials, including President Lyndon B. Johnson, deceased President John F. Kennedy and Attorney General Robert F. Kennedy."[39]

Courtney Evans (Hoover's liaison to Attorney General Robert Kennedy) describes how this was done: "Fortas secured the tape . . . because President Johnson had heard about its existence and asked Fortas to look into it. Fortas told Katzenbach that he had listened to enough of the tape to 'make him sick' and that he would turn it over to the FBI Agents who called at his office."[40] The prostitute later admitted to the FBI that she had lied about having sex with President Johnson, the late President Kennedy, and Robert Kennedy, and that her statements were part of a blackmail plot. She continued to maintain, nonetheless, that she had had sex with three U.S. senators and a congressman, two army generals and a colonel, all of whom she named and were listed in the FBI memos. Cartha DeLoach transmitted this transcript of the tape to the White House.[41]

The incomplete information that has been released suggests that the allegation against Fortas was a fabrication. Although Fortas's statements to DeLoach confirm that he at least knew his accuser, none of Fortas's biographers have mentioned any allegations of homosexuality or bisexuality. Fortas remained married for forty-seven years until his death in 1982. However, for purposes of blackmail and influence, the allegation need not have had any basis in fact. The memorandum had been shown to Fortas and then tucked away in Hoover's secret files rather than investigated. If it ever came to light during Fortas's lifetime, it could result in an embarrassing and possibly damaging inquiry. Why did Hoover have DeLoach show the memo to Fortas instead of reporting it to the attorney general? Why did he keep the memos in his office files rather than destroying them as a friend or ally might do? In the end, we are left with conjecture.[42]

The Fortas memos remained in one of the most safe and secure places in Washington, D.C.—J. Edgar Hoover's office at FBI headquarters.[43] They were locked away from prying eyes in 1967. They survived Hoover, who died in 1972, and were then placed in the FBI's "Special File Room" along with the rest of the O&C files. The memos slipped by the intelligence oversight investigations after Watergate. They were withheld from at least one other FOIA requester who was not in a position to file suit.[44] Not until the summer of 1996, when the censored contents of folder 71 were handed to us in a federal courthouse in Greensboro, North Carolina, did the sexual allegations about Justice Fortas become public.

FBI FOIA officials clearly knew all along, even as they were framing their position that the FBI should not be required to look for this material about Justice Fortas, exactly what they would find if they did look. Particularly troubling is Agent Angus Llewellyn's explanation under penalty of perjury of why the material about Fortas serving as an FBI informer was not located in response to my various FOIA requests:

> One of the "see" references [to Abe Fortas] was file number 62-116606, the "Official and Confidential" files of former FBI Director J. Edgar Hoover. A page by page review of the voluminous file would have been necessary to locate the specific references to Abe Fortas. . . . The "Official and Confidential" files are comprised of approximately 18,000 pages with 164 different subject matters indexed to the general indices to the FBI Central Records System.[45]

At best, this explanation reflects Agent Llewellyn's insufficient personal knowledge about Hooves O&C files. In fact, the Fortas "see" or cross-reference to Hoover's O&C file referred not to materials in the Fred Black folder (number 37) but to a named reference to the *Abe Fortas* folder (number 71).[46] A page-by-page review was *not* necessary to locate this other folder. Agent Llewellyn needed only look at the index at the front of Hoover's O&C file under "F" for "Fortas" to locate folder 71.

With some help from Judge Tilley, we managed to hammer out a settlement of the remaining issues: the FBI would do a page-by-page search of the remaining portions of Hoover's O&C files, would make additional searches for records about the Supreme Court, and would process all other cross-references to Abe Fortas. We would give up the claim to many hundreds of pages of classified electronic surveillance records in which members of the Court such as William O. Douglas had been referenced. The FBI would explain the context of these records, and the documents would be preserved for future researchers.[47] The FBI would pay attorney fees.[48]

CONCLUSION

Has the FOIPA Section returned to the good old days of maximum information disclosure instituted during the Carter administration? Yes and no. Yes, President Clinton and Attorney General Janet Reno have made positive declarations about improving access to government information. There is a new executive order on classified information. Yes, there are many hardworking FOI analysts at the FBI, like Julia Eichhorst, who were always courteous despite having to spend hundreds of hours processing my requests.

No, because today the wait for information is longer than during the late 1970s (longer even than during the 1980s under the restrictive policies of Presidents Reagan and Bush).[49] For example, when Thurgood Marshall's FBI files arrived in my office after a three-year wait,[50] I found that the FBI again ignored my request for electronic surveillance records, as it had earlier ignored my request for information on the Supreme Court. In response to my request for all cross-references to Justice Marshall, the FBI told me that it "will not be able to process them anytime in the foreseeable future."[51] Under this new FOIPA Section policy, none of Hoover's O&C memos about Justice Fortas's role as an informer or the sexual allegations against him would have been processed for release because, according to the FBI, they were indexed to Fortas as cross-references and not as main files.

The FBI has never accepted that the "FOIA is a *disclosure* act, not a *protection of information* act."[52] Until the FBI follows President Clinton's and Attorney General Reno's lead, the decade-long delays and incomplete disclosures will continue.[53] The truth may be out there, but it may take a lifetime to play the FOIA game.[54]

NOTES

1. "I" refers to FOIA requester and author Alex Charns; "we" refers to lawyers Alex Charns and Paul Green.

2. Real "X-Files," known within the FBI as "Do Not File," "June," "Personal & Confidential," or "Official & Confidential" files, may come to current agents' attention for the first time only because they fall within the scope of an FOIA request; or they may have been jealously guarded for some time in a cache of sensitive records designated for special handling at the time they were created. Either way, the FBI's willingness to provide requesters with volumes of records responsive to their FOIA requests is not inconsistent with the agency's simultaneous burial of one or more "X-Files" along the way. Some of the most sensitive records were kept in J. Edgar Hoover's "Official & Confidential" (hereafter "O&C") files. Hoover kept these records in his office, separate from the ordinary FBI information indices. Some of these had been designated by him as "Personal & Confidential," and were slated for posthumous destruction. The full record-destruction plan was not carried out.

3. 5 U.S.C. section 552.

4. The request went on: "including but not limited to FBI surveillance, bugging, wiretapping, efforts to force resignation, attempts to influence decision-making, attempts to gain copies of court documents prior to public release, and use of Court employees as informants, directed at the Court as a body or the above-named Justices including but not limited to files and documents captioned in, or whose captions include . . . 'United States Supreme Court' . . . in the title. This request specifically includes 'main' or 'see reference' files [and the] ELSUR Index." Charns to FBI, May 17, 1984, 190-37116-21x2.

5. FBI to Charns, September 4, 1984, 190-37116-29x3.

6. For an explanation of the FBI Central Records Systems, see e.g., *Federal Register* 54, no. 197 (October 13, 1989): 42066 *et seq.*, and the most recent FOIPA updates in the *Federal Register* and *Code of Federal Regulations*.

7. FBI HQ file 62-27585, serial or document number 74 (62-27585-74).

8. I later learned that such documents are called "High Visibility Memoranda." They are generated as part of the FBI FOIA Section's efforts to anticipate and minimize negative publicity resulting from FOIA releases, including prerelease of information to family members of the subject of the request.

9. Five days before sending the letter denying that any "pertinent" information on the Court existed, some of these files had been described in an internal "Fee Waiver Memorandum," which strongly suggests that the records had been slated for release. This memo, dated August 30, 1984, describes various files that were about to be released to me, for the consideration of a committee, including chief of the Freedom of Information Section, James K. Hall, that would decide whether or not I would be granted a

waiver of the usual copying fees due to the historical interest of the records. The memorandum included the information that three main files comprising about one hundred pages on the Supreme Court had been located, including two files on extortion letters mailed to the court, and one file on a 1974 FBI investigation of leaks to newspapers of sensitive information about Court personnel. The Fee Waiver Committee met on October 30, 1984, decided the records were of substantial public interest, and granted me a 50 percent reduction of the usual copying fees. [XXXX] to Fee Waiver Committee, Re: FOIA request . . . for records pertaining to the United States Supreme Court and [former named justices], August 30, 1984, 190-37116-29.

10. I ultimately requested FBI files on every deceased Supreme Court justice going back to the early part of this century as a way to pry loose whatever records related to the high court as a body. I also requested another large file entitled "Federal Judges," 62-53025, which contained miscellaneous information on relations between the FBI and various members of the judiciary going back some fifty years.

11. FBI Special Agent Angus Llewellyn later explained the bureau's 1984 denial that it possessed any records on the Supreme Court in the following way:

On May 17, 1984, plaintiff requested information on *(inter alia)* the "United States Supreme Court as a body." A search was conducted on August 6, 1984, listing eight references. Upon review of the actual documents by FOIPA personnel, these references were found not to be pertinent to the Supreme Court as a body, thus plaintiff was advised by letter dated September 5, 1984, that the FBI had no responsive records. In handling a related request for plaintiff, an employee in the FOIPA Section became aware that the FBI had records indexed under "Supreme Court." It then became apparent that the indices search done on plaintiff's May 17, 1984, request was not sufficient. It can only be surmised that the search was done on "United States Supreme Court" and not "Supreme Court." This was not according to the way the search should have been conducted. However, once the existence of the files was discovered, an employee of the FBI telephonically notified the plaintiff of the existence of these records on August 11, 1987. It is important to note, the FBI informed plaintiff of this apparent mistake.

Second Declaration of Angus B. Llewellyn, *Charns v. U.S. Department of Justice,* C-88-175-D (U.S. District Court for the Middle District of North Carolina, March 21, 1990). The court ultimately accepted this explanation of an innocent mistake. There are some obvious problems. To begin with, my May 17, 1984, request was clearly intended to be as inclusive as possible, and it was unreasonable for the FBI employee to decide unilaterally that the eight files located were "not pertinent" to my request, without even informing me of their existence. Second, if the actual documents were in fact reviewed in 1984, it must have been seen that the reference to Supreme Court clerks, 62-27585-74, was just a small part of a two-thousand-page file on the Supreme Court, 62-27585. Third, the fact that a fee waiver memorandum was prepared and a fee waiver approved shows that at least someone in the FBI FOIA Section had determined back in 1984 that at least a hundred pages in three main files *were* pertinent to my request and should have been released to me at a reduced copying rate. Finally, although the FBI did ultimately inform me of the existence of the Supreme Court file, 62-27585, this would never have happened had I not requested specific material from that file, thus making discovery of it inevitable. In addition, I requested the Supreme Court file by its exact file number.

12. These included "FBI Kept Secret File on the Supreme Court," *New York Times,* August 21, 1988; "Report on Kennedy Ended a Hoover-Warren Alliance," *New York Times,* November 29, 1985; and "FBI Maintained Close Watch on Justice Douglas," *New York Times,* July 22, 1984; and "How JFK Report Split Warren and Hoover," *San Francisco Examiner,* November 30, 1985.

13. *Charns v. United States Department of Justice,* C-88-175-D (U.S. District Court for the Middle District of North Carolina). A second suit adding more claims relating to specific justices was filed in 1989. *Charns v. United States Department of Justice,* C-89-208-D (U.S. District Court for the Middle District of North Carolina)(hereafter *"Charns v. DOJ I and II"*).

14. *Green v. Federal Bureau of Investigation,* No. 89-699-CIV-5-BR (U.S. District Court for the Eastern District of North Carolina).

15. The authors have donated these documents to Marquette University; the documents are open to researchers.

16. Alexander Charns, "FB-Eyed: Secret Supreme Court Surveillance Began in '30s," *Durham Morning Herald,* August 14, 1988, pp. A1, A9; Alexander Charns, "How the FBI Spied on the High Court," *Washington Post,* December 3, 1989; and Alexander Charns, ed., "U.S. Supreme Court and Federal Judges Subject Files," University Publications of America (1992)(microfilm).

17. Athan Theoharis has been seeking release of Hoover's O&C files since 1977. In that year, he requested release of the eight folders that had been transferred from Hoover's "Personal and Confidential" files to his "Official and Confidential" files shortly before Hoover's death and subsequent destruction of the "Personal and Confidential" files by Hoover's secretary acting on his personal instructions. These eight folders included folder number 37 on the Fred Black case. In response to Theoharis's request, the FBI released 30 or 40 pages of the Fred Black folder, without informing Theoharis that folder 37 contained a total of 437 pages, the remainder of which were withheld entirely. In 1980, Theoharis requested *all* of Hoover's O&C files. In 1983, the FBI released about seven thousand pages, many with large redactions, and withheld another ten thousand pages entirely. Theoharis immediately filed an administrative appeal to the Justice Department's Office of Legal Policy, which was granted in part in 1985; additional records were released in 1987. At the Justice Department's invitation, Theoharis filed a follow-up appeal and specifically noted, among other things, the disparity between the number of pages released to him from the Black folder in 1977 and then in 1983. The FBI continued releasing documents to Theoharis in 1988 and 1989, and continued to advise him that if he was dissatisfied he could appeal again. On December 22, 1989, Theoharis and Charns were simultaneously sent copies of the DeLoach/Fortas memoranda from the Fred Black folder, O&C folder 37.

18. Alexander Charns, *Cloak and Gavel: FBI Wiretaps, Bugs, Informers and the Supreme Court* (Urbana: University of Illinois Press, 1992), pp. 55–62, 65–66, 73–75; and Alexander Charns, "Gavelgate," *Southern Exposure Magazine,* Fall 1990.

19. Fourth Declaration of Angus B. Llewellyn, Attachment 1, Exhibit B, *Charns v. DOJ II*, November 29, 1989.

20. Declaration of Angus Llewellyn, pp. 3–4, *Charns v. DOJ II*, February 16, 1990.

21. Thanks to Woody Voinche.

22. Ms. Eichhorst has been helpful, hardworking, and a pleasure to work with. She works weekends, including Sundays, and should get a big raise for the overtime she put in on our Supreme Court litigation. Maybe a promotion, too.

23. Was that the sound of a brontosaurus grunt?

24. Fred Black Folder, Hoover's O&C files; Athan Theoharis, ed., *From the Secret Files of J. Edgar Hoover* (Chicago: Ivan R. Dee, 1991), pp. 267–75; Charns, *Cloak and Gavel*, 55–62, 65–66, 73–75.

25. Nat Hentoff, "Profile of Justice Brennan," *The New Yorker*, June 12, 1990, 61–62.

26. Alexander Charns (AC) telephone interview with Cartha DeLoach, December 12, 1996; Charns, *Cloak and Gavel*, p. 94.

27. AC telephone interview with Cartha DeLoach, December 2, 1996.

28. Rumors persisted that Hoover and Tolson were homosexual lovers. Hoover required his agents to report anyone who made homosexual allegations against him, and agents were punished for failing to do so. Hoover retaliated against his accusers. He was particularly vicious toward homosexuals. Athan G. Theoharis and John Stuart Cox, *The Boss: J. Edgar Hoover and the Great American Inquisition* (Philadelphia: Temple University Press, 1988), 208–9. Popular writer Anthony Summers' *Official and Confidential. The Secret Life of J. Edgar Hoover* (New York: Putnam, 1993), claimed a mobster and "Roy Cohn involved Edgar in [homosexual] sex orgies." Hoover was also said to dress in drag (253–54). However, the credibility of these stories has been questioned. Athan G. Theoharis, *J. Edgar Hoover, Sex and Crime: An Historical Antidote* (Chicago: Ivan R. Dee, 1995).

29. Theoharis, *From the Secret Files of J. Edgar Hoover*, 292. Hoover's private files included allegations of homosexuality against other high-ranking government officials such as Adlai Stevenson (pp. 284–91).

30. One page of the memo was released in a highly redacted condition, and three pages were withheld entirely on grounds of personal privacy. Black marker redactions are shown as "XXX."

31. Fortas had been at the White House all day advising LBJ on the Detroit riots, during which time he met with FBI Director J. Edgar Hoover, Attorney General Ramsey Clark, and other officials. Bruce Allen Murphy, *Fortas: The Rise and Ruin of a Supreme Court Justice* (New York: William Morrow 1988), 392–405.

32. DeLoach to Hoover, July 24, 1967, Hoover's O&C files, folder 71; Declaration of John M. Kelso, Jr., *Charns v. DOJ I and II*.

33. AC telephone interview with Cartha DeLoach, December 2, 1996.

34. C. A. Evans to Mr. Belmont, the Advisory Committee on Rules of Criminal Procedure, October 23, 1963, 62-10902-1 (Hoover's handwritten comments).

35. DeLoach said that he had no independent recollection of these memos and based his comments to me on the language of his earlier memo to Tolson.

36. David J. Garrow, *The FBI and Martin Luther King, Jr.* (New York: Penguin, 1983), 125–27.

37. Sanford J. Ungar, *FBI* (Boston: Little, Brown, 1975), 357.

38. Hentoff, "Profile of Justice Brennan," pp. 61–62.

39. A. Rosen to Mr. Belmont, XXXXXX Activities in the District of Columbia Information Concerning, January 13, 1964, 62-109231-3.

40. C. A. Evans to Mr. Belmont, XXXX Also Known as Call Girl Activities in the District of Columbia White Slave Traffic Act, January 10, 1964, 62-109231-4.

41. A. Rosen to Mr. Belmont, XXXXXXXX Activities in the District of Columbia Information Concerning, January 14, 1964, 62-109231-6.

42. Why did the FBI withhold the memos about Justice Fortas for so long? In 1969, Fortas was hounded from the Court in a scandal unrelated to his role as an FBI informer. Fortas had returned to private practice. He died in 1982. His wife, Carolyn E. Agger, died on November 7, 1996, leaving no immediate family. Was the FBI protecting the privacy of the surviving wife from inquiries about her husband's sexuality that might embarrass her? If so, why were the memos released four months prior to Carolyn Agger's death?

43. Notations on DeLoach's report confirm that it was given to Hoover, who in turn instructed his personal secretary, Helen Gandy, to place it in his O&C files. It was placed in a folder titled "Fortas, Abe." Hoover's secret files were not indexed to the FBI's main files. They were a special kind of "Do Not File" record that officially did not exist. FBI officials devised other secret filing systems to hide evidence of FBI warrantless wiretapping and burglaries. Additional filing procedures were created in the wake of embarrassing revelations during the trial of Judith Coplon and after the Supreme Court's ruling that gave criminal defendants access to FBI reports for use in cross-examining witnesses. *Jencks v. U.S.*, 353 U.S. 657 (1957). The FBI headquarters file on the *Jencks* case and its legislative and administrative aftermath is 62-104029.

44. Athan Theoharis had requested Hoover's entire O&C files in the late 1970s. Theoharis continues in his attempts to gain the entire, unexpurgated O&C files to this day. The bureau had never released folder 71 (or its subject matter), claiming it was exempt from disclosure.

45. Declaration of Angus B. Llewellyn, *Charns v. DOJ II*, February 16, 1990, p. 3.

46. The FBI claimed that I had abandoned my claim to all cross-references about Abe Fortas because I had not rerequested them after I was provided a random sampling of references during the 1980s. See note 51 for the FBI's current policy of refusing to process cross-references.

47. A copy of the settlement agreement can be found in the court files for *Charns v. DOJ*.

48. Approximately thirteen years after my first FOIA request for records about the Supreme Court, I am still receiving records under the settlement agreement. The records about Abe Fortas's cooperation in the FBI's sexual surveillance program of the early sixties arrived in the mail while this article was in draft form.

49. The FBI explains that it "has over 200 employees assigned full time to comply with the disclosure provisions of the FOIPA.... At the end of May, 1993, our total requests on hand in various stages of processing num-

bered over 10,500. These requests will require the review of an estimated 3.3 million pages." FBI letter to Charns, June 8, 1993.

50. Tony Mauro, "Thurgood Marshall Helped FBI," *USA Today,* December 2, 1996, pp. A1–A2; Alexander Charns, "My Hero Still," *Washington Post,* December 16, 1996, p. A25.

51. "The enclosed material is from the main investigative file(s) in which the subject of your request is indexed. The subject of your request may also be indexed in files relating to other individuals, organizations, activities, or general topics. These additional mentions or references have not been reviewed to determine if, in fact, they are identifiable with the subject of your request. Our experience has shown that such references are frequently similar to information contained in the processed main file(s). We will process these references if you now make a specific request for them. However, because of a significant increase in FOIPA requests and an expanding backlog, we have given priority to the processing of main investigative files and can complete the processing of these additional references only as time and resources permit. Therefore, if you do decide to request these references, we will not be able to process them anytime in the foreseeable future." FBI to Charns, November 25, 1996. As of this writing (April 1997), I have not received any FBI headquarters cross-references on Justice Marshall, nor on the late Justice Arthur Goldberg, although I requested "all records" on Goldberg in January 1990.

52. Harry Hammitt, "Reinventing FOIA," *Access Reports,* November 20, 1996, p. 5 (emphasis in original).

53. Can one ever trust a secretive law enforcement agency whose high-ranking officials sometimes shred documents (Ruby Ridge) and help the White House violate the privacy rights of hundreds of citizens for political purposes (Filegate)? One should not blame the FOIPA section staff for the mismanagement and cover-ups in other parts of the FBI. FOIPA section officials should be blamed for their own mistakes and credited for their own good works.

54. The FBI documents concerning the U.S. Supreme Court and the federal judiciary have been donated to the Southern Historical and Folklife Collections of the Manuscripts Department of the Academic Affairs Library of the University of North Carolina at Chapel Hill, Chapel Hill, NC 27599-3926. It is anticipated that the documents will be available to researchers in 1998.

7

The Endless Saga of the Nixon Tapes

Joan Hoff

As a rule, presidential libraries are a bad idea; they have in the past led to many access and secrecy problems, and will continue to do so in the future. In part, these problems are the result of the National Archives' lack of courage in enforcing pre- and post-Watergate records laws. The time and expense of traveling to far-flung presidential libraries scattered all over the country have also led historians to write monographs and general works that atomize and highly personalize individual administrations rather than the needed comparative studies of the U.S. presidency.

Since Franklin Roosevelt, modern presidents and their families have favored the private funding of presidential libraries and have had the blessing of Congress, which prefers not to fund the processing and storage of presidential papers, with one exception—those of Richard Nixon. In the case of Nixon's presidential papers, moreover, the Justice Department, with the approval of the National Archives, in April 1997 approved a proposed "deal" to turn over all Nixon tapes and papers to the Richard Nixon Presidential Library and Birthplace in Yorba Linda, California, rather than to continue to process and protect them at Archives II in College Park, Maryland.

As the Watergate crisis unfolded in 1973 and 1974, questions about access to, and protection of, the documents the Nixon administration had generated assumed unprecedented national prominence. Ironically, in May 1973, presidential counselor Leonard Garment and Attorney General Elliot Richardson had advised President Nixon to place the papers of White House aides H. R. Haldeman, John Ehrlichman, and John Dean under the protection of the FBI. At the time, Nixon agreed on the condition that no one would have access to these papers "without written presidential consent." Nixon's claimed right of executive privilege to withhold these and other records soon became a powerful issue when Congress demanded and the president refused to produce requested records and tapes. Nixon's refusal precipitated a bitter political controversy and an unprecedented national constitutional crisis centering on his claimed right as president to control access to White House records.

The Supreme Court ultimately overruled Nixon's executive privilege claim.[1] Nonetheless, coinciding with his resignation from the presidency, Nixon signed an agreement with the then head of the General Services Administration (GSA), Arthur F. Sampson, that would have mandated the destruction of the tapes of White House Oval Office conversations and allowed considerable opportunity for destruction of some presidential papers. This September 8, 1974, Nixon-Sampson agreement could be executed because the National Archives and Records Service (NARS, now an independent agency known as the National Archives and Records Administration, or NARA) was at the time under the jurisdiction of the GSA. In consequence, the Archivist of the United States had no role in negotiating this agreement; moreover, neither the Justice Department nor the Special Prosecutor's Office had been consulted about its terms.[2] If the agreement had been carried out, massive destruction of the Nixon presidential tapes and papers would have taken place, and secrecy, rather than the public's right to know, would have prevailed.

Instead, this letter of agreement, approved by President Ford at the urging of White House aide Alexander Haig and the president's personal counsel, Philip Buchen, at the same time he pardoned Nixon, created a firestorm of criticism from Congress and the scholarly community of researchers. Critics decried the wide latitude Nixon would have been granted to control access to his presidential papers and tapes (including deciding which of these papers and tapes should be preserved). The agreement also left in doubt whether Nixon's presidential records would ever be donated through the National Archives to a presidential library and made available for historical research, as had the papers of all other occupants of the White House since Herbert Hoover. Historians had formerly encountered serious problems in researching the records at earlier presidencies. At times they were denied access to certain records; at other times only the most positive material about individual presidents deposited at presidential libraries had been selectively released. Nonetheless, the preservation of an entire documentary record of a single administration had never been an issue; never before had access to records been so personalized for the American public.

In the immediate wake of President Nixon's resignation over Watergate, the Nixon-Sampson agreement precipitated an unprecedented congressional response. Legislation was enacted asserting federal control over Nixon's papers and tapes. Many had come to question the once traditional view that presidential papers were largely the personal property of occupants of the White House. Reflecting these new concerns, Joint Resolution 4016, the Presidential Recordings and Materials Preservation Act (PRMPA), introduced in October 1974, quickly passed both houses on December 19.

Senator Sam Ervin (D-NC), chair of the Senate Government Operations Committee, proved instrumental in ensuring passage of this legislation. Speaking for Ervin and himself, Senator Gaylord Nelson (D-WI) urged President Ford, who had previously approved the Nixon-Sampson agreement on the basis of questionable legal advice, to void it because it was "so contemptuous of the national interest, and perhaps even in violation of the law dealing with Presidential libraries." A week later Senator Ervin argued that in "equity and in good conscience all the official records made by an elected Federal official, at the expense of taxpayers . . . ought to be regarded as public property."[3]

President Gerald Ford did sign this legislation, thereby dramatically altering the control that presidents had previously exercised over materials produced during their tenure in office. New archival procedures were ultimately produced to govern the processing of presidential papers. Title I of the 1974 Presidential Recordings and Materials Preservation Act (44 U.S.C. 2111) explicitly repudiated the Nixon-Sampson agreement and authorized the seizing of all Nixon documents and tapes, to be placed under the control of the federal government. The act further mandated that any information in this presidential material regarding abuses of power was to be made available to the public as soon as possible. Title II established a special commission to examine current policy involving presidential records, the National Study Commission on Records and Documents of Federal Officials (commonly known as the Brownell Commission after its chair, Herbert Brownell, Jr., President Dwight Eisenhower's first attorney general).

Following a two-year inquiry, the Brownell Commission issued its report, released on March 31, 1977, in which it unanimously recommended that "all records and documents accumulated by all Federal officials in the discharge of their official duties should be recognized by Congress to be the property of the United States." The commission's recommendations ultimately led to the passage of the 1978 Presidential Records Act. This legislation, which took effect with Ronald Reagan's presidency, applies to all the papers, tapes, and electronic records of succeeding presidents. It mandated that presidential materials must be made public after twelve years and were subject to the Freedom of Information Act (FOIA). This latter provision, however, was almost immediately successfully challenged in court.

In the interim between 1974 and 1978, senior NARA archivists began to establish guidelines for reviewing all the documents and tapes created during Richard Nixon's presidency. To carry out this task, the National Archives created the Nixon Presidential Materials Project (NPMP), located first in Alexandria, Virginia, and now at Archives II in College Park, Maryland. The name of this project was changed in 1990 to the Nixon Presidential Materials Staff (NPMS), but it is usually cited as simply NPM.

The subsequent review process was complicated by the fact that the 1974 act governed only official records, while the government had custody of both official and unofficial Nixon material. Archivists accordingly had to cull from these presidential papers and tapes private and personal material relating solely to the president's family or other nonpublic activities, including "private-political associations." Defining what constituted the latter category proved particularly troublesome during the processing of both the Special Files and the bulk of the Central Files.[4] Most Nixon documents have some political content, and few are concerned exclusively with the private-political association of the person who wrote or received them.[5]

For three years following passage of the 1974 PRMPA, Nixon fought its implementation in the courts. Then, when the Supreme Court upheld the legislation's constitutionality in 1977, attorneys representing the former president and federal archivists negotiated an agreement to permit the NARA systematically to screen and prepare for research purposes the Special Files and the White House Tapes. In February 1979, this unusual "negotiated agreement" called for the permanent removal of "any political document in the files that did not have a direct connection to President Nixon's constitutional powers or statutory duties." These documents were to be returned to Nixon with the understanding that "he would donate them in the future to the National Archives."[6]

The NARA subsequently interpreted this provision of the PRMPA by applying the standard of "private-political association" to all documents and tapes. This meant, for example, that if a presidential aide wrote that a particular senator should be supported for reelection, this was personal; if the aide suggested that the senator should be supported because he favored the Vietnam War, this became a presidential document that should be opened and not returned to the former president. The archivists' "private-political association" standard to govern the processing of the papers and tapes avoided having to "gut" the Nixon papers, since most presidential papers and tapes mix personal with public remarks. Nixon's lawyers both before and following his death, however, have challenged the use of this unique archival standard, which would not automatically ensure the removal of all personal remarks. Because of this and other unprecedented (and contested) review procedures, processing the Nixon papers did not begin until five years after Nixon's resignation as president.

During this 1974–78 period, Jack Eckerd, who succeeded Sampson as GSA administrator, delayed promulgating regulations that could tackle government secrecy as mandated under the 1974 legislation. Congress had to intervene several times to void proposed GSA actions or regulations until the NARA and Nixon's attorneys eventually reached the February 1979 "negotiated agreement." This seeming resolution paved the way for the promise, detailed in the 1974 Ervin Senate report, "to assure full public access to all facts connected with the Watergate affair, including the fruits of all investigations conducted pursuant thereto, and to afford full public access to all such materials, including papers, documents, memorandums, tapes, and transcripts originating during the period between January 20, 1969, through August 9, 1974, *at the earliest practicable time and in an adequate and effective manner.*"[7]

Since that time, out of the 44 million documents (including 1.5 million of the most sensitive abuse-of-power documents), a little over 7 million documents and twenty-seven hundred pages of transcripts have been made public, as well as sixty-three hours of White House Tapes (out of the four thousand hours). *There are no transcripts for the remaining tapes—only a twenty-seven-thousand-page log to make selective listening easier for researchers and the general public.* A single person would have to spend almost two years of nonstop listening eight hours a day just to hear all the tapes, without taking time to review or analyze them. The NARA, moreover, chose to create tape logs instead of transcriptions, having concluded that preparing such transcripts would take at least 400,000 hours of staff time and that even then the transcripts' accuracy could not be guaranteed.[8]

The National Archives had originally intended to open all the recorded conversations in 1989, only a tiny portion of which (sixty hours) were transcribed, having been prepared earlier at the request of the Watergate special prosecutor. (Not all of these tapes and transcripts had been used as evidence in the various court cases after

1974; hence, they remained closed to the public.) The NARA followed established regulations for screening paper documents while process-ing the four thousand hours of extant secret recordings. Under these regulations, all persons mentioned in the recordings who requested advanced notification would be notified so that they could challenge the release of specific conversations. Even when the extensive twenty-seven-thousand-page Tape Survey Log is finally released, there will invariably be many delays and obstacles before researchers will be able to analyze and interpret this unique documentary source about the internal workings of the Nixon administration.

The four thousand hours of tape recordings pose thornier archi-val and access problems than do Nixon's presidential papers. Although the initial processing of the tapes and creation of the massive finding aid had been completed in 1988, lawyers for Nixon and some of his top advisers claimed that an untold number of violations of the per-sonal privacy of individuals remained. The review process in the 1979 "negotiated agreement," they argued, had not proved feasible for these controversial secret tapings. Stricter privacy standards should govern their review. Nixon project archivists, in response, steadfastly defended the objectivity and fairness of their screening and their finding aid indexing these tapes. This challenge caused the delay. Finally, on June 4, 1991, sixty hours of the initial eighty hours of Watergate Special Prosecution Force File Segment, or White House Tapes, were released, accompanied by twenty-seven hundred pages of transcripts. Occur-ring seventeen years after passage of the 1974 PRMPA, this release did not meet the legislative intent to ensure the earliest possible re-lease of Nixon material.

These tapes and transcripts contain eighty-eight separate entries, eight-six of which were made on recording devices located in the White House, the Old Executive Office Building, and at Camp David. Two others had been recorded on equipment not connected with the White House taping system. Transcripts were prepared for eighty-five of these eighty-eight entries—all made by the Watergate Special Pros-ecution Force (WSPF). (The WSPF had not prepared transcripts for the others.) The NARA did not release two of these, and eighty-eight were not released by the NARA for audio or national security rea-sons. Just as no "smoking guns" emerged from the released papers, the same has proved true for the initial batch of the released secret Oval Office tapes transcripts. The transcribed tapes represent what the WSPF considered to be the best evidence of the Nixon administra-tion's abuse of power for both the impeachment and subsequent trial purposes. These tapes also contain a wealth of anecdotal and substan-tive information about other domestic and foreign policy issues having nothing to do with abuse of power. WSPF transcribers, however, had neglected to follow the stricter review standards that the National Archives later adopted in 1979. Researchers need to use these transcripts with care because, as Maaja Krusten, former archivist with the NPMP, has authoritatively documented, they contain inaccuracies.[9]

In March 1992, Ralph Nader's Public Citizen Group and historian Stanley Kutler filed suit in U.S. District Court demanding the immediate release of the Tape Survey Log and the remaining 3,937 hours of taped conversations. The archivists' review had been completed in 1987, Kutler argued, and as many as 400 hours pertained to Watergate matters. In response to this suit, assistant archivist for presidential libraries John T. Fawcett insisted that the 60 hours that the archives had released in the summer of 1991 represented all of the "integral file segments" related to Watergate. Others, however, estimated that approximately 300 to 400 more hours of abuse-of-power conversations relating to Watergate may exist on the tapes. (Fawcett left the National Archives in 1994 under heavy criticism for his 1989 handling of a list of seventy deletions from Watergate-related tapes and for allowing testimony in the tapes suit to degenerate into slander of individual members of the original NPMS.) Following Fawcett's departure, William H. Cunliffe, then director of the Nixon Presidential Materials Staff at the National Archives, entered into negotiations on behalf of the National Archives with the late president's lawyers, Nader, and Kutler with the goal of releasing in 1995 a block of some 200 hours of tape segments—without transcripts—relating to abuse of power.[10]

During 1992, with Nader's and Kutler's legal challenge pending, two other potentially significant developments occurred. First, the U.S. Court of Appeals for the District of Columbia ruled that Nixon was entitled to payment for documents that the former president claimed were illegally placed under government control following his resignation in 1974. Like every other president before him, Judge Harry Edwards declared, Nixon "had a compensable interest in his presidential papers." This decision reversed an earlier 1991 ruling denying Nixon compensation. Nevertheless, the court concurred that Nixon did not have legal title to his presidential papers. In response, an outraged editorial writer for the *New York Times* queried how much the public will have to pay Nixon's estate after Nixon's attorneys place a dollar value on the "smoking gun" conversation or the eighteen-minute erasure. (Because the Justice Department under President George Bush failed to appeal this November 1992 decision, the amount of compensation will be decided by a lower court.)[11]

The second significant development occurred when Congress and investigative reporter Seymour M. Hersh critically scrutinized the management of the National Archives. In a highly publicized article in the December 1992 issue of the *New Yorker*, Hersh claimed that high-level federal archivists were deliberately thwarting the release of the remaining tapes.[12] Hersh's article was written after he had gone to the Nixon presidential facility under contract to write a book based on the tapes and discovered that, except for sixty hours, the bulk of the White House Tapes had not yet been released to the public. Implying that archivists had leaked information from the withheld tapes to him, Hersh further contended that Nixon had wanted McGovern campaign material planted in the apartment of Arthur Bremer. (Bremer had attempted to assassinate George Wallace on May 15, 1972.) Archivists involved in processing the Nixon tapes have denied leaking any information to Hersh, saying that his information came from depositions taken in the *Kutler and Public Citizen v. Wilson and Nixon* case.[13]

The impact of a negative Senate report, Hersh's article, and the "deal" over National Security Council computer records (the PROFS case, discussed in Scott Armstrong's essay in this volume) that Archives officials struck with President George Bush on January 19, 1993—the last full day that the former president spent in office—contributed to Don W. Wilson's resignation as Archivist of the United States in February 1993.[14] Then, on March 10, 1993, the National Archives announced its plan to make available twenty-five additional taped conversations covering the period May and June 1972. These were the controversial months in which the two Watergate break-ins, the resultant arrests, and the White House cover-up took place. In compliance with federal regulations, Nixon was informed of the National Archives' intention, and in April he filed a cross-claim to prevent the release of these conversations and also to counter the 1992 lawsuit brought by Public Citizen and Kutler. Nonetheless, on May 16, these twenty-five conversations were released, and the news services immediately produced three differing transcripts. The interested public had no way to determine which of these transcripts were accurate or to place them in historical context. The National Archives further announced its plans to release in August four more hours, or thirty-nine additional conversations.[15]

At this point a May 18, 1993, memorandum of Acting Archivist Trudy H. Peterson was leaked to Nixon lawyer R. Stan Mortenson. "We appear to be unilaterally abrogating the [1979] agreement [with the former president]," Peterson wrote. Commenting on the piecemeal release of short segments of conversations—some no longer than ten seconds—she observed that this "takes the conversation out of context of the rest of the activities going on at the time period. This is not fair to the researcher, who is left to puzzle out what else may have gone on in related conversations that month."[16]

Two months later, on August 9, 1993, Federal Judge Royce C. Lamberth ruled that the 1974 Presidential Recordings and Materials Preservation Act prohibited the National Archives from releasing any more of the Nixon White House Tapes. The National Archives could not release any more tapes until the "purely private material [is] returned for [Nixon's] sole custody and use." Furthermore, he ruled, the archives could not release any more tapes except as a "single integral file." (The judge, in this instance, was apparently unaware that the NARA had previously made incremental releases of Nixon material, thereby breaking up integral file segments.) Lamberth's ruling ostensibly voided the painstaking work of the archivists, who, when reviewing the unreleased conversations, had used the standard of "private-political association." In response and to avoid having to rereview the remaining 3,937 hours of unreleased tapes, the National Archives proposed several alternative ways for releasing the tapes.

Nixon, however, sued again. This suit led to the negotiations that, after nearly fourteen months, produced the agreement that eventually led to the 1996 release of all tape references to abuse of power—however cryptic and out of context. After these abuse-of-power tapes were spliced together and released, Nixon Presidential Materials Staff Director Cunliffe affirmed, his staff would complete a chronological review of the remaining tapes and release broad segments of the untranscribed tapes. The staff would first remove privacy and national security information and make spliced cassette copies.[17] Shortly thereafter, however, Cunliffe left the Nixon Presidential Materials Staff and was replaced by senior archivist and acting NPMS Director Karl Weissenbach, who has presided over the release of Nixon tapes in compliance with the April 1996 "negotiated agreement" in *Kutler and Public Citizen v. Carlin.*

On November 18, 1996, 201 hours of these abuse of governmental power (AOGP) tape segments were released, along with a chronological listing and a portion of the twenty-seven-thousand-page Tape Survey Log, the Nixon estate having given up what had been a twenty-one-year battle to preserve their secrecy. Of the original 4,000 hours of tapes, at first 63 and in 1996 an additional 201 hours have been released, with approximately 3,700 hours remaining unreleased. Of these, the National Archives designated 820 hours as relating exclusively to private matters and returned these to Nixon's daughters. Until rereviewed by archivists, 2,880 hours have yet to be released—despite the fact that these tapes had already been reviewed and, according to the staff of the NPMP in 1988, were ready to be opened for research.[18] The delay created by this rereview of the remaining tapes will be further compounded by the requirement that a panel composed of archivists from three presidential libraries will decide whether to honor objections to the release of disputed segments from the Nixon estate and from those individuals whose voices are on the tapes. Presidential libraries are not known for their commitment to release controversial information about modern presidents or their closest aides and, in this instance, "reports circulated in the Archives that Nixon's estate was demanding that archivists serving on the review panel to re-screen the tapes be selected from 'Republican Libraries.' "[19]

Dating from his resignation until his death twenty years later, Nixon (and then his estate) had first challenged the constitutionality of the 1974 Presidential Recordings and Materials Preservation Act, especially concerning the release of the White House Tapes. His heirs have now conceded on the AOGP segments. They apparently plan to continue to contest the release of some of the remaining 2,880 hours of recordings by taking advantage of the negotiated agreement in *Kutler and Public Citizen*, which, in effect, endorsed Nixon's attorneys' long-held position: namely, that the National Archives had not adequately segregated Nixon's private from his purely political statements. The Supreme Court has not ruled definitively on the right of privacy after a person dies, although lower courts have held that privacy does not continue beyond the grave. I do not share the optimism of some archivists and historians that the twenty-year litigious battle over access to Nixon's papers and tapes appears to be nearing an end. The National Archives and a series of administrations have rolled over on this issue too many times in the past.[20]

Furthermore, I fear that the *Kutler and Public Citizen* negotiated agreement will ensure further delays but will not ensure archival integrity. Among other matters, this agreement did not end litigation over the retention and final disposition of the original tapes. Furthermore, underscoring the archives' traditional deference and lack of independent courage when dealing with presidential papers questions, and especially those of Richard Nixon, John W. Carlin, the first Archivist of the United States not to have any professional archival experience, stated when announcing the agreement:

> The National Archives and Records Administration is eager to make public all material that the law allows to be released to document the Nixon Presidency. But we also are sensitive to the concerns of the Nixon family about the material that is legally personal and private, and we recognize the need to treat materials not related to "abuses of power" as we would treat materials

of any other President in our Presidential library system, consistent with the law specifically governing the Nixon materials. We believe that this agreement protects both the Nixon privacy rights and the public interests as defined by law.

Following the opening of these tapes in November 1996, Kutler characterized the agreement as a "victory" and as marking "the transition between Watergate as a story for journalists, to one for historians."[21]

Only a handful of archivists, historians, and journalists have criticized the incredibly fragmentary nature of the supposedly "integral files segments" about Watergate-related matters.[22] A total of 1,900 segments from 931 conversations, many less than a minute long (with some no more than twelve or thirteen seconds), have been released completely out of context. The existence of so many all but unintelligible snippets may represent the fact that the special prosecutor had identified the most significant abuse-of-power recordings in 1974, thereby leading to their release in 1991.

As in the case of the original 63 released hours, the newly released tapes confirm the poor quality of the White House taping system, except for telephone calls. The 201 hours are on 309 individual cassettes, but *only one copy of each is available for research at any given time.* This scarcity of tape copies caused consternation when journalists descended on the NPMS during the first week following the most recent tape release in November 1996, even though twenty listening stations had been set up in a special room. Too few copies remain a problem should more than half a dozen researchers seek to review the tapes on any given day, the number of listening stations having been reduced to six or eight (depending on whether all are operative), with half or more semipermanently staked out by teams of researchers paid by individual historians such as Kutler and news services.

In addition, the tape cassette players of the ultramodern Archives II building's research area perform as if they had been purchased at a rummage sale. The Secret Service might have installed less than state-of-the-art taping equipment in the White House in 1971. Similarly substandard equipment was installed at the archives building. The NARA has also decided that for the time being those AOGP tape recordings for which there are no transcripts cannot be reproduced. As a result, an individual researcher will have to expend months to listen to and take notes on all 201 hours.

Should the remaining 2,880 hours be publicly released by the end of 1999, the NARA will permit researchers to obtain copies *only* of the AOGP segments. Should the rest of the tapes not be released by the end of the year 2002, the NARA will permit copies of all tapes released by that time and of subsequently released ones. The National Archives announced that 278 hours of the Cabinet Room tapes should be released no later than April 1998, with the remaining 2,602 hours released in five segments over the next several years.[23] These delays, mandated under the rereview requirements of *Kutler and Public Citizen v. Carlin,* border on the unconscionable, the more so since the NPMS had earlier concluded that these tapes were ready for release in 1989.

The reality of continued secrecy and delayed research is not public knowledge, most journalists and historians having chosen not to speak out publicly about the fragmentary nature of the latest tapes, the rereview delays, the denial of reproduction rights until the year 2000, and the less than desirable and scarce equipment available for listening to the Nixon tapes. An entire wing of Archives II had been built to accommodate Nixon's presidential material. Nonetheless, the cassette listening area services all of the archives' audio collections— not simply the White House Tapes—ensuring that desk personnel cannot accommodate those clamoring to use the Nixon rationed tapes.

The tape segments released in November 1996 did not prove to be a victory for access to information over secrecy owing to their fragmentary nature and lack, to date, of *new* abuse-of-power information. This latter aspect escaped public notice as journalists made headlines with stories seemingly providing fresh insights into the nefarious ways of the Nixon administration. Perhaps the most transparent of these "new" discoveries had to do with White House conversations recording Nixon's discussion of breaking into, and/or firebombing, the Brookings Institution. Nixon had earlier mentioned this discussion in his memoirs as had other Watergate participants. Regardless, journalists rehashed this unsavory conversation in November 1996, with most failing to indicate that no follow-up, illegal action had been undertaken (as in the case of so many of the other angry statements Nixon uttered or wrote in the margins of presidential documents).[24] The resultant news stories conveyed the distinct impression that such criminal action had actually taken place—in fact, some of Nixon's advisers at the time pointed out the futility of taking any action against Brookings at the very time when Pat Buchanan and Charles Colson, the originator of this firebombing plot, were urging such illegal activities.[25]

This rereporting of the White House conversations about Brookings also ignored their historical context in the immediate wake of the publication of the Pentagon Papers (a classified history of U.S. military and diplomatic conduct in Vietnam) in June 1971. At the time, Nixon had been cajoled by National Security Council aide Henry Kissinger first to try to prevent publication of the Pentagon Papers and then to take punitive action against Daniel Ellsberg, a former student and academic colleague of Kissinger's at Harvard, and any others involving in leaking this classified history. Kissinger was present during at least three of the taped conversations in which Nixon railed against Brookings. In the first one, on June 17, 1971, Kissinger insisted that Brookings "ha[d] no right to have classified documents," but he fed the president's suspicion that the think tank did, indeed, possess such material. Then, on June 30 (after Nixon learned that the Supreme Court had refused to block further publication of the Pentagon Papers), and again on July 1, the head of the National Security Council listened passively to talk about raiding Brookings, which his personal panic over the Pentagon Papers had fanned, insisting that "anyone who [gave] a paper to Ellsberg . . . ought to be out by the end of the day today." Kissinger has since denied remembering any such meeting where breaking into the Brooking Institution was discussed, but the AOGP tapes document his presence.[26]

None of these 1996 stories ever mentioned Nixon's (and other presidents') tendency to "pop off" on topics and in referring to various ethnic groups (but not racial, in Nixon's case) in what John Ehrlichman has called Nixon's "Queen of Hearts" syndrome. Ehrlichman meant by this phrase, "off with their heads," that Nixon's statements usually amounted to venting and nothing more.[27] Nixon's alleged "paranoid anti-Semitism" consisted of a verbal pattern of condemning various ethnic groups and ordering IRS or other investigations of them; almost none of these actions were carried out.

I do not condone the atmosphere that existed in the Nixon White House, which these tapes underscore. Nixon, however, should be given the same benefit of the doubt for angry talk and frustration as other modern presidents (albeit they were wise enough not to tape their ventings indiscriminately, or to write so many of them in marginal notations). Nonetheless, it is shocking to have such specific confirmation of the embattled mind-set within the Nixon White House that led to even the discussion of, let alone the president's ordering, black bag jobs.

I also find disturbing the ahistorical headline-grabbing reports based on the latest release of the White House Tapes to convey the impression that significantly new information was released and that, therefore, the public's right to know had triumphed over secrecy. Only by comparing the released tape material with Nixon's daily diaries, with information already available in Ehrlichman's and Haldeman's written notes of their meetings with Nixon, and with the Haldeman CD-ROM diaries (and the originals the NARA belatedly released following publication of the commercial version) will we be able to determine if this released material enhances our understanding of Nixon's presidency.[28] At this writing (April 1997), the released tapes provide no important new information, with the possible exception of Nixon's April and again May 1973 conversations in which he suggested first to Henry Kissinger and then to Chief of Staff Alexander Haig that perhaps he should resign over Watergate-related matters. But even these statements seem to have been intended to elicit praise and support from Haig, rather than confirming that the president seriously considered resigning. And all headlines (and an A&E Investigative Reports segment, "The Secret White House Tapes," aired on March 29, 1997) implying that these 1996 tapes are laden with swearing and pejorative ethnic remarks may be as exaggerated, as they were in the case of the 1991 releases.

Still another twist in the Watergate saga involving the White House Tapes remains on the horizon, namely, the taped conversations between President Nixon and White House counselor John Dean. Had it not been for Dean's attempts to censor Len Colodny's and Robert Gettlin's controversial 1991 book, *Silent Coup: The Removal of a President,* by filing a multi-million-dollar libel suit, scholars might not have paid attention to the conversations between Dean and Nixon in the AOGP segments. Colodny and Gettlin documented that Dean had more than a passing interest in and knowledge of the two Watergate break-ins. Their research refuted the largely unsubstantiated accounts of Watergate by investigative reporters Bob Woodward and Carl Bernstein. In a word, *Silent Coup* cast doubt on all Watergate studies that have uncritically relied on John Dean's testimony and books.

In their suit, Dean's lawyers attempted to prevent anyone from quoting or relying on *Silent Coup.* Ironically, journalists and historians, who condemn Nixon for constitutional violations, have ignored Dean's attempt to censor those authors who disagree with the former White House aide's versions of his role in Watergate and the virtual monopoly he has exercised over media representations of Watergate.[29]

Newspaper stories about the AOGP segments should have also focused on Dean's conversations with Nixon listed in the Tape Log Survey and those others that Haldeman and other individuals have said he had. The latest tapes release record no conversations for the time that Dean spent at Camp David from March 23 to 28, 1973, during which he was supposedly writing a report about Watergate. Both Haldeman and Ehrlichman report having had telephone conversations with Dean while he was at Camp David, yet these conversations with Dean are "missing" in the tapes recorded for that period. Nixon dismissed Dean from "investigating" Watergate at the end of the month, even though at the time Dean had not yet produced his written report. Moreover, both Haldeman and Nixon refer to having reviewed certain other conversations with Dean in 1973 that were not among the segments released in either 1991 or 1996. We can only assume that Dean reviewed some of these tapes during his stay at Camp David in March.

The most glaring "missing" conversation, however, took place on the evening of April 15, 1973. Nixon was "obviously quite disturbed" by this conversation, according to the Haldeman CD-ROM diary, because it appears that Dean indicated to Nixon he had decided to cut a deal with the Ervin Committee rather than testify before a federal grand jury, as Ehrlichman and others had recommended. Dean had more than likely told the president he would resign only if Nixon's two closest aides, Haldeman and Ehrlichman, did so as well so that it would not look as though he (Dean) was being singled out. If this is correct, Dean came close to blackmailing Nixon by indicating in this missing conversation that Haldeman and Ehrlichman (and possibly the president) were guilty of obstructing justice. For, in all the surrounding phone calls to this missing conversation, Nixon began to use the term "obstruction of justice."

Another curious anomaly emerging from the latest AOGP segments concerns a March 29, 1973, recording between Ehrlichman and Dean, in which Ehrlichman strongly urged Dean to testify before the grand jury because "one can't expect probity, fairness and guarantees of rights before a committee of the Senate that does the kind of things [including asking for raw FBI files] this committee has done in the last couple of days." During his subsequent trial, Ehrlichman's defense could have been helped by this tape. In it Ehrlichman says that his "safe refuge is at the grand jury," and he expressed his willingness to volunteer information in that forum to "cleanse" his name. Dean, however, refused to volunteer to appear before the grand jury.[30]

This conversation was not on the list of events and tapes that Dean prepared for the special prosecutor, a bare-bones outline that cast Dean in the most positive light. Nor is this recording cross-referenced in the Executive Office Building (EOB) or Oval Office tape segments. Since this tape records Ehrlichman's statement that he stepped out of a meeting with the president, it was first thought that Dean may have privately recorded this conversation. National Archives officials, however, maintain that no private Dean dictabelts were found in his papers and thus cannot explain the absence of a cross-reference, unless this conversation was taped in the Lincoln Sitting Room.[31]

When and if the Dean libel suit against Colodny and Gettlin goes to trial, this as well as other tapes containing negative information about Dean will be closely scrutinized, as they should have been in 1974–75. The National Archives now admits that certain conversations (most notably one for the evening of April 15, 1973) had not been recorded because the Secret Service had neglected to change the tape on the system recording conversations taking place in the Oval Office. All telephone conversations that evening with the president before and after Dean's visits, however, were recorded and are not released. Before this latest release, it was also not known that seven of the reel-to-reel tapes in the collection (not all necessarily in the AOGP segments) are completely blank. Four are from Camp David and are most likely to have included conversations with Dean about Watergate at the time he was preparing his report; three are from the Oval Office. Furthermore, none of the tapes scheduled for release include some 950 hours of dictabelt records, which remain locked away. The Nixon Research Project does not plan to process these dictabelts in the near future, no one having sued for their release, but also because many others can be found as typed memorandums in the papers of White House aides.[32] Thus, it remains unclear whether the public's right to know will prevail over the past quarter century of secrecy enshrouding these "missing" recordings.

Finally, because the National Archives (and Congress) have chosen not to make authoritative transcripts of the remaining White House Tapes, Nixon historians and journalists will inevitably wrangle over the meaning of Nixon's individual words, phrases, and intonations well into the next century. Was Nixon, for example, really talking in a "slurred voice" the night he asked Haldeman to resign, as Neil A. Lewis of the *New York Times* insisted in his first story on the new releases? Was he almost in tears in a midnight call of April 16, 1973, when he complained to Kissinger about how he was probably going to have to fire "these good men"? Does the often-used phrase "laced with profanities and ethnic slurs" accurately describe the new tape segments? Such a dispute has already taken place over a September 8, 1971, conversation, with *San Francisco Examiner* Bureau Chief Christopher Matthews claiming that Nixon was ordering IRS investigations of "rich Jews" and Nixon Presidential Library archivist Susan Naulty, claiming that the term "Jew" appears at the beginning of an almost inaudible tape made from the EOB (the least distinct of all the taping sites) and that the word "investigation" is not necessarily related to any of the preceding proper nouns because Nixon proceeded to talk about previous presidents who had used the IRS against their political opponents, including some friends who had supported his 1962 bid for the governorship of California.[33]

The released AOGP segments do underscore the seamy aspects of the Nixon White House and reinforce the conventional view that Nixon was the most evil man ever to occupy the office of the presidency of the United States.[34] As I have argued for a number of years, the degree to which we continue to view Nixon as an aberration rather than the quintessential politician of the last half of the twentieth century, representing the best and worst of modern presidents and our political system, will ensure that we will never learn from Watergate. For this reason, these tapes should not be simply sensationalized out of context but instead used to understand what has happened to presidential discourse.

The story these tape fragments tell goes far beyond the events we now have come to call Watergate. In fact, the story these tapes tell may constitute the best example of the "process disintegration" within the White House that has continued down to the present, as we have witnessed the transition from the modern to the postmodern presidency. In this sense, recent media coverage of the latest tapes releases has not simply been ahistorical; more important, these reports have missed the first signs of the disintegration of the modern presidency. These tapes document the deconstruction of the presidency, as Nixon and his aides created narratives (i.e., stories) that had no basis in reality—where the story of the day over Watergate gradually became reality.

This structural disintegration of the presidency took place on Nixon's watch primarily in relation to Watergate—and not his substantive domestic or foreign policies. While Nixon may have initiated a few now famous Watergate slogans, phrases, and stories, since then such practices have become the predominant mode of operation of presidents. Public and private psychobabble rhetoric now occupies a place "between drama and therapy where deniability reigns" and no one, particularly the president, is responsible for anything.[35]

The tapes are also relevant for understanding the public's greater right to know over the government's (and presidential libraries') desire for secrecy. There are two related issues here. One involves the intentional withholding of information. The second and equally important problem relates to whether declassified documents are then either accurately interpreted or placed in historical context. Incomplete releases will not enhance our understanding of the past. Past secrecy had enabled government officials to re-create or distort the record of their decisions. But selectively released documentation, as has often been practiced by presidential libraries and now with NARA's response to the *Kutler* decision, and then the resultant failure to place the incomplete released information in context, equally distorts our understanding of the past.

The latest examples of this continuing problem with the National Archives over presidential libraries and the Nixon papers and tapes occurred in April 1997. First, U.S. District Judge Norma Holloway Johnson ordered the National Archives to return "all personal and private conversations" on Nixon's tapes "and any copies thereof" to the Nixon estate, along with all portions of the twenty-seven-thousand-page log summarizing those 820 hours of conversations. Federal archivists working with the tapes immediately claimed that the original tapes were too fragile to be cut and spliced to extract such personal material, and thus the original version of the remaining 3,700 hours of tapes would probably have to be surrendered. The National Archives, however, obtained a stay from this order and is currently considering several options. The best recourse would have the National Archives return the original version in its entirety, retaining the entire master (analog) copy it had made (which is of better audio quality) under an elaborate "double-lock vault"—or other system for securing access—to ensure that no one can listen to or copy the private sections without the Nixon family's permission.[36]

While the archival and research communities were deliberating how to implement Judge Johnson's decision, another legal announcement of greater importance made headlines in April 1997 when the Clinton administration (like the Bush administration) did not appeal the 1992 court of appeals decision granting Nixon compensation for the presidential materials seized in 1974. Accordingly, the executors of Nixon's estate continued to litigate over the amount of payment. On January 6, 1997, the parties agreed to remove the case from the lower court's current trial schedule while they attempted to reach an out-of-court settlement. Some observers feared that the NARA, in order to diminish the amount of compensation to Nixon heirs, might classify as strictly "personal" more records and return them to the Nixon estate. Such action would reduce the papers open to research and would perpetuate the seemingly endless secrecy that since 1974 had surrounded the Nixon papers and tapes.[37] As it turned out, an even worse scenario happened.

On April 5, 1997, the Justice Department (representing the NARA) reportedly agreed to a $26 million compensation settlement. The 1992 ruling had granted the Nixon family compensation under the right of eminent domain owing to the "taking" of the president's documents in 1974. Eight million dollars of the total amount would be used to build a new, underground facility at the Nixon Library in Yorba Linda, to house and continue to process the Nixon papers and tapes. Both parties to this settlement, however, publicly denied having reached any agreement.

This proposed out-of-court settlement marks not a victory over secrecy, favoring the unbiased processing and release of more information from the Nixon papers and tapes. Moving this enormous collection across the country will significantly delay research access to the currently open papers and tapes. The Yorba Linda community and the Nixon Library Foundation Board, moreover, have disturbingly expressed little initial enthusiasm over the possible transfer of the Nixon papers to Yorba Linda, indicating that this "deal" between the government and the Nixon estate was pushed by the National Archives, in particular the current Archivist of the United States, who has said it would open the door to a "new partnership" with the Nixon family, rather than more contentious litigation.[38]

The Nixon settlement is one more example of the NARA's less than courageous administration of presidential papers and its insensitivity when allowing the Nixon papers and tapes to be moved in violation of provisions of the 1974 Presidential Recordings and Materials Preservation Act, which requires that custody "shall be maintained in Washington, District of Columbia, or its metropolitan area, except as may otherwise be necessary to carry out the provisions of title." NARA administrators' claim that the research and journalism communities have nothing to fear about future access insofar as archives will exercise archival supervision of the Nixon Library is hollow given the access problems that have already occurred at the Hoover, Roosevelt, Kennedy, Johnson, and Reagan presidential libraries.[39] No director of any of these facilities has ever been appointed without the ex-president's, his family's, or his foundation's explicit approval; these institutions exist to enhance the images of the chief executives whose collections they house.

Page Miller, director of the National Coordinating Committee for the Promotion of History, aptly observed in her monthly *Washington Update*:

> In the presidential library system, Library directors are rarely chosen without the consent of the President's family, who retain some indirect control over the operation of the libraries and over access to records. Some researchers note that many Presidential families have had a tendency to micro-manage the libraries and to polish the President's image. Considering [Nixon's and] the Nixon estate's efforts over the past two decades to keep records closed, there is little evidence that they would facilitate the open-

ing of the large majority of the records that have already been closed for too long.[40]

For those who fought to have the NARA become independent of the GSA to ensure that it could stand up to presidents and their families, the "deal" to return the Nixon papers and tapes to California is another disappointing example of this agency's stance on presidential papers. The National Archives' standard operational procedure governing the Nixon material raises concerns in light of its less than sterling record at most presidential libraries in providing access to controversial material. Ironically, no other presidential papers and tapes have been as controversial as Nixon's. Instead of mitigating further litigation, implementation of this agreement, including the provision to move the papers to the Nixon Library at Yorba Linda, will continue indefinitely the litigious saga of these papers and tapes.

NOTES

1. On July 24, 1974, the Supreme Court unanimously ruled in *United States v. Nixon* that the courts, not the president, could define the limits to an executive privilege claim; that without a valid national security reason, the president could not withhold evidence from a grand jury about possible criminal actions of White House officials.
2. For the full text of this agreement, see *Weekly Compilation of Presidential Documents: Gerald R. Ford, 1974*, 10 (September 9, 1974): 1104–8. A month earlier, on the day of his resignation, Nixon had struck another deal with Sampson changing the terms of his gift of his prepresidential (primarily vice presidential) papers to the National Archives—preventing access to them until January 1, 1985. He had previously donated these papers with the stipulation that access would be denied only so long as he was president. In December 1968, after his election but before taking office, Nixon claimed four hundred thousand dollars in tax deductions for this gift. The IRS disallowed that amount as excessive in April, ruling that Nixon owed more than that amount in back taxes. The IRS also referred this matter to Special Prosecutor Leon Jaworski on the possibility that fraud was involved in arranging this tax deduction. Both the deed of gift for the papers and their appraised value had been backdated to March 27, 1969, enabling Nixon to claim a substantial tax deduction for 1968 in compliance with a congressional tax-reform act making such deductions retroactive to July 1969. See *New York Times*, August 18, 1974, pp. 1, 35; and Stanley I. Kutler, *The Wars of Watergate: The Last Crisis of Richard Nixon* (New York: Knopf, 1990), pp. 431–34.
3. *Congressional Record*, September 18, 1974, S. 31551 (first quotation); October 4, 1974, S. 33976, S. 18240 (second quotation); and U.S. Senate, Committee on Government Operations, *Public Access to Certain Papers, Documents, Memoranda, Tapes, and Transcripts*, 93d Cong., 2d sess., report no. 93-1182 on S.J. 240, September 18, 26, 1974.
4. The most sensitive Watergate-related tapes and documents from the

White House Central Files were known officially as the "Special Files" and informally as the "abuse of [government] power" papers. Ironically, this Special Files Unit had originally been created within the Nixon White House in September 1972 to provide a separate storage location for "sensitive" documents removed from the Central Files and selected staff members' offices. They initially included the complete files of the staff secretary, the President's Office, and the offices of H. R. Haldeman, John Ehrlichman, John Dean, and Charles Colson.

5. The processing problems posed by the Nixon presidential papers and their less than satisfactory resolution are discussed in detail in Joan Hoff, "A Researcher's Nightmare: Researching the Nixon Presidency," *Presidential Studies Quarterly* 26 (Winter 1996): 107–30.

6. Joan Hoff, "Researching the Nixon Presidency," in Leon Friedman and William F. Levantrosser, eds., *Watergate and Afterward: The Legacy of Richard Nixon* (Westport, Conn.: Greenwood Press, 1991), pp. 263–67.

7. U.S. House of Representatives, Committee on House Administration, *Disapproving Certain Regulations Proposed by the General Services Administration Implementing Section 104 of the Presidential Recordings and Materials Preservation Act*, 94th Cong., 2d sess., report no. 94-1485 accompanying H.R. 1505, September 9, 1976; U.S. House of Representatives, Committee on Government Operations, *Public Access to Certain Papers, Documents, Memorandums, Tapes and Transcripts*, report no. 93-1182 accompanying S.J. 240, September 26, 1974 (emphasis added to Ervin quotation); and Congressional Information Service Index, *GSA Regulations Implementing Presidential Recordings and Materials Preservation Act, May 13, 1975*, CIS/MF/7, item 1037.

8. I originally believed that opening more tapes without official NARA transcripts would compound an already professional and litigious battle among scholars and Nixon aides over Watergate. But Maarja Krusten and Frederick J. Graboske, archivists who worked on processing the tapes, convinced me that, however desirable it might be to avoid multiple versions of the same tape, this would require too much time and money. Even with computers, one hundred archival hours would be required to transcribe one hour of one tape to obtain 99 percent accurate transcripts for the released tapes. (In 1979, nearly three hundred hours were needed to transcribe one hour of conversation.) The task of transcribing these tapes is tantamount to translating a document from an ancient language. The thousands of pages of log material, moreover, require cross-references and antecedents to enable researchers to place what they hear within a historical context. Transcripts prepared by the NPMS who were familiar with individual intonation of the voices recorded on the tapes and thoroughly grounded in the history of Watergate are infinitely better than the current situation whereby numerous researchers of varying degrees of expertise all claim to have the "authoritative" transcriptions.

9. Maarja Krusten, "The Nixon Tapes at the National Archives" (unpublished manuscript; updated version, March 1994), and letters to author, November 26, 1993, March 9, 1994. The University Publications of America has microfiched and indexed these transcripts, making them available outside of the Archives II in College Park, Maryland.

10. Maarja Krusten to author, October 1, 1996; *Stanley Kutler and Public Citizen v. Don W. Wilson,* Complaint for Declaratory and Injunctive Relief, Civil Action 92-0662, U.S. District Court, D.C., March 19, 1992; deposition by

Maarja Krusten in Civ. A. 92-0662-NHJ, September 29, 1992; and author's telephone conversations with Cunliffe, January 20 and February 21, 1995. Members of the NPMS created working notes when they originally reviewed all the tapes; these can be used by future researchers to identify the specific sections. Fawcett's role in accepting Nixon's informal list of deletions to Watergate tapes without required public notice and the Justice Department's later defense of this action are fully discussed in Hoff, "A Researcher's Nightmare, pp. 262, 273; and Maarja Krusten, "Watergate's Last Victim," *Presidential Studies Quarterly* 26 (Winter 1996): 273.

11. AP press release, March 19, 1992; *Washington Post,* March 20, 1992, p. A7; December 14, 1991, p. A8; and *International Herald Tribune,* November 20, 1992, p. 6 (quoting the *New York Times*).

12. "Senate Report on Mismanagement at the National Archives," November 2, 1992, and "Action Plan" by Don Wilson—both summarized by National Coordinating Committee for the Promotion of History, November 25, 1993; *Washington Post,* November 4 and November 24, 1992; *Federal Computer Week,* January 4, 1993; *Chronicle of Higher Education,* January 23, 1993, pp. A1, A24; and Seymour M. Hersh, "Nixon's Last Cover-up: The Tapes He Wants the Archives to Suppress," *New Yorker,* December 14, 1992, pp. 82–95.

13. Hersh, "Nixon's Last Cover-up," 76; *New York Times,* December 14, 1992, p. A9; and *OAH Newsletter,* May 1993, p. 10. The most authoritative rebuttal of the insinuation that archivists leaked information to Hersh can be found in Krusten, "The Nixon Tapes at the National Archives."

14. Don W. Wilson, the former Archivist of the United States, became head of the Bush Presidential Center and research professor of presidential studies at Texas A&M University. No conflict of interest influenced his decision to turn jurisdiction over the controversial PROFS tapes to former President Bush, he claimed, at the time he was under consideration for these new positions. Three Democratic senators disagreed and demanded an investigation. *Washington Post,* February 8, 1993, p. A18; and February 17, 18, 1993; *New York Times,* February 17, 1993; and *OAH Newsletter,* May 1993, p. 10. The senators were John Glenn (D-OH), David Pryor (D-AR), and Joseph L. Lieberman (D-CT).

15. *OAH Newsletter,* May 1993, pp. 9–10; W33 Burrelle's News Service for May 17, 19, 25, 1993; and AP Press Release, May 17 and August 4, 1993, NPM, NARA.

16. Maarja Krusten, "The Nixon White House Tapes," (unpublished manuscript, 1993), pp. 5–6; and AP Press Release, August 10, 1993, "Nixon Tries Again to Block Release of Tapes" (byline James Rowley), NPM, NARA.

17. *New York Times,* August 10, 1993, p. A9; April 26, 1994, pp. A1, C19; and author's telephone conversation with Cunliffe, February 21, 1995. The National Archives originally attempted to get around Judge Lamberth's injunction by releasing blocks of sanitized taped conversations as "integral files." The November 1996 release proved to be more fragmentary and out of context than those of May 1993 for reasons discussed later.

18. This rereview should be faster than the initial review because of the availability of the twenty-seven-thousand-page log and working notes prepared by previous archivists. Even so, this process will further delay release of the remaining Nixon tapes for a minimum of four years.

19. Krusten, "Watergate's Last Victim," 280.

20. *OAH Newsletter,* May 1993, pp. 9–10; *New York Times,* April 26, 1994, pp. A1, C19; *The Nation,* May 20, 1996, pp. 23–24.

21. Carlin quoted in NARA press release, April 12, 1996; Kutler quoted in *New York Times,* November 19, 1996, p. A12; *Lingua Franca,* November 1996, p. 90; and Krusten, "Watergate's Last Victim," p. 279. Krusten points out that another potential source for the National Archives' further deference toward presidents occurred when Carlin transferred attorney Elizabeth A. Pugh from the Justice Department, where she had argued "implied support" for concealing National Archives actions restricting certain Nixon tape segments from the public. See note 10.

22. The most concentrated examples of criticism can be found in *Lingua Franca,* November 1996, pp. 86–90.

23. NARA press release, April 12, 1996.

24. See Nixon's memoirs, *RN: The Memoirs of Richard Nixon* (New York: Grosset and Dunlap, 1978), pp. 511–12. In the Brookings case, the 1991 released tapes had also recorded Nixon reiterating that no action was authorized whether using tax returns, cutting off government contracts, breaking and entering, or firebombing. See April 26, 1973, transcript, White House Tapes, Watergate Special Force File Segment (WSPFFS), conversation no. 431-009, NPM, NARA.

25. Clark Mollenhoff to Haldeman, October 17, 1969, Box 53; Colson to Haldeman, May 23, 1970 (suggesting the creation of Republican-oriented Brookings, possibly using money from Ross Perot), Box 60—both in the recently declassified Presidential Materials Review Board Review on Contested Documents, White House Special Files, Haldeman Files, Nixon Presidential Materials, NARA. Mollenhoff's memorandum records his conclusion that "the Brookings Institute [*sic*] is being used [by former Democratic officials] as a kind of shadow government on projects that appear to be aimed at undermining Administration policy and operations at both Defense and State." He then concluded: "It is my considered opinion that the Brookings Institute represents one of the least of our problems. . . . Our problem is . . . that the anti-Nixon people at Brookings still have the widest contacts with highest level policy jobs in almost all departments. . . . If we could wipe out Brookings tomorrow, it would be like putting on a band-aid to cure a cancer."

26. White House Tapes, Abuse of Government Power (AOGP) Segments, conversation nos. 525-001, June 17, 1971; 533-001(1), June 30, 1971; 534-002(3)(4)(5)(6), July 1, 1971; Christopher Matthews, *San Francisco Examiner,* November 21, 1996, p. A1. Matthews is one of the few reporters to note Kissinger's presence (and as well Melvin Laird's and John Mitchell's) at the June 30 meeting. Kissinger attended at least two other meetings where he expressed no opposition during discussions of breaking into Brookings. These new tapes not only document Kissinger's extreme opposition to publication of the Pentagon Papers but that Kissinger (1) sat passively by when anti-Jewish remarks were made; (2) was actively involved in the 1972 political campaign even though he headed the National Security Council; (3) played a decisive role in the decision to fire Ehrlichman and Haldeman; and (4) discussed with Nixon the details of the Watergate break-ins after they occurred—something the president did not do with Secretary of State William Rogers or other cabinet members.

27. Public Broadcasting System, *Lehrer News Hour,* January 2, 1992 (Ehrlichman, Tom Wicker, and Monica Crowley commenting on Nixon tapes). For an analysis of the relative absence of expletives, and ethnic and racial references in the sixty hours of tapes released in 1991, see Joan Hoff, *Nixon*

Reconsidered (New York: Basic Books, 1994), pp. 312–22. I am currently preparing a similar computer analysis of ethnic and racial references in the 1996 tape segments.

28. Hoff, "Researcher's Nightmare," pp. 268–69.

29. For example, lawyers for Basic Books, my publisher, recommended that I alter several sentences in the paperback edition of my book *Nixon Reconsidered*, Dean's lawyers having threatened to sue them and me over my citations to several pages of references in the Colodny-Gettlin book. This interpretative controversy has also carried over to media productions. John Dean has played a major role as consultant and thereby has promoted the conventional interpretation of Watergate. Two television productions exemplify his influence: the 1989 ABC TV movie and the 1994 BBC Watergate production, both based almost exclusively on Bob Woodward's and Carl Bernstein's undocumented, fifteen-year-old book. Dean also served as the principal consultant for Oliver Stone's movie about Nixon. James Rosen, in *Forbes Media Critic* 2 (Spring 1995): 76–83, devastatingly recounts why the BBC first accepted and then rejected the Colodny-Gettlin interpretation despite the protests of some of Nixon's aides who had participated in the production.

30. AOGP Segments, conversation no. 044-80, March 29, 1973.

31. According to the author's conversation with Linda Fischer, tape specialist at Nixon President Material Project in College Park, Maryland, April 15, 1997.

32. Ibid.; and author's telephone conversation with acting director of the Nixon Presidential Materials Project, Karl Weissenbach, April 29 and May 27, 1997. Although no dictabelt transcriptions had been requested during the original Watergate trials, attorneys for Colodny and Gettlin did request all recordings involving Dean, including dictabelts. At this writing it could not be determined if they received any.

33. Christopher Matthews, *San Francisco Examiner*, December 8, 10, 1996, pp. A1 and A17, respectively; and Susan Naulty, *Washington Times*, January 28, 1997.

34. The latest in a long line of exaggerated "Nixon as evil" statements can be found in Gary Taylor, *Cultural Selection* (New York: Basic Books, 1996). Taylor attempts "to control Nixon's image and to make the entire value of America society hinge on it" by saying: "You must remember this: Nixon was evil. If we forget that, his crimes will cease to be crimes; evil will become instead the way of the world." *New York Times Book Review*, May 26, 1996, p. 17. For similar earlier references to Nixon, see Hoff, *Nixon Reconsidered*, pp. 336–38.

35. *New York Times*, March 29, 1997, p. 19, op-ed piece by Charles Baxter (quotation); and Hoff, *Nixon Reconsidered*, pp. 9–13, 341–46.

36. Page Miller, National Co-ordinating Committee, *Washington Update* 3, no. 14 (April 10, 1997); and author's telephone conversation with Louis Bellardo, assistant archivist for presidential libraries, April 10, 1997.

37. The civil action for compensation was *John H. Taylor and William R. Griffin v. United States*, C.A. 80-3227 (JGP). For earlier decisions in this case see *Nixon v. United States*, 782 F. Supp. 634 (D.D.C. 1991); *Nixon v. United States*, 978 F. 2d 1269 (D.D.C. 1992); *Griffin and Taylor v. United States*, memorandum, November 20, 1995, C.A. 80-3227 (JGP); and Maarja Krusten, "The

National Archives: Watergate's Last Victim" (unpublished manuscript, revised November 25, 1995), pp. 26–27.

38. For opinions in the Yorba Linda area see *Los Angeles Times*, April 5, 1997, pp. A1, A28. Carlin quoted in the *Washington Post*, April 5, 1997, p. A1. Several days later, the *Washington Post* reported that the Nixon family, the Nixon Presidential Library staff, and the Center for Peace and Freedom funded by the Nixon Foundation were at odds over whether to accept a $6 million gift from the foundation of Elmer H. Bobst, a close friend of the Nixon family who died in 1978, to establish a Bobst Institute at the Yorba Linda facility. The problem stemmed from Bobst's alleged anti-Jewish sentiments and was temporarily resolved when the foundation decided to halt construction of a building that would have made the Bobst Institute a branch of the Nixon Library, complicating NARA supervision of presidential papers under the proposed agreement (April 9, 1997, pp. D1 ff., and April 10, p. A2, respectively). The Nixon Library already has its hands full without the additional burden of taking on the contentious Nixon presidential papers and tapes.

39. *Washington Post,* April 5, 1997, p. A1; *New York Times*, April 6, 1997, p. A1; and author's telephone conversation with Louis Bellardo, assistant archivist for presidential libraries, April 8, 1997.

40. NCC *Washington Update* 3, no. 14 (April 10, 1997).

8

The War over Secrecy: Democracy's Most Important Low-Intensity Conflict

Scott Armstrong

The U.S. Supreme Court has just refused to grant certiorari in my case against the president.[1] My lawyers had asked the Court to overturn a decision by the Court of Appeals for the District of Columbia Circuit which held that the National Security Council (NSC) is not an agency of the government but merely a group of staff aides who advise the president. The Clinton administration had argued and the court of appeals agreed that the Federal Records Act, and thus the Freedom of Information Act (FOIA), do not apply to the NSC.[2] By leaving that decision in place, the Supreme Court assures that NSC activities will remain secret for twelve years after Clinton leaves office; more important, the president and his national security adviser can decide which records they will and will not retain.[3] As a practical matter, the Clinton administration has successfully made one of the most—if not the most—sweeping assertions of secrecy of the past twenty-five years.

I had shared with my lawyers at the Public Citizen Litigation Group both a skepticism that the justices would take our case and a fear that if they did they might subvert the progress we had made on other issues at a lower level. While we had much to lose, we felt it was important to resist a terrible precedent giving presidents the right to declare an agency of the government a nonagency and, by so doing, ensure that actions behind closed doors would remain as totally secret and as unaccountable as they might wish. We had tried to avoid a higher court ruling by spending months attempting to negotiate with the Clinton administration a compromise that would treat the records of the advisers closest to the president differently from those of the staff who ran the NSC. When that failed, we tried a legislative fix but were forced to take the case to the Supreme Court owing to Congress's unwillingness to address the ever-compounding problems of secrecy and inaccessibility of government information created first by the Reagan and then the Bush and Clinton administrations.[4]

FIGHTING FOR ACCESS TO GOVERNMENT INFORMATION

Most citizens, even seasoned journalists, academics, and politicians who should know better, believe that the battle against excessive government secrecy is fought in alternating volleys of great constitutional moment. In fact there are few such grand battles over principle in the secrecy business. The daily attacks on government secrecy by everyday citizens (often employed as news media professionals) are usually nothing more than routine inquiries about what the government is doing. They are often met by the most customary and mundane of defenses. Where "I don't know" or "I can't tell you" doesn't work, "it is secret" generally does. When someone tries to breach the access barrier with either a Freedom of Information Act request or a similarly formal query, government officials respond that the requested information is "classified."[5]

From time to time, these barriers are informally breached. Journalists or public interest representatives mount isolated assaults on specific government offices, hoping to pick up information piecemeal from several sources and link it together into a more coherent tale.[6] Depending on the subject matter and particularly on its political ramifications, a collaborator within the walled citadel sometimes will "leak" information to the outside. Such additions to the public record are often strategically planned by an official seeking advantage in an internal struggle and willing to leak a selective account into the media. The media may try to verify this "leaked" information, but on deadline the weapons to perfect such information are crude at best. Journalists also find themselves as susceptible to the selective partial truth of a counterleak as to the original leak. At best the journalist keeps the information flowing, hoping that the collective droplets of leaked information constitute the beginning of access to a deeper reservoir of controlled government information.

Given the government's propensity to conquer, control, and manipulate information, individual journalists, scholars, and concerned citizens must fight an ongoing low-intensity, guerrilla war for government information. It is fought sporadically, individually, and in small bands of detached "light troops." These aggressive raids take place behind enemy lines where the spoils—the valuable information otherwise denied—can be secured. Increasingly, these incursions probe the bureaucratic defenses of the government's organizational cantons. Citizen experts, public interest specialists, and beat reporters, targeting critical information issues, go where they know the information exists.

SENDING OUT A RECONNAISSANCE TEAM

My recently rejected Supreme Court petition began with such a routine query. During the week of January 9, 1989, Eddie Becker, one of the most unconventional and creative thinkers employed at the National Security Archive, the nonprofit, nongovernmental organization I founded and directed, returned from a visit to the National Archives and Record Administration (NARA) with some disturbing news. Becker, a professional archival researcher and video journalist, reported that the archives' staff had told him that the Reagan White House intended to purge its entire electronic mail system on the eve of president-elect George Bush's inauguration, the following week. There was little time, Eddie insisted; the White House was determined to destroy these crucial government records.[7]

Such a dastardly act on such a precipitous time frame did not seem likely. I was less convinced that a conspiracy was at hand than bureaucratic ineptitude. But Eddie's concerns were grounded in reality. For included in the White House e-mail was a specific IBM proprietary communications network, known as the PROFS[8] notes system, managed by the White House Communications Agency and used to store the NSC's interoffice e-mail. All NSC officers had personal passwords that enabled them to send and receive secure messages to each other from terminals at their desks.

Our entire staff at the National Security Archive had become familiar with the PROFS system two years earlier. On February 26, 1987, the Tower Commission, appointed by President Reagan to investigate the growing Iran-contra affair and headed by former Senator John Tower (R-TX), issued its three-hundred-page report. This report repeated either verbatim or in paraphrase sections of hundreds of PROFS notes exchanged by the successive NSC advisers Robert "Bud" McFarlane and Vice Admiral John M. Poindexter, and their trusted aide Lieutenant Colonel Oliver L. North. A commission staff member had discovered that the contemporaneous e-mail, which the three NSC officials thought had been erased, was actually recorded on backup tapes.[9] Career staff at the White House Communications Agency had saved the backup tapes of this e-mail. Many of the "erased" PROFS memos were then easily restored and printed out in a four-foot-high stack of memos.[10]

These recovered messages documented the involvement so assiduously denied by the three men in the secret supply of arms to the Iranian military and how they secretly managed and directed the contra war against Nicaragua from the White House throughout 1985 and 1986. The PROFS notes further demonstrated that McFarlane had lied to several members of Congress about the Reagan administration's role in facilitating private donations to the contra rebels fighting the government of Nicaragua and that Poindexter had directed North to conceal and develop cover stories about his "operational" role in that "civil" war. Over the course of the next two years, the PROFS notes became the principal evidence first during the televised congressional hearings and then during the ongoing investigation of the independent counsel.

As more PROFS notes became public, they became critical to an understanding of the NSC's complicated and secret transactions in the Iran-contra affair. The electronic tags on the e-mail revealed precisely who had sent them, at what time, on what day, to whom, whether or not they were read and by which recipient at what time, who else received copies, and whether they had been answered. They were also surviving proof of the ease and casualness by which government officials first succeeded in classifying information and then distributing it through a discrete medium to manage breaking developments, and finally electronically destroying all evidence of the communication without a trace.

The PROFS note evidence was so detailed that investigators could track the complicated role that Oliver L. North played. Detailed to the NSC staff in 1981 to work in the Defense Policy Directorate and a protégé of ex-Marine McFarlane, North rose with McFarlane, who had moved to the NSC from the State Department to become deputy national security adviser and eventually Ronald Reagan's national security adviser. As the contra war grew in Nicaragua, North became first McFarlane's, and then Poindexter's (McFarlane's successor) sole point of contact for the complicated series of the NSC's various covert and semicovert operations.

When the focus of the Reagan administration's covert efforts to retrieve American hostages from Lebanon moved from antiterrorist activity to secret hostage negotiations, North also became operationally in charge of that "account." As a result, North managed both the secret contra resupply operations in Central America and the highly secret arms-for-hostages initiative with Iran. As the complexity of North's operation developed, he turned outside the government to retain deniability inside. He built what came to be known as the "Enterprise," a covert government logistics capability involving Richard Secord, a retired air force general with considerable background in arms sales and such special operations as the planned second (but never executed) Iran hostage rescue mission. North set Secord in motion; in turn, Secord, with Iranian expatriate Albert Hakim, set up a network of shell corporations, offshore bank accounts, arms procurement, air and shipping systems, and an airlift capability.

When Attorney General Edwin Meese publicly broke the Iran-contra scandal on November 25, 1986, North abruptly left the NSC and became the immediate scapegoat for the Reagan administration. North subsequently testified under a grant of immunity before the Iran-contra congressional committee and in March 1988 was indicted on Iran-contra-related charges by a federal grand jury. But as of January 1989, North was yet to be tried. One of the charges he faced was the destruction of government documents, including PROFS notes.[11]

In January 1989, the preserved sections of the PROFS system remained critical to understanding just about everything in the complicated Iran-contra story and its overlap with U.S. relations with Israel, the Saudis, and a variety of European, Latin American, and Asian allies. Much remained undone in the Iran-contra investigations, including the fact that the alleged coconspirators remained to be tried or to testify under plea agreements. Since many other original documents were false when created or were destroyed or altered, the PROFS notes provided the most complete, accurate, and candid account of the decisions of these NSC officials. Most important, these materials could shed light on the controversies about the involvement of departing president Ronald Reagan and of president-elect George Bush.

On hearing Eddie's account, I became highly skeptical about the motivation at the White House. I had filed an FOIA request on behalf of the National Security Archive for the supporting records of the Tower Commission. (The executive order establishing the commission had made it an administrative creature of the State Department.) The material, we were told, was not available under the FOIA because on its final day the commission had turned over all its records to the White House counsel's office, thus making them presidential, and not agency, records.

There was some possibility that such an outrageous decision to destroy unique records would not stand. I did not think there was any doubt at the White House that records of such importance and historical uniqueness as those created or retained by the Tower Commission would have to be preserved. I suspected that the White House had chosen to pretend that the only records that needed to be preserved were the particular PROFS notes that had become evidence before the Tower Commission, during the Iran-contra hearings, or during the Office of the Independent Counsel's preparations for the trial of Oliver North. Since these records would be retained and introduced into the public domain by the respective institutions pursuing the Iran-contra affair, the White House was probably choosing to ignore the fact that any other recovered e-mail, not to mention subsequent e-mail, constituted federal records. My first instinct was that by threatening to make public such an obvious abuse of the Federal Records Act's requirement (mandating the preservation of government agency records), I might force the White House to agree to preserve these electronic records.

I called the office of White House counsel Arthur Culvahouse to inquire about Eddie's find and was told that the computers would be purged on inauguration eve. Anything of record value would already have been printed out by White House or NSC personnel and filed with other paper records. I noted—to no avail—that operating under these very same instructions prior to the revelation of the Iran-contra affair, the NSC staff had preserved virtually no e-mail and had instead deleted the very records that had so articulately provided the principal evidence against the White House, North, Poindexter, and McFarlane.

I was told that the evidentiary material provided to the independent counsel and the congressional committees would be preserved as part of their records. Anything else, including all backups and current e-mails, would be purged. The White House counsel's office alone would define which records would be retained. E-mail was not a record category requiring preservation.

I insisted that to destroy these records would violate the guidance of the NARA for record preservation. Not so, I was informed. NARA's director of presidential libraries had approved the deletion of the electronic mail.

THE OPENING VOLLEY

I wasted no time in calling John Fawcett, the director of the NARA Office of Presidential Libraries, and arranged an appointment for Wednesday afternoon, January 18, the day before the scheduled destruction. I had had intermittent contact with Fawcett over the years as he rose through the ranks of the NARA until he became head of all presidential libraries, with responsibility for overseeing the preservation, appraisal, and accessioning of each administration's records. I knew that in historical circles Fawcett had become notorious for consistently taking the side of former presidents and the entourages they left in charge of the political management of presidential libraries. Many of his colleagues at the archives were also worried that Fawcett's deference to past presidents might lead him to abandon the archives' obligation to ensure the preservation and accessibility of government records. He became known as former president Richard Nixon's principal ally in assisting Nixon's lawyers in keeping the majority of his records and tapes private.

To reinforce my outrage over this pending White House decision, I invited representatives of the American Library Association, the American Historical Association, and the American Newspaper Publisher's Association to join the delegation from the National Security Archive in our meeting with Fawcett.[12] We arrived and each expressed our concern that a loophole was being left open—perhaps inadvertently—that would inevitably lead to great mischief.

At first Fawcett did not seem to grasp the problem. Referring to his office's version of the PROFS e-mail system, Fawcett maintained that the electronic data from e-mail did not differ from the electronic information transmitted over a telephone wire. This was just digital data. Notes of the conversation, not the electronic information, would constitute the record, he insisted: a record would have to be printed out, electronic data need not be retained.

We were incredulous that Fawcett could not understand that e-mail systems also established the time and scope of the message's distribution and response. This additional information, Fawcett argued, was nothing more than the equivalent of a telephone message slip. Substantive information about government business was contained in the paper version (which thus was a record); the only unique feature of the e-mail was the electronic tags placing time and date and distribution (which was not a government record).

We conceded that not every PROFS note needed to be preserved. Some were no doubt trivial, regardless of their form. But others were undoubtedly of critical importance. I compared Fawcett's willingness to allow Reagan administration officials to destroy any electronic record they wished with knowingly allowing the Nixon administration to erase 18½ minutes of tape. Surely, the definition of a permanent agency record should encompass materials created by North, Poindexter, McFarlane, and other NSC staff.[13] Surely, out of an abundance of caution, the archives would act to ensure the preservation of such materials.

The practical reality of boxing up any White House materials, Fawcett responded, meant that secretaries and clerks were often left to decide what was important. That was a fact of life. The archives could do little other than offer general guidance about what was a federal record and what was a presidential record. As a matter of practice, moreover, the archives did not inspect what was retained or destroyed except to figure out how to transport or store it. Archives personnel did not directly supervise or inspect the actions taken by government officials in the disposition of their records.

But this didn't mean that records would not be preserved, Fawcett assured us. Papers would be saved, but not electronic records. These would provide "ample" and "adequate" documentation of everything about which we had raised concerns. As long as a copy of an e-mail was printed out by each office that considered it to be a record, Fawcett questioned whether it mattered that the electronic data documented that three people had had electronic copies of a message. This was a stunningly absurd proposition to anyone who had done research in a presidential library and found documents in a sender's file that were not in the addressee's files. Had they been received? Had they been read? Had they been acted upon? E-mail could answer these questions. Requiring the office of each party to print out their e-mail as each saw fit would continue the existing problem of fuzzy historical documentation.

Most distressing to us was the complete failure of Fawcett and his superiors at the archives to understand the historical importance of independent contemporary records that, owing to their electronic provenance, were more accurate and comprehensive than paper records. In any institutional setting, such records were important and unique. But in the case of the Reagan administration's admission that its staff had destroyed and altered records on several occasions, these records took on special meaning. After reviewing potentially embarrassing records, North and his staff had shredded many of them. In another instance, North had found that five memorandums about his highly secret support of the Nicaraguan resistance indicated that his supervisors knew about his activities.[14] Since these records had been registered in the NSC's official record system and thus could not safely be destroyed, North checked them out of the archives, rewrote them to remove the damaging material, and his secretary, Fawn Hall, retyped them and then returned the doctored documents to the NSC record system.[15]

I asked Fawcett if it wasn't his professional responsibility to ensure that the White House preserved all federal and presidential records in whatever form, whether computer tapes, computer disks, microfiche, paper, or whatever. I inquired whether it wouldn't be simpler to preserve the existing backup tapes and to back up all the information presently on the system.

Fawcett hit us with a shocker, more bluntly put than I had imagined. He claimed that Congress intended the Presidential Records Act of 1978 to cover any materials generated to carry out the constitutional and statutory duties of the president. Congress, in Fawcett's perspective, had deliberately left vague the definitions of what constitutes a presidential record. The president alone could determine what materials were presidential papers. The act specifically exempted the president's personal papers, such as diaries and journals, and the president's activities as leader of his political party. Fawcett pointed out that many documents fall into gray areas. Since Ronald Reagan was the first president to be covered by the act, the applicable standards would no doubt evolve. Besides, Reagan was leaving an enormous body of paper—over 60 million pages, nearly twice that left by any of his predecessors.

Indeed, Fawcett noted, it was permissible to delete both the e-mail and all the hard disks on which word processing files existed. Only the paper copies of files would be preserved, and only those portions that were either federal agency records or presidential records. In either case, the president, through his delegation of authority, would decide what would be preserved in either category.

For the first time it dawned on me that the ground was being laid for the destruction of a lot more than mere e-mail.

For years the NSC had operated on the premise that its "records" consisted only of the minutes of its formal meetings (which were held rarely), those staff memorandums recording official actions and logged into a central registry, and a limited number of formal intelligence findings and other documents. Everyday office files of each NSC staff member were considered "convenience" files. We had learned only the previous year that these records were never searched in response to FOIA requests, ostensibly because they were the personal property of the NSC staff member and thus were not institutional records. Although there were some variations over the years, by the end of the Reagan administration, it was assumed that the staff member would donate these documents to the presidential library. In addition, as the Iran-contra scandal developed, it became clearer that the White House personnel who were responsible for the preservation of records and managing public requests for access to them were in fact systemically allowing records to be destroyed and altered. Moreover, some NSC staff had been actively involved in foreclosing the public release of records responsive to FOIA requests.[16]

Under Fawcett's criteria, the wholesale destruction of paper documents could take place almost as easily as electronic purges. Moreover, documents could (and no doubt would) be transferred from agency records of the NSC to presidential records, making them inaccessible to FOIA requests for a longer time and allowing both President Reagan and President-elect Bush to keep them from successor administrations should a Democrat be elected.

THE FIRST BATTLE FOR THE WHITE HOUSE E-MAIL

We left Fawcett's office without any assurance that he would prevent the destruction and assured, instead, that he would not. We had only two alternatives: allow the destruction to take place or go to court. In the hallway outside the office, I proposed we seek a temporary restraining order (TRO). Representatives from each of the organizations present responded that they would return to their offices to seek authorization to join our suit.[17]

Within a few hours we began working with Kate Martin, counsel to the Center for National Security Studies, to construct our argument in support of our request for a TRO. To get standing to prevent the destruction, we had to show that irreparable harm would come from not granting our motion. To meet that standard, I prepared a series of FOIA requests for the PROFS system e-mail in electronic form. Should the TRO not be granted, the materials would be denied forever. For the remainder of the day and overnight we recruited additional plaintiffs.[18]

Good news followed almost immediately. Senior U.S. District Court Judge Barrington D. Parker set a hearing for 5:15 P.M. Thursday afternoon. It was also good news that Parker would hear the case. Once referred to in the local legal paper as the most cantankerous federal judge in Washington, Parker had a reputation for total independence. I had seen him exercise that independence when he presided over the trials of former CIA Director Richard Helms, the anti-Castro Cuban terrorists who had blown up two activists in Washington, and Represerentative Otto Passman, who accepted bribes from Washington lobbyist and Korean Central Intelligence Agent Tongsun Park.[19] Two years earlier he had heard and dismissed two of North's lawsuits challenging the constitutionality of independent counsel Lawrence E. Walsh's appointment to investigate the Iran-contra affair. We were surprised, however, when the government's lawyer turned out to be the acting attorney general of the United States, John R. Bolton.[20]

Bolton directly challenged our request for a TRO until the judge to whom the case would be assigned could rule on the law. "Your honor," Bolton began, "the outgoing staff members of the White House, who will be leaving tomorrow, are doing what anyone does when they leave one job to go to another. They are taking the pictures off the walls. They are cleaning out their desks and they are eliminating . . ."

"They are not seeking a restraining order against taking pictures off the wall," Parker observed.

"I understand that, Your Honor," Bolton continued. "But what is going on here is not some sinister conspiracy. What is going on here is the normal termination of one staff to give room for the other staff to come in. . . ."

"That may be true, but what is happening to the material that's the subject of this litigation?" Parker asked.

"It is being prepared for deletion," Bolton responded.

"What?" Parker asked incredulously.

"It is being prepared for deletion," Bolton noted, "There's nothing untoward or improper about it. . . . When the new people come into the White House at noon tomorrow, they need to have access to the system and they need to be able to do whatever they are going to do with it. And it would impair that ability, that is to say the ability of the new president of the United States, on his first day in office to get his administration up and running. It would be as if the halls of the White House were filled with furniture from the outgoing administration. It's important for an orderly transition, which is vitally important to the nation as a whole, that we be allowed to go ahead and complete what is nothing more than normal house cleaning," Bolton concluded.[21]

Parker was unpersuaded. "I think that the plaintiffs have made a threshold showing sufficient cause. The world is not going to cave in if I grant a temporary restraining order. This case is assigned to Judge [Charles] Richey, and Judge Richey [to whom the case was assigned after the emergency hearing], I'm sure, will do what is consistent with the law."

At 6:10 P.M. Parker issued a TRO against President Reagan, President-elect Bush, and the NSC staff, prohibiting further destruction or even alteration of tapes in the so-called PROFS system. Bolton then told the court that "some deletions have been made over the course of the last several days," but he promised to tell the White House immediately to stop purging the electronic files.[22]

I was at home that evening when I got a call from lawyers for the NSC and the Department of Justice.[23] The court order was written so tightly, they claimed, that the NSC computer system would have to be totally frozen to avoid altering anything. Not a single keystroke could be entered lest other data be overwritten. In addition, the NSC's computer system and the new president would not be able "to get his administration up and running." Such routine but important functions as responding to incoming congratulatory messages from world leaders—Margaret Thatcher was mentioned—or admitting visiting VIPs arriving at the front gate could not be done without this internal communications system.

Sensitive to the concern that we were interfering with the ordinary conduct of business, I obtained assurances that the material now on the PROFS system could be downloaded to a backup tape without losing any data and could then be reloaded anytime required for the court case.[24]

FROM BATTLE TO WAR

In the wake of our victory in preventing the imminent destruction of the PROFS notes, it did not occur to me at first that we were embarking on a very different type of litigation than in other cases involving our periodic battles with the government under the FOIA. The National Security Archive had continued a tradition I had begun as a journalist at the *Washington Post* in the early 1980s. When the government stonewalled an FOIA request and when the information sought was of a type that should be routinely made available, we filed suit in U.S. District Court. But even when institutions like the *Washington Post* were sufficiently concerned to file such suits, the government's game of delaying resolution discouraged other suits.

When I originally founded the National Security Archive, I continued to litigate the government's most egregious denials. I had been able to obtain pro bono assistance from some of the largest and most prestigious law firms in Washington to assist with our cases. In the PROFS case, we had the good fortune to secure the services of the Public Citizen Litigation Group (PCLG), the litigation branch of the watchdog organization Public Citizen, founded by Ralph Nader. The PCLG's lawyers principally litigate cases in the federal courts involving important public matters, particularly administrative law and separation of powers.[25] The PCLG was the type of group that had the commitment and perseverance for the long haul.

After a very active litigation calendar, the PCLG prevailed on September 15, 1989, when Judge Richey ruled that we had standing to sue to force President Bush's compliance with the retention requirements of the various federal statutes that potentially cover the White House e-mail. Two years after filing the case, we prevailed again when the U.S. Court of Appeals for the District of Columbia Circuit upheld Judge Richey's ruling that we had the right to challenge whether an agency's plans to destroy records violated the Federal Records Act. This, in effect, denied the Bush administration's attempts to have the case dismissed. But we lost on the question of whether a private party could go to court over a president's compliance with the Presidential Records Act during his term of office.

Bill Clinton's election victory over George Bush in 1992 served as a forewarning of further problems. The defeated president might decide to destroy his electronic records. Under any circumstances, his staff was not likely to leave sensitive records in the hands of their Democratic successor. Furthermore, the indictment of former Secretary of Defense Casper Weinberger a few days before the election included quotations from Weinberger's notes about then Vice President Bush's involvement in the original meetings about arms for hostages, an involvement Bush had repeatedly denied.[26] This served as a poignant reminder that while the Reagan-Bush cover story had held up through the Tower Commission and the congressional investigations, it would be sorely tested by evidence the independent counsel would introduce in the remaining prosecutions. On November 19, 1992, Judge Richey allowed us to add the White House e-mail from the lame-duck Bush administration to our case, issuing a restraining order preventing the destruction of the Bush White House backup computer records.

The importance of the injunction became even more obvious when, on Christmas Eve, outgoing President Bush pardoned former Secretary of Defense Casper Weinberger and the remaining officials still under investigation or awaiting trial in the Iran-contra case. Bush's action produced a significant, but ultimately ineffective, outcry. Discredited by the act of pardoning, Bush nonetheless took his lumps secure in the assurance that no materials showing his role in the affair would be introduced into any future trial record. This disposition of the other Reagan-era PROFS and those of his administration was now in the hands of Judge Richey.

On January 6, 1993, Judge Richey found for us on the crucial issue that computer tapes containing copies of e-mail messages by either the Reagan or Bush White House staffs must be preserved like other government records. The electronic versions are not simply duplicates of paper printouts, he held, but contain additional information. The judge also ruled that the archivist of the United States "had failed to fulfill his statutory duties under the Federal Records

Act" after having been told of the White House's intention to delete the material and having taken no preventative action.[27]

The following week, the Bush administration made a last-minute bid to provide a "clean slate for the incoming administration" of President-elect Clinton, proposing that the NSC should be allowed to start erasing its computer records the next day. Justice Department lawyers, representing the Bush White House, contended that the court was impeding "the present administration's ability to leave office with its records dispatched to appropriate federal document depositories consistent with the law."

Judge Richey rejected this proposal and warned in a sharply worded order against any effort to evade his mandate. Richey was "not satisfied" that all "federal records" in the White House computers would be preserved, in part because of "inconsistencies" in the administration's representations to the court and in part because the White House intended to rely on its own staff rather than the National Archives professionals to decide what to save and what to erase. Although the Bush administration had agreed "in part" to abide by the court's orders pending its appeal and preserve computer material on backup tapes, Richey added that the administration had not set out clearly "when backup tapes would be made or have been made." The White House would shoulder a "heavy responsibility," he warned, should officials fail to preserve all the records covered by his order. Some Reagan-era backup tapes had already been recycled "and the information on them lost," in violation of a 1989 order.

So concerned was Judge Richey that the White House would defy him that that afternoon he placed an unsolicited call to *New York Times* reporter Steve Labaton. The court papers filed by the Bush administration led him to believe that despite his rulings, it would begin erasing the material on Friday morning and "write over user data at each work station on all personal computer systems in order to create clean user space for the incoming Administration's N.S.C. staff," Labaton quoted Richey as saying. "This is just outrageous. It's really egregious."[28]

Still unwilling to follow Richey's ruling, the Bush White House filed an immediate appeal and asked the U.S. Court of Appeals for the District of Columbia Circuit to allow them to destroy records while the appeal was pending. The U.S. Court of Appeals refused. But the White House was not done yet.

On the eve of the Clinton inauguration, and unknown to us until later, the Archivist of the United States, Don Wilson, already in secret negotiations to become executive director of the George Bush Center at Texas A&M University,[29] tried to remedy Bush's legal setbacks. At midnight, he signed a secret agreement granting to President Bush exclusive legal control over the e-mail tapes of his administration. Working all night, a National Archive team used rented trucks to cart away from White House offices 4,852 tapes and 135 hard disk drives in cardboard boxes before the incoming Clinton appointees arrived.[30]

A DEMOCRAT ENLISTS ON THE OTHER SIDE OF THE WAR

On May 21, Judge Richey's frustration bubbled over as the same Justice Department and National Archives lawyers, now reporting to the Clinton administration, resisted his authority to rule on the disposition of the tapes and, instead, supported the Bush-Wilson agreement. Richey cited the Clinton White House and the Archivist of the United States for contempt of court for failing to carry out his order to preserve the computer records of the Reagan and Bush administrations. Noting that some of the backup tapes had been damaged and that the Clinton administration had failed to develop guidelines to preserve these materials, Richey warned that should the administration fail to take steps by June 21, he would impose fines of fifty thousand dollars per day for a week and double the daily fines each week thereafter.[31]

Was this just one more instance of career Justice Department staff refusing to buckle under to repeated court rulings that would frustrate their plan to ensure that executive branch officials and presidents could retain maximum control over the documents of their administration?[32] We assumed this did not reflect the new administration's view. After all, when Bush had withheld materials during the presidential campaign, then candidate Clinton had repeatedly attacked him for failing to come clean. And in response to the Christmas Eve pardons, Clinton expressed concern "about any action, which sends a signal that if you work for the government, you are above the law."[33]

The Clinton administration, however, appealed Richey's ruling to the U.S. Court of Appeals for the District of Columbia Circuit. On August 13, 1993, a panel headed by Judge Abner Mikva vacated Judge Richey's contempt orders but affirmed his ruling that the Federal Records Act (FRA) required the preservation of the complete electronic copies of White House e-mail messages, and presumably those of all other agencies. The court of appeals sent the case back to Richey to decide the dividing line between "agency" records (which would be covered by the FRA) and "presidential" records (which would be covered by the Presidential Records Act).

Throughout 1993 and early 1994, we maintained a back channel of communication with various Clinton White House officials and had nearly two dozen settlement conferences with the Justice Department and White House staff, including five meetings with the Civil Division's top appellate counsel. We believed that there were good public policy resolutions to the records issues posed by our case that could be agreed to by more open-minded individuals than the lawyers who had controlled the case for the past four years.

We then believed that most of the resistance came from career Department of Justice attorneys, embarrassed by their continual attempts to allow the destruction of the materials, and whose delays in resolving the case were exposed as partisan moves on behalf of two Republican presidents. The Justice Department's role in the PROFS case had become intertwined with the Iran-contra affair in general, in which Attorney General Edwin Meese had orchestrated a successful cover-up of presidential responsibility. This was baggage that the Clinton administration's political appointees need not carry forward.

Frustrated that the Justice Department lawyers were still able to scuttle any reasonable settlement, we had another half dozen meetings with Clinton White House counsel and senior presidential aides[34] without the presence of Justice Department attorneys. At one point, we thought we had worked out the critical principles for a settlement. In short order, however, career lawyers at the Justice Department prevented the plan from being fleshed out by raising an endless series of objections.[35]

Before long, we thought we had reached another agreement in principle which we were determined not to share with the Justice Department before its approval by Clinton national security adviser and NSC Director Tony Lake and White House counsel (formerly Judge) Abner Mikva. But as reasonable as I thought our compromise might be, I soon had indications that Tony Lake was less sanguine.

At a social gathering following a White House function one evening, Lake, a personal friend, jokingly poked me in the chest and accused me of "ruining his life" by requiring that the White House observe unrealistic record retention practices. One of the founding members of our board,[36] Lake had, during the 1980s, used the National Security Archive's extensive collection of declassified records in the research for his own scholarly publications. Grateful for the access, he was a happy user when he left our board to become Clinton's national security adviser.

But on this evening Lake was not really joking. He produced from his pocket a white index card, elegantly framed by a leather holder, with seven lines of notes of three to six words each. These, he told me, were his notes from one of his longest and most substantive meetings with the president. The codified lack of detail was an effort to avoid creating any record that could be subject to an FOIA request. I reminded Lake that because he was a personal aide to Clinton, any records of his meetings with the president were exempt from disclosure under the FOIA (because they were presidential records as opposed to agency records) until at least five years after President Clinton's departure from office. For matters that warranted national security classification, the time frame was a minimum of twelve years and, given recent patterns, for all practical purposes would be indefinitely inaccessible.

Lake in turn assured me that he was determined to limit the records of his meetings with the president to these extremely cryptic references. He could match these memory joggers with the briefing agendas he took into the Oval Office, but no one else could. He was extremely belligerent about protecting presidential prerogatives and was particularly concerned that a successor administration bent on misconstruing and attacking President Clinton's foreign policy would secure access to the records upon Clinton's departure from office. At the time, I thought Lake's concerns were unreasonable given the practical limits on public access to presidential papers. As the dynamic of constant congressional demands and subpoenas for Clinton administration records grew in the mid-1990s, and as the Clinton administration failed repeatedly to assert any resistance to these demands for fear of being accused of a cover-up, I developed a greater sympathy for the bureaucrats' concern that anything they wrote or recorded could become fodder for a political attack by a hostile Congress.[37]

THE PREEMPTIVE STRIKE

Although I should have seen it coming, on March 25, 1994, the Clinton administration threw us a curve, declaring in a brief before Judge Richey that the NSC is not an agency but a group of personal advisers to the president, and thus its records were exempt from the FOIA. This logic would remove the entire Clinton administration's White House e-mail from the reach of the Federal Records Act; the president alone could decide whether or not to preserve these records under the Presidential Records Act (PRA). Because the PRA cannot be contested by a private citizen while the president is still in office, Clinton would succeed in doing what Reagan and Bush had failed to do—escape any challenge to his decision to purge White House records.

In further debriefing the White House and NSC staff, who had encouraged us to believe we were close to a deal, it appeared that

Lake could not live with the prospect of losing control over materials that he felt needed to be kept private. He was willing to roll the dice on the judicable question of whether the NSC was an agency at all. Created in 1947, through nine presidents the NSC until this moment had always been treated as an agency. The most senior personnel, the national security adviser and his deputy, were considered to be presidential aides when they advised the president directly but agency officials when administering the NSC staff.[38] Had the Reagan or Bush administration succeeded in asserting that the NSC was not an agency, the original PROFS notes would have been declared presidential records subject to the sole discretion of the president and would have been long gone, with virtually no recourse for us or other researchers.[39]

On February 15, 1995, Judge Richey rejected the Clinton administration's characterization of the NSC's nonagency status as "arbitrary and capricious . . . contrary to history, past practice and the law." He declared the NSC an agency. The Clinton administration immediately appealed the decision to the court of appeals.

While awaiting Judge Richey's pending ruling on the Clinton administration's assertion that the NSC was not a federal agency, on December 13, 1994, we filed suit contesting the Bush-Wilson agreement.[40] The Clinton administration also decided to defend this agreement. The following February Judge Richey declared the Bush-Wilson agreement "null and void," ruling that it violated the Presidential Records Act. "No one, not even a President, is above the law," Richey wrote.[41]

In March 1995, the National Archives published proposed guidelines to govern how federal agencies should maintain e-mail records. The agencies lobbied against "the burdens" of the proposed new requirements. The new archivist, John Carlin, responded that while the regulations "stress that the Federal Records Act applies to e-mail just as it does to records created in other ways," the regulations "do not impose new burdens on agencies."* Our hard fought victory with

---

*In 1984, because of the lack of independence of previous archivists, the Congress enacted legislation that requires the archivist to be a professional without strong political connections selected "solely on the basis of professional qualifications required to perform the duties and responsibilities of the office." The current archivist, John Carlin, was governor of Kansas from 1979 to 1988. He ran President Clinton's 1992 presidential campaign in Kansas and was appointed by Clinton in June 1995. According to the *Baltimore Sun* (January 3, 1997, p. 1E) the records of his term as governor were opened a year after he left office and hurt him in subsequent political campaigns. "I just felt like I had nothing to hide and I wanted to make it clear that anybody that wanted to see the papers could," Carlin said. "I had a couple more campaigns later and it turned out to be not too wise a move, because [oppo-

Judge Richey had been reduced by Carlin to allowing agencies to simply print out any e-mail or any other electronic information they feel is a record. In practice, the e-mail would not be preserved in its electronic form, and as a result, most often it would not be preserved at all.

On August 2, 1996, eleven months after oral argument, a three-judge panel of the U.S. Court of Appeals for the District of Columbia reversed Richey's ruling by a vote of 2 to 1. The majority opinion, written by Judge Douglas Ginsburg,[42] sided with the government in holding that the NSC is not an agency subject to the Federal Records Act. NSC records, instead, are presidential records governed by the Presidential Records Act and could not be subject to judicial review. Under current law, FOIA requests for NSC records may not be filed until five years after the president has left office (unless the archivist has processed the records, an event that almost never occurs) or twelve years if the records are classified—which most are.

Judge David S. Tatel wrote a lengthy dissent explaining that for twenty years the NSC had been treated and in many significant ways had acted as an agency. Tatel accordingly endorsed Judge Richey's conclusion that the NSC "must maintain and preserve its records in accordance with the Federal Records Act, except when high level officials of the National Security Council are acting solely in their capacity to advise and assist the President."

In February 1997, we petitioned the Supreme Court to review the court of appeals decisions. Failing to get at least four of the nine justices to grant Supreme Court review, we have come full circle.

FACING THE GOVERNMENT'S ARMY OF LAWYERS

The best measure of how dearly government officials protect something from becoming public is how energetically they defend it. When Judge Parker granted our first TRO, I should have recognized that this was no ordinary case. After all, none of us had ever seen an attorney general—albeit only an acting attorney general—appear on

---

nents] dug through and took out of context and twisted and so forth. So maybe what I learned is there's a reasonable time before records are released." The American Historical Association, the Society of American Archivists' Council, and the Organization of American Historians opposed both Carlin's professional qualifications and his partisan background. Although he was accused of being a crony of Clinton, in fact he has difficulty in getting anyone from the White House to return his calls.

an FOIA case before. It soon became apparent that the Justice Department, the Bush White House, and the National Archives were going to extend this battle into a war. I realized later that in my twenty-four years in Washington, only a few cases received such high-level attention. While there are no indications that any president was transfixed by our case, three presidents had more than a passing awareness of it. Three vice presidents saw fit to comment unfavorably to the press on aspects of our lawsuit.[43] Three former and five active national security advisers to the president became actively involved in scheming to thwart our efforts.[44]

Another measure of the intensity of resistance is the hours the government devoted to avoiding the relatively reasonable and quick options for settling the case. As of early 1997, there had been thirty-five hearings before Judge Richey, seventeen depositions, four trips to the court of appeals, and a trip to the Supreme Court. Between 1989 and September 1995, government lawyers devoted 30,169 hours, 37 minutes, and 48 seconds litigating and appealing decisions in the case.[45] In 1996 and early 1997, in appeals first to the court of appeals and then to the Supreme Court, this number increased by over 5,000 hours. Using 35,000 hours as a basis and taking the Justice Department's lowest average rate[46] to calculate the value of government lawyers, the government spent over $4,200,000. If the calculations were based on the customary charges for the market rate value of such services,[47] the figure becomes an astounding $9,275,000!

Cynics might view these figures as the cost to the taxpayer of career lawyers keeping the old business of prior administrations covered up; in fact, most of the litigation costs (29,000 of the 35,000 hours) came during the Clinton administration. What is it that three successive administrations intend to protect? Why would three administrations devote extraordinary resources to frustrate what would seem to be mundane attempts to obtain government records? There was no threat that the information would find its way immediately into the public domain. And why would the Clinton administration join the two prior Republican administrations in denying these records to the public?

BEHIND THE LINES: FRONTIER BORDERS DIVIDE SECRECY VERSUS PUBLIC RIGHT TO KNOW

The PROFS case involves a series of component issues, beginning with seemingly small bureaucratic disputes, initially handled by lower-level political appointees and career employees. As John Fawcett told me before the case began, clerks and secretaries had been doing things this way for a long time. John Bolton, the acting attorney general, was also right. At the time the first decisions were made to destroy or recycle electronic tapes, there was no master conspiracy to subvert the public's right to know. In its beginnings this case began as an everyday attempt to take advantage of bureaucratic prerogatives.

But as the issues ratcheted up to systemwide consequences, resisting our minor query became a major issue for three successive administrations. Only after the principles on which the lower-level battles were being fought highlighted the broader implications for presidential secrecy did successive administrations initiate an energetic defense to ensure their own PROFS would never become public.

A significant majority of formal classification and security clearance decisions are made in good faith. But beneath this level, a range of minor bureaucratic maneuvers permit officials to tie up documents. At the lowest level is the central principle that what doesn't exist is de facto secret. At an intermediate level, it matters less that such records are destroyed than that they simply be inaccessible. In the higher orders of secrecy, classification works to screen out and discourage outsiders, while security clearance restrictions and compartmentalizing secret programs limit awareness about similar decisions by other government employees.

Top-level political appointees quickly became vigilant in seeking to preserve three main bureaucratic prerogatives of secrecy: control over preservation, control over custody, and control over access. The political appointee has opportunities to expand these bureaucratic prerogatives from time to time. For example, putting restrictions on the date when the records can be publicly viewed before they are deeded to the government has the same practical effect as overclassification, with fewer risks of being overruled by a successor in office. In recent years, removing one's own records from the executive branch at the end of a term of office has proved a remarkably effective way to maintain secrecy.[48]

Government employees have been granted extraordinary latitude by their superiors over record classification and preservation. The prohibitions and penalties—even criminal penalties—against abuse of record standards are lax and ineffectual, with the result that the minimum standards for secrecy are often set by the lowest-level bureaucrat with access to the information. The result: virtually anything can be kept secret by anyone who wants to obstruct public access—at least for a short time.

Inevitably cabinet officers, senior agency personnel, and political

appointees become persuaded by the proven efficacy of tactical bureaucratic secrecy. As aspirants to power, they might swear that their
administration will never stonewall the press or the public. But once
in office, the same behavior is repeated. What was deemed unacceptable becomes acceptable. Each new administration develops an interest, agency by agency, in using bureaucratic techniques to expand the
boundaries of secrecy.

THE BUREAUCRACY'S COST-BENEFIT ANALYSIS
OF THE WAR OVER SECRECY

The use of government secrecy has a public and statutorily codified rationale—the protection of the national security. In my experience, however, bureaucratic rationales most often define the actual
usage patterns of secrecy. Because there are so few formal challenges,
appeals, or lawsuits resulting from legitimate claims of national security, the most frequent—and thus most important—rationales for secrecy are bureaucratic.[49]

For example, claims that technical information in the areas of
intelligence sources and methods and of weapon system specifica-
tions and performance characteristics must be protected are often used
to withhold information that could challenge the fiscal responsibility
of departments and their closest contractors. In the Gulf War, the
ability to protect technical capabilities allowed government officials
to manipulate the media through selected graphics that seemingly
demonstrated the success of weapons systems beyond their actual
abilities.[50]

For many political appointees and top career bureaucrats, secrecy's most compelling benefit is to control the argument. To restrict
direct access to raw information ensures that one side in the internal
policy debate dominates. This is often a matter of timing. For those
managing a weapon system, keeping Congress dependent on selectively released information is most important during the test stage
when investments are made, although information about many a failed
system becomes increasingly more difficult to obtain when the system's failures—and thus the likelihood of cancellation—increase. In
this instance, other agencies and contractors competing for the same
resources are perceived to be at least as dangerous as foreign foes.

The Commission on Protecting and Reducing Government Secrecy recently evaluated the annual cost of protecting national security information as $5.6 billion,[51] a figure including $2.6 billion in
government security classification costs and $2.9 billion in contrac-

tors' costs. The true costs are at least ten times larger, according to those who manage security systems for the defense and intelligence agencies. Another uncalculated cost involves the enormous expense of litigation to ensure nondisclosure, which is absorbed by the Department of Justice within its own budget.

NO SIGN OF A THEATERWIDE TRUCE IN THE WAR OVER SECRECY

Despite substantially improved rhetoric, the Clinton administration's record is as bad as those of most of its predecessors and worse than some. With the lone exception of the Department of Energy, no department in the Clinton administration has significantly improved its openness or made more than a beginning in curtailing secrecy excesses.

It is ironic that the Clinton administration's overall performance on openness should be so uniformly poor. In those matters where presidential privilege and personal presidential privacy have been most at stake (i.e., Whitewater and related scandals), Clinton's cooperation in providing records to congressional investigators has by and large been more forthcoming than that of any prior administration. This may be attributed to the White House's sensitive press monitoring and finely tuned polling, revealing that Clinton's public and media credibility is badly hurt if he is perceived to be stonewalling for his own benefit.

Traditionally, the NSC has overseen the development of secrecy policy within each administration, and it did so during the first two years of the Clinton administration. During that time, it issued a revamped executive order on classification, 12958, which was then promoted as a major reform to reduce the number of items classified and to more quickly declassify archival material. Little, however, was accomplished beyond insisting that all agencies address the task over the next five years when automatically declassifying all classified documents over twenty-five years old.[52] Some agencies immediately began disgorging the innocuous, but many sought exceptions for vast quantities of material twenty-five years old and older.[53]

The initial NSC spin was that the executive order would stem the proliferation of classified information. However, no mechanisms were instituted to make this promise a reality. Even before the executive order took effect in October 1995, its key advocates left the NSC staff. With their departures, the Justice Department assumed responsibility in the fight over secrecy. In furtherance of this disengagement, the NSC dispatched the Information Security Oversight Office (ISOO) to the NARA. The ISOO was responsible for monitoring the use and abuse of security classification and determining the appropriateness of security actions taken by the contractor community.[54] An Interagency Security Classification Appeals Panel was created on October 14, 1995, to hear appeals to agency decisions on mandatory declassification review requests and to review internal challenges to classification decisions and agency determinations to exempt twenty-five-year-old information from automatic declassification. But after an eighteen-month existence, the panel reportedly considered few decisions and overturned even fewer.[55]

The Department of Justice retained its role as the counterinsurgency troops in the battle over secrecy.[56] Attorney General Janet Reno has frequently and sincerely extolled the need for openness and has insisted that the Department of Justice is committed to facilitating the release of information under the FOIA. She has encouraged all federal agencies to make discretionary releases whenever possible and has announced her intention not to defend agencies seeking to deny release on inappropriate grounds. But at the same time, the department's Civil Division has effectively resisted openness.

Civil Division lawyers are "the keepers of the Grail," according to a career government lawyer who believes that the government should designate special masters to settle litigation where secrecy is at issue. After Justice's Civil Division prevented the appointment of such an outside expert, he said that "few of the professionals in the worlds of defense, intelligence and diplomacy care as deeply about keeping the courts out of the secrecy game as the civil division. They argue at every chance they get that one chink in the armor will lose the war." Another government lawyer says, "For those of us defending the government from the range of legal assaults, openness is like AIDS. One brief exposure can lead to the collapse of the entire immune system. Take away national security secrecy and the government is just one more litigant, winning some and losing some. Now we can always play the trump card—state secrets—and close down the game."[57]

The Justice Department's Civil Division also supervises the Office of Information and Privacy, which manages FOIA and Privacy Act responsibilities, including assisting in deciding all appeals from denials by any Justice Department office of access to information under those acts.[58] This office has traditionally coordinated government policies to thwart the release of classified information sought under the FOIA and provides the training to ensure that every government employee handling FOIA requests understands the potential "adverse" impact of their actions as precedents for disclosure. More than any other factor, it has been this office's directives that have created the agency adage "When in doubt litigate."

After an initial rhetorical flourish suggesting that it would become a participating advocate of openness, particularly where nuclear weapon and stockpile transparency were concerned, the Department of Defense has initiated few changes on the secrecy front, largely acceding to the Justice Department's willingness to litigate any challenges.[59] Nonetheless, the Office of the Secretary of Defense still runs the most efficiently and honestly administered FOIA shop in government, apparently taking the statute seriously except when overruled from above. The declassification programs of some military components also hold promise of providing significant insight into the structural mandates of organizations that persist through today.[60]

Even so, the Defense Department's desire to retain a general lack of accountability, notably in the Gulf War syndrome debate, has served to strengthen public suspicions and distrust of government. The military's initial refusal to open up classified records except in piecemeal form and later efforts to locate and declassify more arcane and sensitive intelligence reports came to be perceived by veterans, the press, and even Congress as part of an elaborate and persistent cover-up. The Pentagon's attempts to refute the proposition that U.S. troops had been exposed to chemical or biological agents were frustrated by its refusal first to declassify all field reports and then even to identify the systemic intelligence reporting systems involved.[61]

As the story unfolded, no military or intelligence official could produce either the official log of chemical/biological incidents or even a chain of custody for such records. The Pentagon was eventually forced to admit that a comprehensive, detailed log of General Norman Schwarzkopf's official actions and of the reports and communications the general had received and reviewed had been kept by his senior military aide. The Pentagon then acknowledged that Schwarzkopf had been permitted to remove this log as his personal property when he retired to write his memoirs. This official record remains Schwarzkopf's private property.[62]

In the military services and in the defense/intelligence contractor community, the secrecy situation continues to worsen. The thousands of special access program compartments have created a nightmare of inefficiency and lack of accountability.[63] "Clearances" awarded under highly unusual and often subjective conditions are used to control information without regard to classification, ensuring that only a handful of people gain access to information the department needs for any major secrecy reforms.[64] The CIA has also sidestepped most secrecy confrontations by relying on statutes that specifically exempt its records from disclosure.[65]

The Departments of State, Treasury, and Commerce share this

compulsion to hide their records of international dealings from view as much for reasons of convenience as for diplomatic, commercial, or banking considerations. All three agencies habitually delay resolution of requests for information, relying on the fact that agencies, such as the CIA, have a stake in foreclosing the release of information and must review it before it can be released. Even historical materials are withheld on this basis.[66]

Other examples of tardy releases demonstrate the questionable basis for the State Department's secrecy decisions. Not until May 1997 did the U.S. government[67] release a highly critical analysis of the Swiss government's and banking communities' post–World War II policies involving Nazi Germany. While some of the information was already or would have been available shortly under the fifty-year rule, the most important documentation had been held back on the basis that its release would interfere with foreign relations.[68] In September 1996, Representative Carolyn Maloney (D-NY) introduced the "War Crimes Disclosure Act," which would have made intelligence records concerning Nazi war crimes during World War II subject to the FOIA, thus adding the ability to seek judicial review of FOIA requests for denied CIA operational documents. But "the CIA strenuously objected to the legislation and has effectively killed it in this Congress," Representative Maloney protested.[69]

These delays in record declassification reflect a bureaucratic stratagem. A de facto policy is to avoid releasing "linchpin" documents that can provide overviews or analyses that pull together information contained in already released documents. Without the "linchpin," previously disclosed materials are often difficult to locate, link up with other disclosed materials, correlate with appropriate human sources, and fit into an analytical framework. The pattern of FOIA withholding by agencies often indicates the willingness of bureaucracies to most vigorously object to the disclosure of otherwise largely unclassified "linchpin" documents.[70] For the same reason, government agencies tend to refuse to release most indices and listings of documents, including those of previously declassified and released documents.

THE GOVERNMENT SUES FOR PEACE

There are a few bright spots in the Clinton administration's conduct of its War over Secrecy. A new cost-benefit analysis was undertaken at the Department of Energy in the first weeks of Secretary Hazel O'Leary's tenure. Based on her prior government service at the

Federal Energy Regulatory Commission, O'Leary was familiar with the Enegy Department's institutionalized obfuscation, particularly where the department had fouled the landscape with radioactive materials or otherwise endangered citizens living in the neighborhood of one of its weapon complexes. She was keenly aware of how deeply the Energy Department was hated by nuclear researchers involved in tracing the history of nuclear weapons policy and design.

Seeking to confront the issue head-on, O'Leary recruited an experienced staff on the premise that to reestablish trust throughout the country, the Department of Energy must overcome the distrust of various "stakeholders." She defined stakeholders as the following: citizens who lived near, worked for, or depended on nuclear weapons facilities owned by the Department of Energy; public interest groups that had long documented the dissembling of department officials; the contractors who had dominated the department's decision making and operations since its founding; the far-flung fiefdoms of federal laboratories administered by contractors and universities; and whistle-blowers who had challenged the department or its contractors. To establish accountability, O'Leary issued orders requiring cooperation with her aggressive staff over questions relating to releasing information and in resolving ongoing stakeholder problems.[71] She also went out of her way to meet with the whistle-blower community.

As O'Leary prepared to launch an Openness Initiative, a series of news stories was published about victims of government radiation experiments.[72] Virtually all the "secret" details had been revealed earlier during 1985 congressional hearings but had not then made a public splash.[73] The first public outcry over the published revelations in 1993 provided O'Leary with a potential organizing tool for reforms. At her behest, President Clinton appointed an Advisory Committee on Human Radiation Experiments.

O'Leary sold the Advisory Committee to Clinton on the basis that "this committee as an indispensable part of our effort to restore the confidence of the American people in the integrity of their government [and] to increase the confidence of the American people so that . . . they could trust the government to tell the truth and to do the right things."[74] Under the leadership of scientific ethicist Ruth Fagen and the day-to-day direction of regulatory reformer Daniel Guttman, the commission uncovered the most cynical possible record of why materials were classified. A 1947 letter of an official at what was then called the Atomic Energy Commission was made public in 1994. This letter opposed the release of any document "which refers to experiments with humans and might have adverse effect on public opinion or result in legal suits."[75] In another case, the committee disclosed that the Veterans Administration (VA), which for decades has denied benefits to veterans exposed to radiation during cold war testing in the Pacific, knew as early as 1947 that veterans might have valid claims stemming from those tests. That year, in response to Operation Crossroads, the code name for the 1946 detonations of two atomic weapons at Bikini atoll in the Marshall Islands, the VA created the secret "Atomic Medicine Division" to study widespread contamination of servicemen at the Bikini tests and in the occupation of Hiroshima and Nagasaki, both hit by the atomic blasts that ended World War II. Ever since 1947, the VA had denied the vast bulk of nuclear test–related claims filed by veterans, who in 1979 created the National Association of Atomic Veterans to press for service-related benefits from the government.[76]

The committee's revelations were triggered by its unprecedented access to government documents. The committee retrieved and reviewed approximately four hundred thousand government documents. When agencies could not locate information responsive to the committee's request, the Advisory Committee staff went to the National Archives and often found what the agencies had said did not exist. Many of these documents were then retroactively classified as secret, although they had not originally been classified or handled as classified, and the Advisory Committee had to fight to have them declassified.

Over her four-year tenure, ending in January 1997, O'Leary reduced the amount of information classified, sped up the declassification process, and genuinely sought the input of public interest groups for declassification priorities. She established a Fundamental Classification Policy Review for the Department of Energy headed by Dr. Al Narath, formerly president of Sandia Laboratories, one of the national consulting labs. Narath and other nuclear weapon specialists recommended constructing higher security standards for the most sensitive material and opening a vast amount of material currently classified but not sensitive. The process of reviewing and updating classification policies and guidance was also begun, and an interagency process was established to expedite the declassification and release of shared information. O'Leary also created an Openness Advisory Panel to draft legal changes in classification policy and strategies to declassify the enormous mountain of old classified documents. She insisted on the declassification of significant amounts of information that had previously been withheld from the public. Over three hundred thousand pages were made accessible on OpenNet, an Energy Department Web site on the Internet.[77]

But most significantly, O'Leary ordered her general counsel to reduce litigation over Department of Energy practices. By releasing previously secret materials to public interest organizations, whistle-blowers, and their counsel, and by acknowledging their well-founded claims, which were often based on leaked information, O'Leary moved to resolve underlying problems rather than using secrecy for an advantage in litigation. Every pending case might not have resulted in a settlement; nonetheless, significant progress was achieved. O'Leary had difficulty institutionalizing this approach within her department's general counsel's office. It remained an open question at the point of her departure whether the policy of openness would continue.

PEACEMAKERS? THE MOYNIHAN COMMISSION AND THE CONGRESS

At the insistence of Senator Daniel Patrick Moynihan (D-NY), on April 30, 1994, Congress authorized the appointment of a federal commission to investigate secrecy. Called the Commission on Protecting and Reducing Government Secrecy (the Moynihan Commission), it spent nearly three years completing its mission, ultimately issuing a report that decried the current situation. The commission's report declared that secrecy was a form of bureaucratic regulation without statutory authorization. The report offered few details about how the system actually failed other than from the sheer weight of grotesque overclassification, and it recommended a very few general changes.

As its predecessors had done,[78] the Moynihan Commission came to the right, and obvious, conclusions. First it found that too much is classified, and it attributed this underlying problem to the fact that nearly all current incentives encourage secrecy. Officials were not properly trained to weigh the costs and benefits of secrecy, officials were not held accountable for their classification decisions, there was no penalty for overclassifying, and the president and the Congress made a double entendre of the phrase "oversight of classification." Second, declassification proceeded too slowly because agencies did not consider declassification an important mission and did not want to pay for it while Congress and the president did not provide sufficient resources to do the job right. Third, the commission focused on calculating the time frame needed to ensure the "safe" release of classified documents, concluding that the current fifty-year standard was too long.

Relying on the ISOO data, the commission estimated that just over half the secrets are created by the military, with the CIA contributing another 30 percent, the Justice Department fully 10 percent, the

State Department 3 percent, and all other agencies 1 percent. In fact, the ratios may be vastly different. Many of the military secrecy holdings involve contractor documents for intelligence and sensitive, high-tech weapons systems. Other commission numbers appear to be seriously flawed, and the estimates of the amount of information under government secrecy control is remarkably low (although it is unclear where in a range of from 2 to 10 billion pages these estimates fall). Estimating that about 1.5 billion classified documents are more than twenty-five years old, the commission proved unable to deal with ISOO figures about contemporary classification decisions. At the latest official count for the year 1995, the U.S. government made 3.6 million decisions to classify something—from a word or phrase to an entire document. That's roughly 10,000 new secrets a day. If each decision involved a single document that would be one thing; in fact, many decisions involve thousands of distinct records. Furthermore, many records start as one electronic file but are subsequently copied or printed out dozens, hundreds, or even thousands of times.[79]

The commission's approach, moreover, was based on a particular vantage point. The report adopted the analytical frame of Edward Shils's book *The Torment of Secrecy*,[80] a minor classic of the cold war years of anti-Communism and McCarthyism. Adopting Shils's sociological analysis and underlying disdain for a McCarthyite preoccupation with espionage, sabotage, and subversion at home, Moynihan and the commission concluded that significant national security threats were rare, and yet that legislators, investigators, and bureaucrats felt compelled to denounce and protect against a wildly inflated "enemy." Perhaps because Moynihan's prescription was so deeply rooted in Shils's forty-year-old analysis, the commission's principal focus appeared to be overcoming the historical origins of the "torment of secrecy" by extricating the historical record.[81]

The commission's report was discussed on May 9, 1997, at a public hearing of the Senate Governmental Affairs Committee. Fred Thompson (R-TN), the committee chair, and Senator John Glenn (D-OH), the ranking minority member alone attended the hearing. Attendance may reflect the attention that will be given to the "Government Secrecy Act of 1997," legislation introduced that day by Senators Patrick Moynihan and Jesse Helms (R-NC) in the Senate and Representatives Larry Combest (R-TX) and Lee Hamilton (D-IN) in the House. Their bill would establish the general principles that should govern federal classification and declassification programs and contains only the vaguest outline for needed reforms. Acknowledging that secrecy is an essential component of U.S. foreign policy, the bill proposes to limit classification to prevent a threat to the United States.

A balancing test is recommended to weigh the benefit from public disclosure of information against the need for protection of the information. "If there is significant doubt as to whether the information requires such protection, it shall not be classified." Unfortunately, the bill does not clarify how immediate, material, or demonstrable a threat to the United States need be to require protection.[82]

In general, the bill reaffirms the current policies of Executive Order 12958, whereby authority for classification decisions is delegated through agency heads. In other ways, it slips backward by proposing a thirty-year time frame for declassification of sensitive information, whereas the executive order sets twenty-five years. The bill also calls for a National Declassification Center to coordinate and oversee policies and practices.[83] Appearing on the *Jim Lehrer Newshour,* Moynihan stated that the National Archives would probably be the agency where the declassification center would be located. The NARA, which already regrets having the ISOO, is unlikely to be interested or able to handle such a new responsibility.[84]

The Moynihan Commission's emphasis on releasing historical information was a pleasant surprise for secrecy bureaucrats. This emphasis drove a further wedge between historians and those who make use of contemporary government information, primarily journalists and public policy analysts. Historians appear to be so concerned to obtain access to dated historical records on a regular basis in as complete a form as possible that many of them are willing to accept limits on contemporary information. They have avoided the bureaucratic rationale for secrecy and have confined their argument to the fact that the sensitivity of documents diminishes over time.[85] Highlighting these contrasting priorities, author and former journalist David Wise opposed the proposed Moynihan legislation. Wise objected that establishing a statutory basis for classification could in turn criminalize leaks, making it a crime both for a federal official to leak classified information to journalists and for journalists and their publishers to possess or communicate the information. The result would be a U.S. version of the British "Official Secrets Act" and an abandonment of the First Amendment right to publish "secrets."[86]

The testimony and discussion that day before Thompson's committee and the soon-to-be-filed bill nonetheless typify Congress's ambivalence. Congress is easily distracted from reforming secrecy every time a major leak of classified information is prominently reported in the press. The most likely legislative outcome might be to criminalize leaks and thereby increase unwarranted secrecy. By coincidence, the day before the hearing on the Moynihan Commission legislation, the *Washington Post* carried a front-page leaked story about a possible

Israeli mole in the U.S. government. Citing U.S. government officials as sources, the story quoted verbatim from National Security Agency intercepts of a conversation between an Israeli intelligence officer and his superior in Tel Aviv. The conversation included a request by Eliayahu Ben Elissar, Israel's ambassador to Washington, that the embassy intelligence officer seek to obtain from a well-placed source known as Mega a letter from Secretary of State Warren Christopher to Palestinian leader Yassir Arafat. The Israelis claimed that the reference was to the CIA desk officer for Israel, with whom they had a formal liaison relationship.[87]

CONGRESS AND THE INFORMATION WAR POWERS ACT

Despite the Moynihan Commission's findings and the possibility that some vague legislation may pass, Congress has traditionally had little interest in confronting secrecy issues, reflecting its own tacit understanding with the executive branch about secrecy. Congress can have a major impact on secrecy by enacting legislation to make more information available; generally members of Congress have respected claimed presidential prerogatives of secrecy and control over records. Occasional confrontations occur around withheld information,[88] but by and large Congress has been unwilling to institutionalize standards that would ensure disclosure. Congress could legislate information access but more often limits what the executive needs to release. Whether in deference to the commander-in-chief powers of the president or as a result of political caution, congressional leaders—even those in the party of opposition—prefer not to know certain secrets. In so doing, they reserve their right to complain about government policy or actions later if the administration is publicly discredited, while retaining their own deniability. At the very best, congressional oversight is a double entendre.[89]

Virtually the only exception to this rule has been for historical information, and then only when the degree of public skepticism reaches epic proportions. The corrosive public skepticism about the Warren Commission's "one shooter" theory eventually pressured Congress to create the Kennedy Assassination Records Review Board and to grant it unprecedented authority. Even then, age and the undisputed historical relevance of the documents in that exception made their mandated disclosure by means of an independent board easier to justify than extending this requirement to other sensitive records of the same period.

Although that degree of pressure is not likely be repeated on any other issue, the legislation creating this board can be a useful precedent. The board's mandate included having jurisdiction and declassification authority to address the question: Did the evidence of the harm that would result from the release of the information outweigh the public interest in the information? Second, President Clinton appointed professional historians and archivists (not present or former agency officials or politicians) to a board headed by a lawyer (who was appointed a federal judge during his tenure). This model can be improved and strengthened by institutionalizing any similar board's access to presidential authority. More than any other single factor, the careful bureaucratic skill of the board's chair, John R. Tunheim, in dealing with White House counsel prevented the CIA and FBI from succeeding either by stalling or through direct appeals to the president. Whether or not this process will endure in the final year of the board's extended term, the model appears to be the best yet designed.

From time to time, federal courts have expanded the right to know when deciding in favor of access. Their rulings have been most helpful when courts have conducted detailed inquiries into the reasons for withholding, often intimidating the executive branch into releasing documents.[90] The use of special masters and aggressive inquiry into the adequacy of government reasons for withholding documents, whether in litigation or in response to FOIA requests, have proved critical to ensuring government accountability.[91]

PEACEKEEPING: WHO MUST DO WHAT TO END THE WAR OVER SECRECY

Citizens need to challenge government secrecy daily by asking questions of their elected officials, of the administration in power, of the press, of scholars and public interest watchdogs. Each question loosens a grain of sand in the bricks of secrecy. The principal benefit of the resulting greater openness is good government through accountability to the people. Citizens must become their own information militia responsive to appropriate calls to arms by public interest organizations, journalists, or their elected representatives.

Reporters do their part by probing, by encouraging openness, by assuming skullduggery whenever secrecy does not make eminent sense. When they succeed in getting a leak, journalists remove one brick from the wall of inaccessible government. But they also need to ask themselves, "Who benefits from this secrecy, and who benefits from the leak?" The answers to these questions can begin to challenge the upper-level political actors who find it convenient to escape accountability, to shape their own story without the inconvenient intrusion of a curious press or citizens.

Elected officials should also be skeptical about assertions of secrecy. They should assume the worst and be willing to be disproved by disgorged facts. And most of all, rather than fulminating about "leaks" and press intrusions into public business, they would do better to address openly the questions revealed by leaks. For them, the first among these is also: Who benefited from the secrecy, national security or the national security bureaucrat? History has confirmed that the public and their government do better when the maximum amount of information is available for public review and debate. When an agency or an administration cannot be persuaded to put things into the open, members of Congress should do so. Woodrow Wilson, a professor at the time and later a president, aptly observed that "the informing function of Congress should be preferred even to its legislative function. The argument is not only that discussed and interrogated administration is the only pure and efficient administration, but, more than that, that the only really self-governing people is that people which discusses and interrogates its administration."[92]

Most of all, the Congress should also remember that openness promotes good government through accountability. Congress must encourage citizens (and the public interest organizations who represent them as information militias) to demand openness and must be willing to protect the guerrilla force in the war over secrecy, the journalist who pursues information for the public when no one else will or can.

NOTES

1. *Scott Armstrong v. Reagan* became *Armstrong v. Bush* and is now styled *Scott Armstrong et al. v. Executive Office of the President et al.* The "et al." includes: the organization I founded, the National Security Archive; the colleague who first brought the problem to my attention, Eddie Becker; the American Library Association; the American Historical Association; and the Center for National Security Studies. As a practical matter, the most important participants have been our attorneys at the Public Citizen Litigation Group, Michael Tankersley, Alan Morrison, David Vladeck, and Kathy Meyer, and, before them, Kate Martin of the Center for National Security Studies. For dramatic purposes alone, I have used the pronoun "I" when "we" is almost always more accurate.

2. *Armstrong v. Executive Office of the President*, 90 F. 3d 553 (D.C. Cir. 1996).

3. See the explanations of the effects of the Federal Records Act versus

the Presidential Records Act, the National Archives and Records Administration's interpretations of those statutes, and the application of the Freedom of Information Act to records under each law.

4. While the Republican chairman of the Technology, Terrorism, and Government Information subcommittee of the Senate Judiciary Committee (as well as chair of the Senate Intelligence Committee), Senator Arlen Specter (R-PA), was willing to insert language explicitly establishing the NSC's agency status into the Electronic Freedom of Information Act (which passed the Senate on September 17, 1996) or another piece of legislation, his Democratic colleague, ranking member Patrick Leahy (D-VT), previously an unparalleled advocate of openness in government, rejected the proposal on the basis that judicial appeals should first be exhausted before Congress addressed the issue. His staff cited his concern that attaching an NSC provision to the Electronic Information Act would only ensure a veto and destroy Leahy's carefully constructed consensus on the bill.

5. Until 1981, the secretary of defense instructed Pentagon personnel to treat all press inquiries promptly and to provide all available information or a reason why something could not be provided as if the request had formally been filed under the Freedom of Information Act (FOIA). Beginning with the first year of the Reagan administration, and to discourage requests, the Pentagon press office then told reporters with detailed or probing questions to file an FOIA request, ensuring significant delays and prohibitively high fees.

6. My personal favorite use of classification is the "aggregation" or "mosaic" theory. I first heard of it when an assistant secretary of defense told Bob Woodward, "We know what your friend Armstrong is up to. He's trying to piece together individually unclassified bits of information into a coherent whole so he can see what we are doing. Well that 'mosaic' is classified, so we are going to have to deny him the individual pieces even though right now they are unclassified." True to their word, the Pentagon soon issued its first denial of information based on the "aggregation" or "mosaic" theory that it could be used to deduce an accurate picture of "classified" information.

7. An accessible account of this case can be found in Tom Blanton, ed., *The White House E-Mail* (New Press, 1995).

8. Professional Office System (PROFS).

9. At the beginning of its work, I conferred with the staff director of the Tower Commission and suggested that certain files were critical to review, including the e-mail. I was told within a day or two that few, if any, relevant records remained. Most had been destroyed. This turned out to be incorrect. A few weeks later, Tower Commission staff member Kenneth J. Kreig, a 1985 graduate of Harvard University's John F. Kennedy School of Government, who had been assigned temporarily to the NSC's Crisis Management Center before being detailed as a Pentagon intern to the commission, found the backup tapes.

10. John Poindexter and Oliver North electronically shredded more than five thousand e-mail notes in the memory banks of their computer systems. Not all were eventually recovered.

11. In addition to shredding and erasing memorandums and PROFS notes, North had his secretary, Fawn Hall, retrieve memorandums from the NSC files and forge substitute memorandums omitting incriminating de-

tails. Only the PROFS allowed a reconstruction of what had been destroyed. On May 4, 1989, North was found guilty on the charge of destroying NSC documents, as well as assisting in the preparation of a false chronology for congressional testimony of Poindexter and Director of Central Intelligence William Casey and accepting an illegal gratuity (a $13,800 security system from Secord). On July 5, 1989, he was sentenced to a suspended three-year prison term, two years' probation, twelve hundred hours of community service, and a fine of $150,000. North appealed, and on July 20, 1990, a three-judge court of appeals panel vacated all counts.

12. Respectively Ann Heanue, Page Miller, Dick Schmidt (general counsel of the American Society of Newspapers Editors), and Eddie Becker and Tom Blanton of the National Security Archive.

13. In subsequent negotiations with the White House, we considered the possibility that the president's zone of protection extended to those aides—the national security adviser, the deputy national security adviser, and certain others who were working directly for the president when they prepared materials for him or acted solely on his behalf (as opposed to acting as an agency head of the NSC). There was a similar protection for the president's senior political aides such as chief of staff and White House counsel.

14. Some had handwritten annotations by Admiral Poindexter showing he had read the material.

15. Fawn Hall testified during North's trial that she shredded the originals after typing altered versions. But because she had not had time to remove copies of the originals from North's files before he was fired on November 25, she smuggled them out stuffed in her boots and the back of her skirt and gave them to North and his lawyer outside the Old Executive Office Building. *Washington Post*, March 24, 1989, p. A9. At the trial of Admiral Poindexter, she testified that North told her to remove references to McFarlane's and Poindexter's knowledge of his activities in arms deals with Iran and supporting the Nicaraguan contras, activities that Admiral Poindexter hid from Congress. *Washington Times*, March 15, 1990, P. A3 .

16. The most energetic of these obstructionists was a career archivist, Brenda S. Reger, who after three years on the NSC staff was promoted in 1983 from the position of director of the Freedom of Information Office to NSC senior director of the Office of Information Policy and Security Review. It was Reger who was found responsible for the faulty retrieval and declassification of documents and materials when responding to congressional and outside inquiries. See Final Report of the Independent Counsel for Iran/Contra matters, pp. 84, 142, and 145. It was Reger who, under intense scrutiny from the Tower Commission, began the process of collecting and processing the materials for the Iran-contra investigations by congressional committees and by the independent counsel. See August 20, 1985, memo ("Working files in staff members' offices are not subject to this or any other kind of searches since they are 'convenience files' generally made up of drafts, and/or copies of documentation in the institutional and presidential advisory files") written by Reger to Poindexter and quoted in the *New York Times*, April 14, 1989, p. A16; see also *Washington Post*, June 6, 1989, p. A21.

17. We had little time to recruit. The American Library Association always quick to defend openness in government and decry secrecy, joined at once. The American Historical Association took a bit longer but joined. No journalistic organization would join us, most claiming they did not litigate.

The Society of American Archivists (SAA) was unwilling to consider joining until we had won several lower court cases. The SAA remained reluctant to take an unabashed stance against the National Archives despite the archives' horrible track record on such issues.

18. By the time we filed, we had added the coauthor of the Presidential Records Act, former Senator Gaylord Nelson (D-WI).

19. I had written the original stories about Korean influence peddling and hoped that Parker would recognize the National Security Archive's status as a representative of journalism and journalists in general.

20. At the time, John R. Bolton was the assistant attorney general of the Civil Rights Division; Attorney General Richard Thornburg was occupied with the Pennsylvania delegation to the inaugural, and the position of deputy attorney general remained open.

21. See the transcript of Oral Argument in author's possession.

22. *Washington Post,* January 20, 1989, p. A4.

23. Interestingly enough, the NSC lawyer was Nicholas Rostow. Two years earlier, Rostow had been detailed by the State Department to the Tower Commission and wrote the 185-page narrative heart of the commission report, which concluded that the president and vice president were not culpable. This conclusion had been substantially eroded by subsequent evidence from the PROFS notes. Over the next four years as the NSC's in-house lawyer, Rostow became the most energetic NSC staff member to resist disclosure of the PROFS. *Washington Post,* February 28, 1987, p. A10.

24. The first requirement appears to have been met, but the second became a source of continued delay when the Justice Department repeatedly refused to allow the tape to be remounted so that materials could be retrieved.

25. Katherine Meyer pursued the case from January 1989 to August 1990, when she left to found her own firm; since 1990, Michael Tankersley has taken on the principal burden. PCLG litigation directors Alan Morrison and David Vladeck have guided the case throughout its life. Lucinda Sikes has handled the FOIA case matters.

26. The Weinberger notes were among thirteen thousand documents he transferred to the Library of Congress that had been either hidden from, or overlooked by, the independent counsel and the FBI. The likelihood that PROFS notes remained which had still not been carefully examined was obvious.

27. *New York Times,* January 7, 1993, p. 15.

28. *New York Times,* January 15, 1993, p. 1.

29. *Washington Post,* February 13, 1993.

30. The career NARA staff who managed the "midnight ride" described in a later February 16, 1993, memo how they had violated the NARA's rules for records transfers and how several of the sets of tapes Judge Richey had ordered preserved were lost, erased, or damaged.

31. *New York Times,* May 22, 1993, p. 6.

32. We also saw the Civil Division's customary hostility toward citizen litigants rather than partisanship in the Justice Department's behavior. When finally releasing the list of forty-two thousand White House PROFS notes covered by the litigation, the department attorneys insisted on giving it to us in paper printouts rather than the infinitely more useful electronic form. Using scanners and optical character readers, we converted the paper index into electronic form so we could use computers to prioritize and identify

what we needed. It was no surprise that after the time and expense of converting the database, the Justice Department asked for a copy to ease its own processing efforts. Presumably they did not want to use the electronic data in their possession to create an electronic database because then, even under their own interpretations, they would have had to provide us with a copy.

33. As quoted in Lawrence Walsh, *Firewall* (New York: Norton, 1996), p. 493, from a CNN interview.

34. Some of the most interesting back-channel negotiations over the case began when John Podesta, then staff secretary to President Clinton and later deputy chief of staff, and I shared assistant coaching duties for our Little League–age sons. Podesta, an ardent supporter of openness, worked diligently and ultimately unsuccessfully within the White House to urge a more open and reasonable approach. On a related humorous note, one Justice Department attorney expressed concern that I was discussing the case and gathering information during social interactions with senior White House and NSC officials. I rebuffed the suggestion that I had arranged meetings for these purposes. I was bound to know a number of White House staff after nearly two decades of practicing journalism in a relatively small town like Washington. But he soon learned that in addition to baseball, I also coached soccer and basketball teams on which the children of senior White House and NSC officials played. He suggested to another government official that I was arranging to coach these teams to curry access and favor with these officials. I don't believe he was persuaded otherwise when he learned that at the time the case began my oldest son was playing for the Chicago Bears and that my commitment to children's athletics started considerably earlier and without any political connotations.

35. We may have been naive to assume that those with whom we negotiated in the Clinton administration favored a good public policy resolution. Many were deeply involved in the Whitewater, Travel Office, and other budding Clinton-era problems, which, while not involving questions of national security, did involve questions of presidential control over the disposition of records generally.

36. The original board of the National Security Archive in 1985, during the second Reagan term, included a number of individuals who accepted prominent positions in the Clinton administration. The board was chaired in succession by John Shattuck, who became assistant secretary of state for humanitarian affairs, and Walter Slocomb, undersecretary of defense. Other board members included Deputy Secretary of State Strobe Talbott and Morton Halperin, an assistant to the president and senior staff member of the NSC.

37. "Washington Writer's Block," *Washington Post,* May 16, 1997, p. A25, a column by Lloyd N. Cutler, a Washington lawyer who has been White House counsel for Presidents Jimmy Carter and Bill Clinton. Cutler argues that the Supreme Court must overrule a lower court and reestablish the attorney work paper privilege, which the Clinton administration had asserted over a debriefing of First Lady Hillary Clinton by White House counsel. In his words, within the Clinton administration "taking notes of a meeting on a sensitive subject has become the rare exception, rather than the rule."

38. Most of the compromise proposals discussed with the NSC and the White House attempted to allow the president to separate "presidential ad-

vice" from other agency functions without drawing every NSC employee into the presidential adviser tent. Agency records would be defined as those that were not held for the exclusive use of the president and his closest aides. A practical resolution that reflects the realities of life on the NSC staff is admittedly difficult. Creating loopholes to allow senior NSC staff to give advice to the president can invite abuse. Denying the president such confidentiality for his closest aides on activities so central to his commander-in-chief role is similarly problematic. Highly principled arguments exist on both sides. The difficult but not impossible task is to design a workable system that allows the president confidential advice but retains accountability in the administration of the government.

39. To his credit, Lake publicly committed the NSC to informally process requests for information. He could have sought an exemption from having to "waste" time by meeting the obligation to search for, retrieve, and review classified records having an extremely low likelihood of release.

40. *American Historical Association et al. v. Peterson*, 876 F. Supp. 1300 (D.D.C. 1995). Wilson was represented by former Reagan White House counsel Fred Fielding.

41. The *New York Times* headlined an editorial "A Special Place in History for Mr. Bush," saying that "no President has the right to corner official records in an effort to control his place in history." *New York Times*, March 1, 1995, p. 18.

42. *Armstrong v. Executive Office of the President*, 90 F. 3d 553 (D.C. Cir. 1996).

43. In each instance, we received calls from reporters or others present. Each time, the vice president had the facts of the case wrong. All three, with Gore taking the most extreme view, asserted that we were asking that all electronic mail be retained permanently, a position we had never taken. In no instance did the press find the comments sufficiently interesting to report.

44. Clark, McFarlane, Poindexter, Carlucci, Powell, Scowcroft, Lake, and Berger.

45. Chart provided by the Department of Justice in response to a Public Citizen Litigation Group FOIA request. (This chart excludes thousands of hours provided by nonattorneys advising the government attorneys and the considerable time of attorneys outside the Justice Department.) This includes both hours in the series of PROFS notes cases known as *Armstrong v. Executive Office of the President* (29,284.13 hours), as well as the Bush-Wilson case against the National Archives (*AHA v. Peterson*) over the midnight attempt to shift custody of various materials to the Bush Library (885.5 hours).

46. The Equal Access to Justice Act provides rates each year for the government's reimbursement of certain legal fees to private attorneys, basing this figure on the cost of government representation. Averaging from the lowest rate ($102.89 in 1989) to the highest rate ($125.48 in 1995), with most of the hours spent in the last four years, I am conservatively using $120 (120 x 35,000 = 4,200,000).

47. The attorneys involved in the case were largely experienced and very senior attorneys whose officially calculated rates under the Laffey matrix would fall between $225 and $260 for 1989 and between $280 and $325 for 1996. Using the lower of these rates for the median year would give a rate of $265 per hour (265 x 35,000 = 9,275,000).

48. Former Secretary of State Kissinger was the master of this strategy.

Kissinger donated many of his official records to the Library of Congress with a restriction on access for fifty years and thereby ensured that his memoir of Nixon foreign policy was the only definitive one available, since only he (and presumably Nixon) had access to the papers. See *Kissinger v. Reporters Committee for Freedom of the Press*, 445 U.S. 136 (1980). Former Secretary of State Haig and Secretary of Defense Weinberger also donated their papers to the Library of Congress with restrictive deeds. Former Secretary of State Shultz gave his to the Hoover Institution at Stanford under similar circumstances. Weinberger, moreover, put some of his most sensitive notes in with his personal papers. This hiding in plain view worked until the independent counsel, concluding Weinberger had deliberately withheld materials to obstruct their investigation, was prepared to indict him, at which time he coughed up the materials. Such manipulations succeed if the former official defines narrowly what are the official papers that constitute records that must be left behind at the agency involved while defining broadly the category of "convenience files," which are considered personal. These often include the only copies of notes, calendars, briefing papers, and other materials that deserve more careful preservation as government records. Even Lake's comments above show a candor about controlling the near-term historical and policy debates about the actions of the Clinton administrations.

49. In reality their concerns involve not foreign governments and their spies and protection of the national security but a list of greater threats to bureaucratic security. For the professional government bureaucrat, the benefits of withholding follow the potential for negative impact should information be disclosed to the U.S. media and public interest organizations; internal auditors; competing military services, other federal departments and agencies; competing federal and international contractors; the Congress; and allied intelligence organizations. Because keeping secrets from these institutions allows deniability, organizations and individuals can escape accountability for virtually every form of governmental misfeasance, malfeasance, and nonfeasance. Keeping information out of the public domain makes the most routine task easier. The traditional exemption for information that could compromise relations with foreign governments allows American diplomats to avoid domestic and international second-guessing, difficult questions from allies and enemies alike, and public commitments to policies that may be overtaken by events.

50. See Michael R. Gordon and Bernard E. Trainor, *The General's War: The Inside Story of the Conflict in the Gulf* (Boston: Little Brown, 1996).

51. This estimate is for fiscal year 1995 and is based on information gathered by the Information Security Oversight Office.

52. Some Clinton insiders are not surprised by the failure to follow through on the executive order, given Clinton's unwillingness to confront virtually any opposition from the military or national security professionals on controversial matters. Journalists with long tenure around the White House contend that Clinton's top advisers see government information policy less as a matter of national security secrecy than as simply one more forum for manipulation by the same ploys of presenting hermetically sealed, tardy packages of largely irrelevant information tightly spun into propaganda nuggets.

53. See *New York Times*, January 3, 1996, p. A14, "The Struggle Against Secrecy" (editorial), which enthused that "too little has been made of a land-

mark victory for open government. Hundreds of millions of classified documents will soon become public thanks to Executive Order 12958, which came into force Oct. 15 and requires the automatic declassification of most U.S. Government files more than 25 years old. The struggle against obsessive secrecy is far from over, but President Clinton has honored his promise to let more sunshine in. It has begun to shine even at the Central Intelligence Agency."

54. It does this through the National Industrial Security Program Policy Advisory Committee.

55. The panel is composed of senior-level representatives appointed by the secretary of state, the secretary of defense, the attorney general, the director of Central Intelligence, the Archivist of the United States and the assistant to the president for National Security Affairs. The first chair has been the Justice Department representative.

56. The federal "police" power to keep the peace in the secrecy wars is vested in three institutions: the Office of Management and Budget (OMB), the National Archives and Record Administration (NARA), and the Department of Justice. The OMB and NARA manage the secrecy housekeeping, using the most time-honored bureaucratic mechanism that preserves secrecy—denial of access—to frustrate citizens' ability to find out what is going on in their government. Much of their institutional behavior is driven by the constraint that today's compromise over information access may become tomorrow's required and costly mandate for an information entitlement. The OMB and NARA help preserve secrecy not only by making access more difficult but also by deflecting citizen and journalistic information demands away from internal government files to the more superficial databases meant for public consumption.

The OMB monitors the implementation of general information access procedures across government agencies. Despite its important bureaucratic role, the OMB has sought to avoid responsibility to coordinate the most successful information access programs in the federal government, the creation of Internet Web sites. Many departments have taken these programs seriously, resulting in easy public access to otherwise arcane information. In addition, the recently passed Electronic Freedom of Information Act creates an obligation to provide consistently sought information in electronic form over the Internet.

The OMB has pushed the Government Information Locator Service (GILS), which is a virtually voluntary effort to have agencies report the scope and existence of their internal electronic information systems in a standardized format. The requirement is virtually identical to a similar, and theoretically compulsory, obligation to provide the same information to the NARA. The GILS appears to have initially been designed by the OMB to encourage the creation of electronic information systems by agencies that would offer government propaganda publications while discouraging the use of the FOIA to get government records. But because the GILS has provided an architecture of existing Web sites, it has in fact facilitated the flow of information to the public.

Despite the legislative mandate to act as the independent czar of federal information, national archivists have traditionally acted as if their ten-year statutory tenure was designed not to give independence from presidential administrations but to allow the perfection of subservience to them seriatim.

The NARA has declined to set a national policy on standards for and preservation of electronic records. Despite having absorbed the Information Security Oversight Office, the NARA has also done little to change the contemporary mechanisms by which federal records are classified so that declassification can go forward more smoothly in the future. By far the most underfunded of federal agencies, the NARA seems incapable of setting standards that other agencies must follow to reduce information management costs through decentralized maintenance of electronic information.

57. *Washington Post,* February 16, 1997.

58. The office had been managed for more than a decade by codirectors Richard L. Huff and Daniel J. Metcalfe, who in the early years assisted recalcitrant agencies with every possible alternative to release of information. In the years of the Clinton administration, they have maintained a more positive approach to the release of information through their office's publications and official guidance (see particularly *FOIA Update*). Department attorneys still credit them with framing arguments to resist disclosure whenever an agency decides to litigate.

59. *Washington Post,* February 16, 1997.

60. As an order of magnitude, USAF security officials announced in March 1995 that over the next five years the service would review 176 million pages of historical classified documents for possible declassification. *Air Force Magazine,* May 1996, p. 32.

61. "Marines Tell Gulf War Panel 'Fox' Detection Vehicles Warned of Gas," *Washington Post,* May 8, 1997, p. A6.

62. Schwarzkopf was given permission to maintain a Sensitive Compartmented Information Facility (SCIF), which was deemed by the government to have sufficient security to protect the "classified" information in his documents. The NARA allowed the proposition to stand that "classified" information, which portions of Schwarzkopf's logs clearly contained, remained personal materials. See Federal News Service, January 29, 1997, Hearing of the Senate Veterans Affairs Committee on Persian Gulf War Illnesses, chaired by Senator Arlen Specter (R-PA), Witness: Gen. Norman H. Schwarzkopf, U.S. Army retired.

63. *Washington Post,* February 16, 1997.

64. As a result of the Joint Security Commission's call for reforms in 1993, the U.S. Security Policy Board (SPB) was formed in September 1994 and was directed to recommend major improvements in all phases of government security. After thirty months, little had happened.

65. See the essay by James Dempsey in this volume.

66. See the essay by Page Putnam Miller in this volume.

67. The study was prepared by an Interagency Group on Nazi Assets chaired by Stuart Eizenstat, who was undersecretary of the Department of Commerce when the report was begun and undersecretary of state for economic affairs when it was concluded.

68. *Washington Post,* November 6, 1996, p. A18. Steve Aftergood, the director of the Project on Government Secrecy at the Federation of American Scientists, an advocacy group concerned with national security issues, notes that "the recent allegations that assets of Holocaust victims are still being held by Swiss banks and are inaccessible to survivors reflect badly on Switzerland [referring to front page *Washington Post* stories of October 26 and October 29, 1996]. But they also suggest the corruption of the U.S. national security classification system, which made it possible

for the Swiss banks to deny their responsibilities for so long. Documentary evidence that would have ended this injustice remained classified in U.S. archives for five decades with no apparent valid national security justification. Fourteen crates of records concerning looted World War II assets were withheld from the public until this year while survivors languished or died. Even with the belated release of these records, surprisingly little has changed." "Waiting for Disclosure" (Letter to the Editor).

69. U.S. *Congressional Record,* September 24, 1996, p. H10818.

70. One example of this is the FOIA request by James Mann (of the *Los Angeles Times*) for a Rand study of twenty years of U.S. diplomatic relations with the government of China. Although most sections and much of the supporting documentation of the study were unclassified, the air force litigated unsuccessfully for three years to prevent the release of the Rand overview. I have experienced similar denials for such overview, linchpin, and historical summary reports issued by Rand and other government-sponsored consulting firms precisely on the basis that they provide a coherent picture of policy where one is not otherwise available. Another example is an FOIA request for cumulative information about the Treasury Department's issuance of individual licenses for the export of humanitarian food and medicine, which was frustrated when the department refused to provide anything other than summary information.

71. Three of the most significant players were Dan Reicher, O'Leary's chief of staff by the end of her term, who came from the Natural Resources Defense Council; Bob Alvarez, who as the staff director of Senator John Glenn's committee with oversight responsibilities for nuclear materials had worked directly with the most important government and contractor whistle-blowers; and Brian Siebert, the head of the Office of Classification (renamed the Office of Declassification under O'Leary), who as a whistle-blower in the Bush administration had run afoul of the Energy Department brass.

72. See Eileen Welsome's December 1993 series in the *Albuquerque Tribune,* which reported that prisoners, mental patients, and even pregnant women were given plutonium and other radioactive material in government-supported research after World War II.

73. There was no follow-up or public outcry when a congressional subcommittee headed by Representative Edward Markey released the first federal report on human radiation experiments, "American Nuclear Guinea Pigs: Three Decades of Radiation Experiments on U.S. Citizens," largely because the federal government refused to make any more information available. Markey lost interest, the press lost interest, and all but the most affected members of the public lost interest. Once the government clammed up, even the bioethicians who had a keen interest in informed consent and research ethics did not vigorously pursue the allegations that unwitting human subjects had been used in secret government research. The government treated the secrets as if they were limited in number, fully disclosed, and not fit for further comment. See U.S. House of Representatives, Committee on Energy and Commerce, Subcommittee on Energy Conservation and Power, November 1986, "American Nuclear Guinea Pigs: Three Decades of Radiation Experiments on U.S. Citizens," ACHRE No. Con-050594-A-1.)

74. Human Radiation Final Report, *The Human Radiation Experiments: Final Report of the President's Advisory Committee* (New York: Oxford University Press, 1996), p. xix.

75. See Human Radiation Final Report, *The Human Radiation Experiments;* and Chair Ruth Faden's article in *The Hastings Center Report* 26, No. 5 (September 19, 1996): *(The Advisory Committee on Human Radiation Experiments: Reflections on a Presidential Commission. Trusting Science: Nuremberg and the Human Radiation Experiments).*

76. *Washington Post,* June 9, 1994, p. 3; *Gannett News Services,* June 12, 1994.

77. Much of the credit should go to Bryan Siebert, head of the Office of Declassification, who put in place many practical, bureaucratic solutions to the problems that bog down openness initiatives throughout the agency. Although most of the changes that O'Leary and Siebert instituted do not call for a major shift in existing policy (as published in a Proposed Rule: 10 CFR Part 1045, "Information Classification"), they do streamline some new procedures, formalize the systematic review process for restricted data, and provide a mandate for public participation in the development of classification policy. Siebert has also instituted bureaucratic routines that greatly reduce the manpower needed to declassify. The most significant of these is an electronic security classification guide. See particularly the work of David Bearman of the Carnegie-Mellon Institute, "Electronic Evidence: Strategies for Managing Records in Contemporary Organizations," and his paper with Ken Scochats, "Metadata Requirements for Evidence," available at www.lis.pitt.edu/~nhprc/papers/pub/David Bearman & Ken Sochats publication.

78. There have been six earlier, major reviews of the contemporary U.S. secrecy system: the Coolidge Committee in 1956, the Wright Commission in 1957, the Moss Special Government Information Subcommittee of the House Government Operations Committee in 1958, the Seitz Task Force of 1970, the Stilwell Commission of 1985, and the Joint Security Commission of 1994.

79. In fact, the number of secrets is lower and the amount of information covered by classification is much higher and may be uncountable.

80. Edward Shils, *The Torment of Secrecy* (1956; reprinted, Chicago: Ivan R. Dee, 1996, with a new introduction by Daniel Patrick Moynihan).

81. The commission called for a thirty-year automatic declassification rule, far better than the de facto standard of fifty years but inexplicably worse than the specification of a twenty-five-year rule in Executive Order 12958. Commission members attribute the difference to the desire of former CIA Director John Deutch to delay the release of agency materials as long as possible. At one commission public meeting, Deutch said he was shocked to learn that even after fifty years a discussion between heads of intelligence agencies might be declassified and that given such a rule, it would cause him to be more careful about what he discussed.

82. House Resolution 1546 and S. 712.

83. The prospect of systemwide coordination or even interagency or international declassification reviews have their own perils. In November 1947, the top atomic bomb researchers and policy makers from the United States, Britain, and Canada gathered in Washington "to determine which wartime secrets could now be declassified" by common agreement rather than piecemeal and inconsistently. One of the participants was Donald Mac-Lean, the Soviet spy extraordinaire who served as the British representative to the Combined Policy Committee. Another was Klaus Fuchs, who while working at Los Alamos provided the Soviets with details of atomic bomb

production and helped jump-start the Soviet program. In the closed sessions, Fuchs was so obstinate in probing the effects of public release of scientific information that he forced those present to provide a checklist of which secrets were most valuable and deserved the greatest protection. See Richard Rhodes, *Dark Sun: The Making of the Hydrogen Bomb* (New York: Simon and Schuster, 1995), p. 300.

This tale once more makes the subtle point that when everything is classified, nothing is classified. National security mavens were so interested in protecting virtually everything that they offered a point-by-point justification to a comparatively broad audience about the damaging effects of each disclosure. It is not clear that either spy gained any specific information from the meetings that they did not already have. Whether MacLean gleaned much of value from these sessions is less clear, since the secret information the United States officially shared with the British was often purposely incorrect (ibid., pp. 294, 301). Thus, following MacLean's defection to the Soviet Union in 1951, the Atomic Energy Commission told the FBI that even "the estimates of raw materials supply that were used in the Combined Policy Committee calculations of 1947 were much under the actual supplies received in that period." But as Rhodes goes on to point out in *Dark Sun*, the purpose was not to fool the Soviets alone. "By 1947, with fewer than 1.5 million men under arms, the United States had made the atomic bomb its first line of defense (however thin the line) as it began to mount a broad, worldwide, challenge to what it perceived to be Soviet expansionism; under such conditions, as it inevitably does for sovereign states, the end of national security justified almost any means." Few in the Congress and virtually none of the general public understood the change in U.S. strategy in 1947; they particularly did not know that the U.S. stockpile of atomic bombs was negligible (ibid., p. 301). By the sheer act of having to review with a large group of people the full range of technology which national security planners sought to keep secret, the project jeopardized the information that truly did require protection.

84. NCC *Washington Update*, 3, no. 18 (May 8, 1997).

85. Unfortunately for historians as well as for the rest of us, this argument ignores the fact that most of the historical record consists of officials making public or private (through inter- or intraagency correspondence or memos to the files) comments when responding to issues raised by journalists and public policy commentators. I recently noted in the course of my professional reading that historical books rarely contain more references to documents than to contemporary journalistic accounts and public quotations. Even those tend to rely heavily on memoirs, which make selective and manipulative use of secret information in the context of the contemporaneous state of knowledge. Exposing lies after fifty years is not just a question of releasing a records group. It is also a question of removing fifty years of rhetorical varnish from those lies.

86. Wise testified that "the classification system is controlled by an executive order and applies to those in the government. It does not apply to journalists, writers, historians and others, who may, in the course of their research, learn of classified information. A statute could lead down the road to criminalizing news stories and prosecuting reporters and writers. Although, I'm sure that is the opposite of the commission's intent, but a statute could be the first step down the road to a draconian British-style, official secrets

act and so, I would be strongly opposed to a law. I think there are certain benefits to the present, somewhat sloppy, system where the classification system is not meshed with any statute and there's a gap between them." Federal News Service, May 7, 1997, *Hearing of the Senate Governmental Affairs Committee on Government Secrecy.*

87. *Washington Post,* May 7, 1997, p. A1, as well as follow-up stories on May 9, 1997, p. A27, and May 17, 1997, p. A1.

88. The failure of the administration to notify the congressional intelligence committees that it was tacitly sanctioning Iranian arms to Bosnia.

89. Indeed, despite the rhetoric of House Speaker Newt Gingrich and other congressional leaders about making congressional proceedings more accessible and open, the 104th and 105th Congresses conducted few oversight hearings and published far fewer committee transcripts, much less materials made available to them by the executive branch. In addition, they often dodge issues involving abuses of secrecy. A case in point has been the Senate Intelligence Committee's recent failure to act in the case of government secrecy abuses surrounding whistle-blower suits against favored government contractors. "We can't touch the cases while they are being litigated," a senior Senate committee staff member told me. "We have to wait until the litigation is over, by which time the issue will be moot and we won't pursue it." See *Washington Post,* February 16, 1997.

90. The Department of Justice prides itself on never having had a federal court rule against it when it has invoked a national security privilege against disclosure. But as a practical matter in many instances, when federal courts appeared prepared to rule against the government, Department of Justice lawyers abruptly arranged for release of the contested materials, thus avoiding an unfortunate precedent.

91. I filed an FOIA request while at the *Washington Post* for materials from the Iran rescue mission aftermath investigations. During litigation, Judge Louis Oberdorfer granted our motion to appoint a "special master" to assist him in conducting de novo review of the withheld fourteen thousand pages of highly classified documents and to develop a representative sample and summarize the arguments for and against disclosure. The government unsuccessfully appealed to the D.C. Circuit, which denied a mandamus petition to require Oberdorfer to revoke his appointment. The special master, Kenneth Bass, who had been the executive secretary of the national wiretap court, conducted a review that resulted in the disclosure of an additional several thousand documents. See *Washington Post Co. v. Department of Defense,* 84-3400 (D.D.C. January 15, 1988), affirmed sub. Nom. *In Re Department of Defense,* 848 F. 2d 232 (D.C. Cir. 1988). See also *Washington Post Co. v. Department of Defense,* 766 F. Supp. 1, 9–14 (D.D.C 1991), which held, "It is a matter of common sense that the presence of information in the public domain makes the disclosure of that information less likely to 'cause damage to the national security.' "

92. Woodrow Wilson, *Congressional Government: A Study in American Politics* (boston: Houghton Mifflin, 1925), pp. 303–4.

9

We Can't Yet Read Our Own Mail: Access to the Records of the Department of State

Page Putnam Miller

On February 15, 1990, Warren I. Cohen, chairman of the State Department's Advisory Committee on Historical Diplomatic Documentation, submitted his resignation to Secretary of State James Baker. "The Department has reneged on the agreement I spent two years negotiating," he explained, and has "undermined my credibility with the professional organizations to whom I report." He continued that "the entire process by which the committee attempts to serve the Department by insuring the integrity of the historical record has been brought into question." At issue, Cohen contended the *Foreign Relations of the United States* (FRUS), the State Department's respected documentary record of U.S. diplomacy, had been compromised, and the advisory committee was in no position to remedy this situation. He concluded: "I cannot protect the integrity of the series, the reputation of the Department, or testify to the concern of this administration for providing an honest historical record." In an attachment to his letter, Cohen summarized the advisory committee's efforts over the previous two years to establish an acceptable review procedure for ensuring the credibility of the FRUS.[1]

Cohen's resignation focused attention anew on questions concerning the State Department's handling of its historical records and the difficulties the historians at the State Department encountered in gaining access to, and ensuring the declassification of, high-level policy and intelligence records in other agencies' custody. The very secretive national security information policy that evolved during the cold war period had severely restricted access by both the public and the State Department historians who had security clearance.

Cohen's resignation highlighted these problems and became a catalyst for the passage of legislation designed to ensure the integrity of the Department of State's historical series and to make available to researchers all but the most sensitive of the department's documents over thirty years old. This essay explores the history of this crisis, one that had been building for many decades. In addition, it examines the legislative history and legacy of Title IV of Public Law 102-138—the Foreign Relations Authorization Act, Fiscal Years 1992 and 1993— passed in 1991.

Publication of the FRUS documentary series has, over the years, been closely tied to the opening of State Department records. At the time or shortly after the FRUS volumes were published, the State Department transferred to the National Archives most of the office files that corresponded to the period of the volume. Thus, the FRUS also became an invaluable aid, enabling scholars to locate—within the National Archives' massive collection of State Department office files— records of special interest. The key documents selected by the Office of the Historian for inclusion in FRUS served as pointers for other documents that fleshed out the formation of specific U.S. foreign policy decisions.

The first FRUS volume appeared on December 3, 1861, and was a supplement to President Abraham Lincoln's annual message to Congress. The 441-page executive document included circulars, notes, instructions, and dispatches related to foreign policy. Until 1906, the FRUS volumes were released the year following the events recorded in the documents. By 1914, personnel shortages and constraints on access to pertinent records stretched the one-year time gap to four years; by 1921 it had grown to eight years. Following World War I, a fifteen-year time gap between the date of the documents and their publication became the practice, and this continued for a number of years.[2]

The 1920s proved to be an important decade for the series, with the establishment of a scholarly staff to prepare the volumes and the issuance of a high-level directive to ensure their historical integrity. In 1925 Secretary of State Frank Kellogg ordered that the volumes contain the correspondence "relating to all major policies and decisions of the Department . . . together with events which contributed to the formation of each decision or policy." Kellogg's order included four points that are still printed at the beginning of each volume. These make clear that there are to be no deletions without an indication of where the deletion occurred, no omissions to conceal or gloss over what might be regarded as a defect of policy, and no facts omitted that were of major importance in reaching a decision. Kellogg's final point specified the criteria under which omissions are permissible: if the published information would impede current diplomatic negotiations or would contravene the confidences U.S. officials had given to foreign governments.[3]

The decade of the 1950s became a difficult period for the FRUS. In addition to a shortage of funds, Republican control of both the presidency and the Congress led, according to Richard Leopold, to "demands that the true story of Franklin D. Roosevelt's alleged wartime bungling and of Harry S. Truman's alleged postwar fumbling be disclosed." Members of Congress accused the State Department's Historical Division of suppressing papers and of delaying publication to conceal mistakes of earlier administrations. In reality, the delay resulted primarily from the Historical Office's need to rely on military records and other sources that were not located in State Department files. For example, the volume on the Yalta Conference included much military as well as diplomatic material. Thus, the editors' need to access and include non–State Department material, created "vexing problems of clearance," exposing them to charges that "they should have gone even farther afield to run down possibly pertinent papers in private hands."[4]

To deal with the various problems delaying the publication of FRUS, in 1957 the State Department formed the Advisory Committee on Foreign Relations. This committee was composed of representatives of the American Historical Association, the American Political Science Association, and the American Society of International Law. This began a tradition wherein the department sought outside expertise to deal with conflicting political pressures and other problems that delayed opening the documents necessary to understand American foreign policy.[5]

In 1961, on the centennial anniversary of the series, President John Kennedy issued a National Security Action Memorandum, observing that "in recent years the publication of the 'Foreign Relations' series has fallen farther and farther behind in currency." Kennedy characterized the time gap approaching twenty years "as unfortunate and undesirable," given the need for a democracy to have an informed citizenry. Delays in disclosure must be kept to a minimum, Kennedy insisted, and "any official should have a clear and precise case involving the national interest before seeking to withhold from publication documents or papers fifteen or more years old."[6]

Richard Leopold further assessed the FRUS series in 1973 on the occasion of its 110th anniversary, observing that, while having its problems, the United States still made available its diplomatic papers "sooner and more extensively than any other nation." By this time more records from other agencies were included and the volumes were enriched by including records from "overseas posts and a rapidly accumulating number of miscellaneous records known as lot files." As "an eloquent testimonial" to the value of the recent volumes, Leopold cited the footnotes to historians Gabriel and Joyce Kolko's books on U.S. foreign policy. "They could not possibly have produced their two impressive and critical studies in so short a time," he observed, "if the Foreign Relations series had not made easily available archival materials from numerous, scattered, and often gargantuan collections." Publication of the 1940s volumes was also important, Leopold emphasized, enabling the "scholar for the first time to check the reliability of [President] Truman's Memoirs, on which rest so many generalizations about the start of the Cold War."[7]

Ironically, Leopold concluded, instead of benefiting from the improvements, the FRUS series was less highly regarded in 1973 than it had been in 1961. He attributed this decreasing prestige to the public's increasing distrust of leaders in Washington, to allegations of executive duplicity on Vietnam matters, and to the growing time lag between the date of the documents and the year in which they are published. "The most subtle, and in the long run perhaps the most serious, danger facing the *Foreign Relations*," Leopold added, "is the declining quality and quantity of reviews the volumes receive." The growing number of volumes produced each year (over twelve) meant that journal editors cut back on reviews of the published volumes. Leopold urged editors of professional journals to ensure more frequent and informed evaluations. The successes and failures of the series required more reviews and more information about the selection and work of the Advisory Committee. "At a time when 'establishments' are viewed with suspicion and 'generation gaps' are taken for granted," Leopold concluded, "the Advisory Committee, created in 1957, runs the risk of being regarded as a defender of and lobbyist for the State Department, rather than as the champion of scholars." Leopold's 1973 evaluation foresaw the impasse that Warren Cohen faced in 1990.[8]

The FRUS's declassification problems became exacerbated in the 1980s. In her annual report of 1980, Betty Miller Unterberger, professor of history at Texas A&M University and the chairperson of the State Department's Advisory Committee, attributed the current delay in publication "not so much to preparation of the volumes as to the institution of the system of re-reviewing of volumes which had already been carefully reviewed for declassification in the department, following time tested procedures." The State Department historians, who had the needed clearances, had already exercised considerable discretion when selecting the documents required for an accurate and comprehensive account of American foreign policy in a given area and time period. A new State Department division, the Classification/Declassification Center (CDC), however, had been established in 1978 and was reviewing the classified documents that the department's historians had selected for inclusion in the volumes. The Advisory Committee asked the Department of State to reconsider the need for this rereview, protesting that this process had resulted in extensive deletions of many documents that should have been included in the volumes. Unterberger specifically noted that the "CDC review of the 1951 volume on China and Korea resulted in deletion of eighty documents, or portions of documents, approaching approximately ten percent of the China material."[9]

The 1980 Annual Report of the Advisory Committee on Historical Diplomatic Documentation concluded that "a critical situation has developed, one which threatens the integrity of the *Foreign Relations* series and the opening of historical documentation." The committee made several recommendations and specifically urged the State Department's Office of the Historian to appeal questionable denials of material that the State Department historians had selected for inclusion in the volumes. Excessive deletions, delays, and the withholding of documents, however, continued.

In 1983, Ernest R. May, a professor of history at Harvard University and chair of the Advisory Committee, reiterated these complaints about the issue of timely access to accurate and comprehensive material. Writing to Secretary of State George Shultz on December 21, 1983, May recommended changes, observing that the State Department had "withheld from serious scholars the sources necessary for writing fair and comprehensive histories." American foreign policy after World War II is poorly understood, May contended, and "the department [of State] is partly to blame." The FRUS volumes "should continue to be reflective of the whole record, with any necessary omission specifically identified so that the international scholarly community can retain confidence in the integrity of the series."[10]

That same year, Congress took note of the problems with the FRUS and the related issue of access to historical records of the State Department. Senator Charles Mathias included in the proposed 1983 Foreign Relations Authorization Act a section on the "Foreign Relations Publications." Mathias's insertion stressed congressional concern about the excessive delays in the publication of the FRUS and recommended a maximum gap of twenty-five years between the historical events recorded by the series and publication. His proposed legislation would have required the State Department's historian to prepare a report for the Senate Foreign Relations Committee explaining the reasons for the current delays and a plan for addressing this problem.[11]

The delays, however, continued. By the mid-1980s, some volumes were not published until thirty to thirty-five years after the events they documented. In a memorandum of November 12, 1985, to the secretaries of state and defense, the director of Central Intelligence, and other key leaders in the administration, President Ronald Reagan addressed this problem of the timeliness of publication of the FRUS. The need for full disclosure, Reagan observed, "must be balanced carefully against the needs of national security and the expectations of confidentiality in the diplomatic process." As a consequence, he established a thirty-year publication time frame and directed that "the Secretary of State take necessary measures to ensure the publication by 1990 of the foreign affairs volumes through 1960." His memorandum had little impact on the continued increasing delays in the publication of the FRUS.[12]

Instead, President Reagan's 1982 Executive Order 12356 on classification and declassification further complicated the release of State Department records in a timely fashion. Unlike President Carter's order, which it replaced, Reagan's order provided no timetable for declassification and, moreover, encouraged stricter standards for withholding material. At the time the Reagan order was issued, many expressed concern about the implications of its section on "classification categories" that required the protection of information that "by itself or in the context of other information" could cause damage to the national security. Anna K. Nelson, representing the American Historical Association and the Organization of American Historians, testified before a House Committee on Government Operations that "the very purpose of historical research is to gather together information from a variety of sources which will have meaning in the context of other information. Perhaps those who wrote that line did so over concern that an intelligence source might emerge from a 'mosaic' of information. If so, the section is a clear case of overkill." Nelson concluded that such ambiguous phrases in the executive order are "open invitations to close any information so desired by the declassifier."[13]

The Carter order, in contrast, had worked from a presumption of nonclassification. Under the Carter order, any doubt over whether to classify was to be resolved in favor of openness. Reagan's order made a presumption in favor of classification. As Steven Aftergood, a key advocate for reform of the declassification system, observed, "The Reagan order makes it plain that, when in doubt, information is to be classified."[14]

Nonetheless, during this period the State Department's Advisory Committee walked a fine line, both praising the work of the State Department's Historical Office in preparing the volumes and criticizing those procedures and policies that were overly restrictive and secretive. The Advisory Committee's 1986 annual report, prepared by Chairman Bradford Perkins, professor of history at the University of Michigan, stated: "We recognize, all reasonable scholars do, that some material cannot be made public even after the passage of thirty years, but we believe that the number of such documents is small." The committee focused on the serious problem of overclassification. "Classification should not be used to obscure the fundamental records of American foreign relations," the 1986 report stated, "and it is our most basic responsibility to assure our professional constituencies, and by extension the American people, that such is not the case." This report further alerted the State Department that the outside scholars could not assure their colleagues that the FRUS was as complete and open a record as it had been historically.[15]

Frustrated by the inability of the State Department to take necessary measures to ensure the integrity of the FRUS, the American Historical Association, the Organization of American Historians (OAH), the Society for Historians of American Foreign Relations, and the National Coordinating Committee for the Promotion of History began in 1988 to solicit support from Congress. They specifically asked Senator John Glenn, who chaired the Senate Governmental Affairs Committee, to review and to enact needed reforms of the State Department's handling of FRUS and declassification procedures. The historical associations offered several specific recommendations. The Advisory Committee was simply being used to rubber-stamp rather than to advise and accordingly should be accorded access to the pertinent classified information to ensure an informed role. New declassification procedures should be adopted to replace the overly cautious guidelines used by the State Department's Classification/Declassification Center for page-by-page review of documents over thirty years old.[16]

Following up on conversations between his staff and the historical community, Senator Glenn posed a series of questions to the Department of State. Instead of addressing Glenn's concerns, however, the department chose to revise the composition of the Advisory Committee in an effort to dilute the voice of its historian members. In 1989 the State Department added representatives from several new organizations, including the Society of American Archivists and the American Association of Economists.[17]

Despite this dilution, the newly constructed Advisory Committee on Historical Diplomatic Documentation, chaired by historian Warren Cohen, continued to question whether the committee could give advice about the integrity of the FRUS if it was denied the opportunity to review the material excised by the department's declassification process. Cohen continued the negotiations initiated by his predecessor, Bradford Perkins, and met with various assistant secretaries of state to solicit their support to allow the Advisory Committee to review those portions of the volumes that the department's declassifiers concluded had to be deleted.

Cohen's insistence that the Advisory Committee could not approve the integrity of the volumes without reviewing the deleted portions had been based in part on the committee's conclusion that the recently released volume on Iran had omitted material that distorted the history of U.S. foreign policy. On November 17, 1989, about three months before Cohen's resignation as chairman of the Advisory Committee, Bruce R. Kuniholm, a professor of public policy studies and history at Duke University and a former member of the State Department's Policy Planning Staff, briefed the Advisory Committee in a closed session on his analysis of the 1952–54 volume on Iran.[18]

In a subsequent article in the American Historical Association's newsletter, Kuniholm wrote that "if the purpose of the series is to provide a record of what was thought, what was done, and why it was done, in order to explain what happened and to instruct those who would learn from the past, such a purpose is not served by this volume, which purports to constitute 'the official records of the foreign policy of the United States.' " Kuniholm's criticism focused on the elimination of any material on the desire of U.S. officials to see Iranian prime minster Mosaddeq deposed, and on the CIA's role in the subsequent coup against Mosaddeq. Kuniholm's criticism appeared against the backdrop of publications by a number of former participants in the British and the American intelligence operations in Iran during this period. For example, in Kermit Roosevelt's *Countercoup: The Struggle for Control in Iran,* the former CIA operations deputy for the Middle East who was responsible for the United States' participation in the coup overthrowing Mosaddeq and who received permission from the CIA to publish his book, presented a very different picture from that of the FRUS. This egregious omission of the CIA's role in the FRUS volume was readily noticed by scholars of American diplomatic history.[19]

The controversy surrounding publication of the Iran volume underscored the inadequacy of the State Department's declassification policy. Cohen pinpointed this problem: "Delays [with the FRUS series] have been caused by an overly elaborate, costly declassification process that encourages distortion and coverup." Cohen emphasized the harmful effect of this declassification process. Furthermore, he noted at just the time that Moscow and Eastern European archives are opening records, "our Government has undermined the reputation of its own documentation."[20]

The problem of maintaining the integrity of the FRUS became the focus of the March 1990 annual meeting of the OAH, held only a month after Cohen's resignation. The OAH Executive Board approved a strongly worded resolution charging that changes in the process for reviewing sensitive material for inclusion in FRUS threatened to undermine the series' credibility. The resolution urged Secretary of State James A. Baker to "take necessary steps to restore the integrity" of the FRUS.[21]

In May 1990, Arnita A. Jones, then acting executive secretary of the OAH, alerted all members of the Senate Foreign Relations Committee and the House Foreign Affairs Committee to problems resulting from changes in the editorial and review process in the publication of FRUS. "The problem is now exacerbated," she wrote, "by the recent failure of efforts to negotiate a process by which the U.S. Department of State Advisory Committee on Historical Diplomatic Documentation could maintain its traditional role in reviewing material excised in the course of the Department's declassification process." She attached to her letter both the "Resolution on the Integrity of the Foreign Relations of the United States Documentary History Volumes," passed by the organization's leadership, and Cohen's letter of resignation.[22]

A number of news articles and editorials endorsed the historians' concern about the integrity of the FRUS. Following publication in the *Chronicle of Higher Education* of a lengthy article that examined these concerns and the events leading up to the OAH resolution, the *Washington Post* and the *New York Times* published articles or editorials on this controversy. The *Washington Post* reported that the problem was not confined to the FRUS volume on Iran; other volumes had been compromised. Roger Dingman of the University of Southern California expressed dismay that 60 percent of the documents published in the recently released 1952 volume on Southeast Asia concerning Thailand had excisions, and that this was repeated for more than 30 percent of the documents for the Philippines in 1953. In the preceding volume on Southeast Asia, Dingman observed, almost all of the documents had been printed in their entirety with no deletions. In its editorial "History Bleached at State," the *New York Times* charged, "The blame lies with State's reluctance to go to the mat with the C.I.A.'s fussy custodians of intelligence secrets."[23]

A few months following Cohen's resignation, Senator Claiborne Pell, the chairman of the Senate Foreign Relations Committee, became the chief architect of an effort to provide a statutory solution to the problems that plagued the FRUS. He was joined by Senator Jesse Helms, the ranking minority member of the Foreign Relations Committee, and Senator David Boren, the chairman of the Senate Select Committee on Intelligence. A powerful Senate coalition had formed to enact legislation that would empower the Advisory Committee to review the deletions from the FRUS and put the volumes on a thirty-year publication schedule. Agreement among these three leaders minimized any potential battle among the Democrats and the Republicans, as well as any prospective turf battles between the Foreign Relations Committee and the Senate Select Committee on Intelligence.

Senator Boren played a key role in the ensuing efforts to ensure enactment of remedial legislation. The heart of the problem of excessive deletions that in turn resulted in distorted accounts, he pointed out, was the fact that the State Department was no longer the sole agency involved in U.S. foreign policy activities. Were an accurate and comprehensive account of U.S. foreign policy to be assured, then the intelligence agencies, particularly the CIA and the National Security Council, would have to be both more open and more cooperative with the State Department's publication of the FRUS.

State Department officials had counted on the CIA to oppose this legislation; Boren's support weakened that strategy. Senator Boren and his staff successfully diffused the objections of the intelligence agencies and offered minor adjustments in the proposed legislation in response to the issues they raised. The proposed legislation included provisions to ensure that State Department historians would have access to the CIA records over twenty-five years old and specified procedures for declassifying pertinent documents.[24]

In a May 1990 article in the *Boston Globe* titled "Why U.S. Foreign Policy Records Are 'A Fraud,'" Senators Pell and Boren laid out the problem and their proposal for dealing with it. They cited both the distortion of the Iran volume for 1952–54 and the volume covering the Guatemalan coup of 1954. The CIA's role in these operations was well known, they observed, yet "the only CIA documents in this section suggest the contrary: that there was no CIA involvement in the coup." While acknowledging the need to control access to classified documents when their release would be damaging to the United States or its allies, they criticized the omission of so many very old documents from the Foreign Relations series. Pell and Boren concluded: "To some people, the accuracy of the historical record may appear to be a peripheral issue. We disagree. In a democracy, where the people make policy, it is essential for all of us to know accurately our own past."[25]

By 1990, a formidable coalition of senators had emerged to support legislation; they were supported by a significant working group of Senate legislative aides who believed strongly in the value and the need to preserve the integrity of the Foreign Relations series. Frank Sieverts, Pell's staff person, was a former State Department employee who well understood the importance of an accurate historical record. James Currie, a historian on Boren's staff, and Cliff Kiracofe of Helms's staff, had both used the Foreign Relations volumes during their graduate studies at the University of Virginia, where they had taken courses with Norman Graebner, a distinguished professor of American diplomatic history. For these aides, this was not an abstract issue but one with which they were quite familiar and to which they were personally committed.

Their initial strategy was to attach a section dealing with FRUS and declassification to the Supplemental Foreign Relations Authorization Act of 1990. This provision gained the support of the Senate Foreign Relations Committee, although the proposed supplemental authorization act encountered opposition over its other portions. When it became clear that this bill would not be brought to the Senate for a vote, Senators Pell, Helms, and Boren decided to prepare a standalone bill.

On October 2, 1990, Senator Pell introduced for himself and Senators Helms, Boren, and William Cohen S. 3225, an amendment to the State Department Basic Authorities Act of 1956 to ensure publication of a thorough, accurate, and reliable documentary record of major U.S. foreign policy activities. This bill specified that the FRUS should be published no more than thirty years after the events documented. It established statutory authority for an advisory committee of outside scholars, and introduced for the first time in legislation the principle of automatic declassification, requiring that most State Department documents were to be available after thirty years. To ensure that the State Department would not continue to withhold large numbers of records over thirty years old under the exceptions provisions, the legislation empowered the Advisory Committee to review both declassification guidelines and procedures and documents that remained classified. The Advisory Committee, in addition, was to report its findings annually to Congress.

The Senate passed S. 3225 two weeks later by unanimous consent. In his floor statement Pell stressed that it is "the essence of the proper formulation of our foreign policy that we should know the history of that policy." Deficiencies in the FRUS volumes will ensure that the American people run the same risk as a builder who constructs his foundations on sand. "The bedrock for foreign policy formulation," Pell asserted, "and for the conduct of foreign policy itself, is an accurate record of what has gone before."[26]

The State Department's immediate response to Senate passage of the bill was to lay the groundwork to prevent enactment of any legislation in the next Congress that would be directed at the FRUS or declassification (based on the likelihood that the House would not enact legislation that session). On October 25, 1990, Janet G. Mullins, assistant secretary for legislative affairs of the State Department, wrote Representative Dante Fascell, chairman of the House Committee on Foreign Affairs, that the State Department had no interest in negotiating any specific points in the legislation, and opposed its passage. Her letter's recurring theme was that "the proposed legislation potentially compromises United States foreign policy interest and would likely make more difficult and costly the future publication of the series."[27]

On October 26, 1990, Representative Stephen Solarz, a Democrat from New York, introduced H.R. 5954, similar to the bill passed by the Senate. However, there was little time left in the 101st Congress for the House of Representatives to consider his proposal.

By then, however, sufficient momentum had developed in support of this issue that at the beginning of the 102nd Congress legislation was reintroduced. On the Senate side, the major coordination was conducted at the full Foreign Relations Committee level by Senator Pell. On the House side, Representative Howard L. Berman, a Democrat from California and the chairman of the House Foreign Affairs Subcommittee on International Operations, took the lead. Berman's chief staff person on this legislation, Amit A. Pandya, worked closely with Frank Sieverts of Pell's staff.

Although the last Congress had not passed the supplemental authorization of the State Department, authorization legislation would likely pass in 1991. Accordingly, instead of a stand-alone bill, the proposed legislative remedy was incorporated as a section of the State Department reauthorization legislation. Major efforts were taken to adjust the language of the 1990 bill to win over support from the leadership of the State Department. As Mullins had explained, the State Department was concerned that the Advisory Committee would no longer advise but would make final decisions, and that the legislation created a wholly different classification procedure for the Department of State than for other agencies. In addition, the Department of State remained troubled about the added resources and personnel that would be required to implement the legislation.[28]

Some of the proposed changes to the 1990 bill included a grace period for compliance with the proposed requirements to cover both the publications of the FRUS and the declassification program. The revisions also responded to the criticism that the earlier version had not protected continued classification of records covered under the Privacy Act. In addition, the role of the Advisory Committee was clarified. The revised legislation made clear that the Advisory Committee could only offer recommendations and not review all documents. Finally, a new section was included defining such terms as "originating agency" and "record."[29]

While the Senate was refining the legislation, the House of Representatives passed H.R. 1415 on May 15, 1991, the State Department Authorization Act of 1992 and 1993. Representative William Broomfield, a Michigan Republican and the ranking minority member on the Foreign Affairs Committee, and Representative Olympia Snowe, a member of the House Foreign Affairs Committee and the ranking minority member on the Subcommittee on International Operations, which had major responsibility in the House for this legislation, responded to pressure from the Bush White House and led an effort to dilute the proposed legislative remedy. Their bill would have put the FRUS on a thirty-year timetable and mandated that other agencies cooperate with the State Department's Historical Office in the preparation of the volumes. At the same time, their bill eliminated the role of the professional associations in selecting Advisory Committee members and introduced a provision allowing the president to claim a special privilege to withhold information from the series. The proposed systematic declassification program was replaced by a call for a study.

Throughout the two-year period when this legislation was under consideration, the historical community—operating through the National Coordinating Committee for the Promotion of History—maintained constant contact with key legislative aides to refine and secure needed support for passage of a strong bill. Through "NCC Briefing Sheets" historians were fully informed about the latest developments and were provided needed background to write their members of Congress to urge its passage. With the help of the Organization of American Historians and the American Historical Association, the NCC targeted mailings to historians in the districts of key Republicans on the House Foreign Affairs Committee. After the House passed the weak Broomfield-Snowe version, the focus of this lobbying effort shifted to a Conference Committee, where the differences between the House and Senate bills would be reconciled.[30]

On July 29, the Senate enacted an amended version of H.R. 1415.

The Senate bill contained much of the refined language hammered out over the past several months and reinforced all of the House attempts to dilute the bill. When the bill came to a Senate vote, Senator Pell summarized the criteria to permit continued classification of sensitive records beyond thirty years. "It is my strong hope and belief," Pell asserted, that the provisions for continued declassification "will be used sparingly on an item-by-item and document-by-document basis rather than serving as a reason for wholesale withholding of entire categories or lots of records." Although Senator Helms expressed his preference for a fifteen- or twenty-year standard over the thirty-year one, he supported this measure because, as he put it, "too much about our foreign policy is hidden for too long from public scrutiny."[31]

A House/Senate Conference Committee met in September to reconcile the differences between the two bills. After much discussion and negotiation, and much drafting and redrafting of legislative language, the Conference Committee completed its work on October 3, 1991. The major differences of the two bills centered on the role of professional associations in selecting the Advisory Committee members and the establishment of a systematic declassification program for all but the most sensitive State Department records.

The House bill included no requirement that Advisory Committee members were to be chosen from lists of names provided by the scholarly associations, the practice for many years. The Senate bill, in contrast, specified that all the Advisory Committee members were to be selected from recommendations of scholarly associations. The agreed-upon compromise language authorized the secretary of state to select six of the nine members of the Advisory Committee from lists provided by the specified professional associations. One member was to be appointed from each list provided by the American Historical Association, the Organization of American Historians, the American Political Science Association, the Society of American Archivists, the American Society of International Law, and the Society for Historians of American Foreign Relations. The secretary of state would select the remaining three individuals.

The Conference Committee resolved the second area of contention over the proposed systematic declassification program by merging the two bills. The new version included the House provision requiring a study on declassification to be completed within 180 days and the Senate requirement that within one year—with an extension to two years if the secretary of state could not reasonably meet the one-year requirement—the State Department must establish a systematic declassification program for all but the most sensitive records, with thirty-year-old records available for research in the National Archives.

The Senate approved the Conference Report on October 4 and the House on October 8, 1991. On October 28, President George Bush signed Public Law 102-138, the State Department Authorization Act of 1992 and 1993.

The president, however, emphasized that although he was signing this bill into law, he had grave reservations about specific sections. He specifically objected to the section on the FRUS and the declassification of State Department records: "This section also must be interpreted in conformity with my constitutional responsibility and authority to protect the national security of the United States by preventing the disclosure of state secrets and to protect deliberative communication within the executive branch." Bush stressed that he would interpret this law in light of the existing executive order on national security information. For Bush, the constitutional issue involved the separation of powers; Congress could not pass legislation that would diminish the president's authority as commander in chief to protect the national security of the United States. Signing statements, however, had no statutory authority. Ironically, it was the abuse of claimed presidential powers to protect "deliberative communication" and "state secrets" that had led to this law's passage.[32]

Enactment of Public Law 102-138 marked a major step forward in a decades-long effort to stop the erosion of access to the historical records of the State Department and ensure the accurate and timely publication of the FRUS. This law, moreover, did not depend on the executive order as does the Freedom of Information Act for the criteria that would govern continued classification. Instead it stipulated its own, less restrictive criteria. The law stipulated that excepting those records that met these criteria and therefore must remain closed for national security reasons, State Department records "shall be declassified not later than 30 years after the record was prepared." Continued classification was permitted for records wholly prepared by a foreign government. The law listed four criteria exempting other records from automatic declassification. These involve records (1) that would compromise weapons technology important to the national defense of the United States, reveal sensitive information relating to the design of U.S. or foreign military equipment or U.S. cryptologic systems or activities; (2) that would disclose the names or identities of living persons who provided confidential information to the United States and who would be subject to a substantial risk of harm; (3) that would demonstrably impede current diplomatic negotiations, other ongoing official activities of the U.S. government, or demonstrably impair the national security of the United States; and (4) that would disclose matters related solely to the internal personnel rules and practices of the Department of State or are contained in personnel, medical, or similar files the disclosure of which would constitute a clearly unwarranted invasion of personal privacy.

The legislated declassification standards significantly expanded access to historical government documents, in comparison with President Reagan's Executive Order 12356 on classification/declassification. Under Reagan's order, information "shall be classified as long as required by national security considerations"; further, "if there is reasonable doubt," records should remain classified.[33] The new legislation confirmed an increasing awareness that the post–cold war environment required a new declassification policy. .

The full legacy of this legislation may not be known for some time. In the five years since its enactment, it has ensured a more accurate, timely, and comprehensive FRUS. Furthermore, as the movement for declassification reforms has gained momentum, it offers specific strategies to promote increased access to older historical records.

Armed with clearances and with "the need to know," the members of the statutorily mandated Advisory Committee were able to review the volumes of the FRUS with greatly enhanced authority. There was now no question whether they could see the portions of those documents that the State Department's declassification office had deleted. The Advisory Committee quickly began to explore ways to deal with those records that were omitted for claimed national security considerations.

One of the committee's important early steps was to insist that whenever important documents were omitted that the FRUS's editors provide a summary of the deleted information. The preface to the 1958–60 volume on Indonesia spells out this new practice. After noting that 1.7 percent of the documents originally selected by the historians of the Department of State for inclusion in the volume had been omitted for national security considerations, the omitted documents are briefly described. These documents were described as including "those relating to the details of U.S. covert support of the Indonesian rebellion in Sumatra and Sulawesi (Celebes) and to liaison with other countries interested and involved in this operation." William Z. Slany, the Historian of the State Department and the author of the preface, aptly describes this as "a transitional volume on the road to fuller release of information of important intelligence operations."[34]

The Advisory Committee further decided to identify omissions that were significant but that would not distort the released record sufficiently to merit withholding the volume from publication. At the same time, the committee wanted a disclaimer included, stating that the volume was an accurate and comprehensive account of U.S. foreign policy. Such a disclaimer appeared in the preface to the Japan and Korea volume for 1958–60. In this volume, approximately 10 percent of the original documentary text selected by the Department of State historians and proposed for publication in the Japan compilation was omitted for reasons of national security. The preface, prepared by William Z. Slany, identifies the most important portion of the withheld documents as relating to the negotiation of the United States–Japan Treaty of Mutual Cooperation and Security of 1960. Furthermore the preface included the Advisory Committee's specific disclaimer that "the complete official record of policy toward Japan cannot be published here" and that the omitted treaty and "its related arrangements was integral and essential to a comprehensive and accurate record of the U.S.-Japan relations."[35]

Another of the Advisory Committee's significant innovations was its insistence that the volumes provide information in the text about any omitted documents—identifying their location and length. The preface to the 1958–60 Korea and Japan volume reflected this practice: "The withheld documentation relating to Korea consisted largely of material pertaining to the introduction of certain modern weapons into Korea and the related question of South Korean military force levels, as well as some intelligence analyses and material concerning intelligence activities, sources, and methods." The preface continued: "Those documents omitted in their entirety from this volume are identified (by description, date, and archival provenance) in the text where they would have been printed. Excisions from printed texts are identified by suitable editorial devices." The Advisory Committee then identified the location of the omitted documents.[36]

In some cases, summaries of omitted material were deemed insufficient. In its 1994 annual report, the Advisory Committee unanimously concluded that Department of State and CIA refusals of declassification will "seriously distort the record of foreign policy with at least two nations during the Kennedy presidency—over 30 years ago." The State Department's Historical Advisory Committee recommended against publication of the FRUS volumes for these two countries—subsequently identified as Guyana and Japan—because the proposed omissions would result in a distorted account.[37]

Tim Weiner, a reporter for the *New York Times,* inferred from the minutes of the committee's quarterly meetings, which are available in the State Department Reading Room, that the two volumes in question dealt with Japan and British Guiana, now Guyana. In two articles

Weiner shed light on these omissions. Following months of intensive research with the assistance of reporters abroad, Weiner pieced together aspects of two CIA covert operations of the cold war involving Japan and Guyana. In doing so, he relied heavily on interviews with surviving participants, discovering in Guyana particularly that there was considerable public knowledge about the events the State Department and the CIA had attempted to continue to keep secret.[38]

Although current national security policy rests in part on the assumption that much information must remain secret because its release would be embarrassing, keeping documents secret can also prove to be embarrassing. Weiner's article reporting on this effort to keep secret CIA activity in Guyana during the 1960s proved to be just such an embarrassment for the Clinton administration. During the 1960s, the CIA succeeded in destabilizing the government of Dr. Cheddi Jagan in Guyana. In 1992, however, Jagan returned to power in that country's first democratic election in thirty years. In June, the Clinton administration considered as its nominee for ambassador to Guyana a person who had been involved in the destabilization efforts of the 1960s. According to Weiner, the administration was "apparently unaware that the prospective nominee had helped to undermine the restored leader." In an interview with Tim Weiner, President Jagan said he was flabbergasted by this nomination and conveyed his unhappiness to the Clinton administration. Furthermore, Jagan emphasized, "Everybody in Guyana knows what happened, I don't understand why they should be left secret." Because of the earlier policy of secrecy, current U.S. officials were ignorant about the activities of CIA representatives during the 1960s. This ignorance caused embarrassment in the 1990s.[39]

The Advisory Committee's concerns over the handling of deletions in the volumes dealing with Japan and Guyana led to new high-level review and appeals procedures. After lengthy negotiations, the State Department and the CIA eventually consented to declassify documents for the Guyana volume. The documents dealing with Japan for the Northeast Asia volume for 1961–63, however, remain classified, and the high-level panel has held only one subsequent meeting. This impasse led the Advisory Committee to report in the preface for the Northeast Asia volume that having "examined the denied documents . . . [the committee] concluded that this published compilation does not constitute a 'thorough, accurate, and reliable documentary record of major United States foreign policy decisions,' the standard set by Public Law 102-138. . . . the Advisory Committee will continue to seek declassification of the documents withheld."[40]

On May 10, 1996, Warren F. Kimball, the chairman of the Advisory Committee on Historical Diplomatic Documentation to the U.S. Department of State, submitted the committee's annual report to Secretary Warren Christopher. The committee's major preoccupation, the report noted, has been "the lengthy appeals regarding documents needed to provide the 'thorough, accurate, and reliable record' required by the statute." The report specifically objected to the decision of the Interagency Appeals Panel not to declassify the records on Japan and announced its "plans to appeal that and similar decisions after a two year period, with the purpose of publishing those important documents in retrospective volumes of FRUS."[41]

The law's requirement that volumes be published thirty years after the events, moreover, presented a formidable goal for the State Department's Historical Office. The office has pressed hard but has been unable to meet this target. At the December 1995 meeting of the Advisory Committee, William Slany reported some slippage in meeting the thirty-year targets for publishing the FRUS volumes. Staff shortage and declassification hurdles have slowed down the preparation of the Johnson-era volumes, Slany conceded, adding that these volumes take longer to prepare because material previously unavailable must be included. The Johnson volumes will be the first to include documents from the president's Foreign Policy Advisory Board, an independent presidential body administered through the National Security Council. The National Security Council's cooperation and that of other agencies, Slany observed, has resulted in the inclusion of more documents in the volumes, notably intelligence material, in order to ensure the required comprehensive documentation of American foreign policy activities. This desire to include more material from other agencies has also resulted in lengthy delays in declassifying requested documents. Although Public Law 102-138 provides specific procedures to promote interagency coordination, these have not been fully observed. In its 1996 annual report, the Advisory Committee attributed "the delays" primarily to decisions by the Historical Office, upon the recommendations of the Historical Advisory Committee, "to allow time to incorporate additional documents only recently declassified by the Central Intelligence Agency."[42]

In addition to ensuring that the FRUS is an accurate and comprehensive account of U.S. foreign policy, Public Law 102-138 has promoted other efforts to reform national security information policy and to making more historical records available to researchers. Some of its most important contributions have been streamlining the Department of State's own declassification system, promoting increased openness in the Clinton executive order, and serving as a model of how an effective Advisory Committee can work.

The Advisory Committee appointed a subcommittee of three of its members to implement its monitoring of the State Department's declassification program. The subcommittee functioned as a real working group, and its members went to the National Archives to examine documents in various randomly selected boxes of still-classified records. The subcommittee focused its work not so much on challenging the continued classification of specific documents but on questioning the declassifying system, which it found exceedingly cumbersome and labor-intensive. Emily S. Rosenberg, a professor of history at Macalester College who served on the subcommittee from 1992 to 1995, noted that the State Department was aware that a restrictive culture had to be changed if it were to work with the Advisory Committee's subcommittee on declassification. New ways of doing things had to be devised if the State Department were to meet the legislation's requirement to make available for researchers in the National Archives all but the most sensitive records over thirty years old. The subcommittee questioned the need for rereviews and why certain records groups had not been reviewed. It also questioned why a large number of records were withheld because a CIA designation appeared on the document and nothing else in the document required continued classification. As such, one of the Advisory Committee's major contributions was increased interagency cooperation, not only among foreign policy–related agencies but also with the National Archives.[43]

Warren Kimball, a professor of history at Rutgers and the chair of the Advisory Committee from 1992 to 1996, observed that by examining boxes of still-classified records, the subcommittee members learned of a number of practices and problems about which they would otherwise have been unaware. As a result, they could question procedures to seek more efficient ways to declassify older records. Furthermore, Kimball added, the fact that "somebody was looking" gave the State Department's declassification unit added incentive to comply with the law and to deal with a large backlog of classified records over thirty years old. No other agency had an outside panel of specialists looking over its shoulder, and Kimball concluded that this definitely had a positive effect.[44]

Although the State Department's declassification program has been streamlined, problems continue. In the 1994 report to the secretary of state, the State Department's Advisory Committee on Diplomatic Documentation expressed concern "about the progress of systematic declassification review and transfer to the National Archives and opening of 30-year-old State Department documents." The Advisory Committee's 1996 report reiterated this concern: "The Historical Advisory Committee remains troubled by the overly restrictive declassification standards used by many within and outside the State Department." The committee recommended that the department adopt new "risk assessment" techniques and rely on the expensive page-by-page reviews only for documents known to be quite sensitive. Exploiting the leverage of Public Law 102-138, the Advisory Committee has successfully pressed State Department declassifiers, as well as other agencies, to initiate further reforms in cumbersome and restrictive procedures and policies.[45]

One of the continuing declassification problems has been the lack of cooperation between agencies who have interests or "equity" in the documents in State Department files. Agencies that frequently exchange information have "equity agreements" that extend each agency's authority over material it did not create or possess but in which the agency had some interest. As such, "equity agreements" are part of a patchwork of policies and authorities that increase declassification costs, cause delays, and frustrate those seeking access to historically valuable information.

The most troubling, unresolved barrier to ensuring publication of an accurate and comprehensive account of U.S. foreign policy remains the CIA's lack of cooperation. Although Central Intelligence Director Robert M. Gates announced an openness initiative in 1992 and subsequently referred frequently to plans to declassify documents concerning major CIA covert operations of the 1950s and 1960s, the CIA has not lifted the veil of secrecy on these operations. Furthermore, the CIA has made only marginal efforts to ensure that the State Department Historical Office will have access to the records required for an accurate and comprehensive history of American foreign policy. Almost a dozen upcoming volumes may be withheld from publication unless CIA covert operations are adequately documented.[46]

At the time Public Law 102-138 was passed in 1991, policy makers concurred that the declassification system was broken. This law represented one of the first attempts to address some of the overclassification problems posed by the huge backlog of classified records over thirty years old and by the lack of interagency coordination. Soon after President Clinton's election in 1993, efforts began to revise President Reagan's Executive Order 12356. The drafting, redrafting, and consultations on language for the new Clinton order continued for two years. During this period the State Department's Advisory Committee helped convince Secretary of State Warren Christopher and other high-level State Department officials to institute major changes in the time frame for material to remained classified, in the criteria used for continued classification, and the role of an Advisory Committee composed of disinterested experts outside of government.

Public Law 102-138 through its Advisory Committee succeeded in encouraging the State Department to take the lead in convincing other agencies of the importance of increased openness. One of its results, the Clinton Executive Order 12958 on classified national security information, signed on April 17, 1995, signaled a definite shift to increased openness. Following a grace period of five years, all but the most sensitive agency records over twenty-five years old should be open and available for research.[47]

More important, the State Department's Advisory Committee can serve as a model for other agencies. Since passage of Public Law 102-138, the Departments of Energy and Defense have instituted their own advisory committees on classification and declassification policy, and the CIA has reconstituted, enlarged, and made more active its advisory committee.

Warren Kimball, the chairman of the Department of State's Advisory Committee on Historical Documentation, was invited to brief the Department of Defense Historical Records Declassification Advisory Panel during its November 15, 1996, meeting. Kimball stressed the key reasons for the successful operation of the State Department's Advisory Committee, all of which he attributed to the statutory authority provided by Public Law 102-138. No law, Kimball observed, governs the other advisory committees. Furthermore, Public Law 102-138 requires the Advisory Committee to be composed of scholars who have the respect of their scholarly associations and assures them the clearance needed to examine pertinent classified records. The committee's status assures access to leaders at the agency's highest policy level, focuses the tasks of the committee, and specifies procedures for interagency coordination. Furthermore, the committee is mandated to prepare an annual report for the secretary of state to be made available to congressional oversight committees. If advisory committees are to be more than window dressing, then they must have authority to review classified documents and have access to high-level officials.

Despite its positive contributions, Public Law 102-138's legacy will be a limited one unless there is a breakthrough in the CIA's continued restrictive policies on access to intelligence records. The State Department's Advisory Committee has expended considerable energy on this lingering problem and has met repeatedly with CIA representatives. In its 1996 annual report, the committee wrote that it is "unpersuaded by arguments recently advanced by the CIA to the effect that disclosure of 30-year-old documents will jeopardize current intelligence liaison with friendly nations."[48]

Henry L. Stimson once said that gentlemen don't read other people's mail. This essay has described the drastic decline of historians' and the American public's ability to read our nation's thirty-year-old mail. As a result, we are denied the information essential to analyze and understand much of what has shaped current U.S. foreign policy and has ensured an officially unadmitted faulty history of the Eisenhower administration's cold war intrigues in Iran. As the Advisory Committee made clear in the preface to the FRUS volume on Northeast Asia 1961–63, the published documents dealing with U.S. policy toward Japan neither accurately nor comprehensively describe U.S. policy.

This nation's declassification policy remains overly restrictive. At the most basic level, the concern of many historians reflects a broader concern for responsible government. Only if assured of access to government records will citizens be able to hold officials accountable for their actions. American foreign and military policy decisions of the cold war era remain poorly understood. Public Law 102-138 in large part grew out of an untenable situation wherein scholars were being asked to rubber-stamp distorted history. The passage of Public Law 102-138 in 1991 and the 1995 Clinton executive order on classification policy point toward increased openness. We still have a long way to go, however, before we can read our thirty-year-old mail.

NOTES

1. Warren I. Cohen, letter to Secretary of State Baker, February 15, 1990 (files of the National Coordinating Committee for the Promotion of History).
2. Richard W. Leopold, "The Foreign Relations Series: A Centennial Estimate," *Mississippi Valley Historical Review* 49 (March 1963): 595–601.
3. Ibid., pp. 600–603.
4. Ibid., pp. 607–8.
5. Ibid., p. 609.
6. National Security Action Memorandum No. 91, President John Kennedy, September 6, 1961.
7. Richard W. Leopold, "The *Foreign Relations* Series Revisited: One Hundred Plus Ten," *Journal of American History* 59 (March 1973): 948–49.
8. Ibid., pp. 951–57.
9. Betty Miller Unterberger, "Annual Report (1980) of the Advisory Committee on Historical Diplomatic Documentation," *Perspectives* 19 (March 1981): 11–12.
10. Ernest R. May, letter to Secretary of State George Shultz, December 21, 1983.
11. U.S. Senate, Committee on Foreign Relations, Foreign Relations Authorization Act Fiscal Years 1984 and 1985: Report, 98th Cong., 1st sess., 1983, S. Rpt. 143, Serial 13507, 29.
12. President Ronald Reagan, memorandum for the Secretary of State, the Secretary of Defense, et al., November 12, 1985.
13. President, Executive Order 12356, "National Security Information,"

Sec. 1.3 (b), April 2, 1982; Anna Nelson, *Hearings Before a Subcommittee of the Committee on Government Operations House of Representatives* (March 10 and May 5, 1982), pp. 109, 110.

14. Steven Aftergood, "The Perils of Government Secrecy," *Issues In Science and Technology* 8 (Summer 1992): 84.

15. Bradford Perkins, "The Advisory Committee on Historical Diplomatic Documentation Report, March 1987," *Perspectives* 25 (May/June, 1987): 11–12.

16. Page Putnam Miller, letter to Senator John Glenn, May 20, 1988 (files of the National Coordinating Committee for the Promotion of History).

17. Internal State Department Memorandum, Office of the Under Secretary of State for Management, Mr. Redman to Ronald I. Spiers, September 16, 1988 (files of the National Coordinating Committee for the Promotion of History).

18. U.S. Department of State, *Foreign Relations of the United States, 1952–1954*, vol. 10, Iran, ed. Carl N. Raether and Charles S. Sampson (Washington, D.C.: Government Printing Office, 1989).

19. Bruce R. Kuniholm, "Foreign Relations, Public Relations, Accountability, and Understanding," *Perspectives* 28 (May/June 1990): 11–12; Kermit Roosevelt, *Countercoup: The Struggle for Control in Iran* (New York: McGraw-Hill, 1979).

20. Warren I. Cohen, "At the State Dept., Historygate," *New York Times,* May 8, 1990.

21. "Resolution on the Integrity of the Foreign Relations of the United States Documentary History Volumes," passed at the Executive Board of the Organization of American Historians on March 22, 1990.

22. Arnita A. Jones, letter to members of the Senate Foreign Relations Committee and the House Foreign Affairs Committee, May 30, 1990 (files of the National Coordinating Committee for the Promotion of History).

23. Karen J. Winkler, "Historians Criticize State Department for 'Distortions' and 'Deletions' in Its Record of U.S. Foreign Policy," *Chronicle of Higher Education,* April 4, 1990, pp. A6, 12; Al Kamen, "Historians Say Secrecy Distorts Foreign Policy Chronicle," *Washington Post,* April 16, 1990; "History Bleached at State," *New York Times,* May 16, 1990.

24. Claiborne Pell and David L. Boren, "Why U.S. Foreign Policy Records Are 'A Fraud,' " *Boston Globe,* May 27, 1990.

25. Ibid.

26. U.S. Senate, Senator Pell of Rhode Island speaking for an Amendment to the State Department Basic Authorities Act of 1956, S. 3225, 101st Cong., 2nd sess., *Congressional Record* (October 19, 1990), vol. 136, no. 142, pt. 2, S16289.

27. Janet G. Mullins, letter to Representative Dante B. Fascell, October 25, 1990 (files of the National Coordinating Committee for the Promotion of History).

28. Ibid.

29. Memorandum from Page Putnam Miller to the members of the Advisory Committee on Historical Diplomatic Documentation, March 1, 1991 (files of the National Coordinating Committee for the Promotion of History).

30. NCC Briefing Sheet, "Integrity of the Foreign Relations of U.S. Documentary Historical Series and Automatic Declassification," March 14, 1991 (files of the National Coordinating Committee for the Promotion of History).

31. *Congressional Record* (July 29, 1991), pp. S11209–11225.

32. "Statement by the President," the White House Office of the Press Secretary, October 28, 1991.

33. 22 U.S.C., sec. 4354 October 28, 1991, pp. 687–88; President, Executive Order 12356.

34. U.S. Department of State, *Foreign Relations of the United States, 1958–1960, vol. 17, Indonesia,* ed. Roberts J. McMahon (Washington, D.C.: Government Printing Office, 1994), vii–viii.

35. U.S. Department of State, *Foreign Relations of the United States, 1958–1960, vol. 18, Japan; Korea,* ed. Madeline Chi and Louis J. Smith (Washington, DC: Government Printing Office, 1994).

36. Ibid., p. viii.

37. Letter from Warren F. Kimball, chair of the Advisory Committee on Historical Diplomatic Documentation, to Warren Christopher, July 1, 1994, with attached 1994 annual report.

38. Tim Weiner, "CIA Spent Millions to Support Japanese Right in 50s and 60s," *New York Times,* October 9, 1994; Tim Weiner, "A Kennedy-CIA Plot Returns to Haunt Clinton," *New York Times,* October 30, 1994.

39. Weiner, *New York Times,* October 30, 1994.

40. U.S. Department of State, *Foreign Relations of the United States, 1961–1963, vol. 22, Northeast Asia,* ed. Edward C. Keefer, David W. Mabon, and Harriet Dashiell Schwar (Washington, D.C.: Government Printing Office, 1996), ix–x.

41. Letter from Warren F. Kimball, chairman of the Advisory Committee on Historical Diplomatic Documentation, to Secretary of State Warren Christopher, May 10, 1996 (files of the National Coordinating Committee for the Promotion of History).

42. Ibid.

43. Telephone conversation, November 21, 1996, between Page Putnam Miller and Emily S. Rosenberg, a member of the State Department Advisory Committee on Historical Diplomatic Documentation.

44. Telephone conversation, November 27, 1996, with Warren Kimball, chair of the State Department Advisory Committee on Historical Diplomatic Documentation.

45. Letter from Warren F. Kimball, chair of the Advisory Committee on Historical Diplomatic Documentation, to Warren Christopher, July 1, 1994, with attached 1994 annual report. Letter from Warren F. Kimball, chair of the Advisory Committee on Historical Diplomatic Documentation, to Secretary of State Warren Christopher, May 10, 1996, which includes 1996 annual report (files of the National Coordinating Committee for the Promotion of History).

46. Telephone conversation on December 4, 1996, with William Slany, historian of the State Department.

47. Memorandum on the Executive Order on Classified National Security Information, from the Advisory Committee on Historical Diplomatic Documentation to Anthony C. E. Quainton, assistant secretary for diplomatic security, January 1, 1994 (files of the National Coordinating Committee for the Promotion of History). Telephone conversation, December 2, 1996, with William Slany, historian of the State Department.

48. Letter from Warren F. Kimball, chair of the Advisory Committee on Historical Diplomatic Documentation, to Secretary of State Warren Christopher, May 10, 1996, which includes 1996 annual report (files of the National Coordinating Committee for the Promotion of History).

10

The John F. Kennedy Assassination Records Review Board

Anna Kasten Nelson

I've never seen any information released that ever did anyone any good.
Agency representative, ARRB briefing

The John F. Kennedy Assassination Records Collection Act of 1992[1] marked an important milestone in the ongoing conflict between the public's need to know and the culture of secrecy that evolved during fifty years of the cold war. The act was designed to strip away theories that implicated federal agencies in a conspiracy to murder the young president. Its unintended consequence has been to crack open the doors to the inner sanctums of the CIA, FBI, and other intelligence agencies.

Following the murders in 1963 of both President Kennedy and Lee Harvey Oswald, President Lyndon Johnson quickly established a "blue ribbon" commission, headed by Supreme Court Chief Justice Earl Warren, to reassure the American public that neither the Soviet Union nor any other foreign power was behind the tragic events in Dallas. The Warren Commission accumulated a host of exhibits and heard testimony from 552 individuals. It requested and received documents from the FBI and CIA that officials heading these agencies deemed pertinent to the assassination inquiry. However, neither the commission members nor the commission's staff were able to search the files of the federal intelligence agencies to ensure the completeness of the record. Eager to dispel any public suspicion of conspiracy, the commissioners issued their report on September 24, 1964, after only ten months of work.[2]

The Warren Commission Report concluded that President Kennedy had been killed by bullets fired by only one assassin, Lee Harvey

Oswald, from the sixth floor of the Texas Book Depository. Three shots had been fired; one hit the president but did not kill him, one went astray, and the third killed Kennedy and wounded Governor John Connally of Texas, who shared the president's limousine as it slowly moved through downtown Dallas. The commission further concluded that, while Oswald was influenced by Marxist ideology and was sympathetic to Fidel Castro's government in Cuba, his decision to kill the president came from internal demons, not an external conspiracy.[3]

Within three years, a number of widely read books appeared that sought to refute the Warren Commission's conclusions. By 1966 a Gallup Poll found that 50 percent of the American people did not believe in the lone assassin conclusion. A Harris Poll of 1975 noted that this number had risen to 65 percent. A year later, a Gallup Poll found that the number of disbelievers had grown to 81 percent.[4] The very rapidity with which the Warren Commission completed its work undermined its conclusions. The lingering doubts contributed to the proliferation of conspiracy theories.

From 1975 to 1978, new revelations about the abuses of power of federal intelligence agencies (notably, disclosures about their intrusive methods and sometimes illegal activities) revived interest in the Kennedy assassination and in the conclusions of the Warren Report. Three independent inquiries, based on research in formerly highly classified agency records, revealed the dark side of the FBI and CIA, which, as the polls indicate, further heightened suspicion of government complicity in Kennedy's death. From 1975 to 1976, the Senate Select Committee to Study Governmental Operations with Respect to Intelligence Activities (the Church Committee) revealed, among other disclosures, the bizarre details of CIA assassination attempts on the life of Fidel Castro and the FBI's illegal surveillance and harassment of dissidents and radicals. Concurrently, in 1975 President Gerald Ford appointed Vice President Nelson Rockefeller to direct the Presidential Commission to Investigate CIA Activities Within the United States. The Rockefeller Commission's report raised more questions than it answered about the CIA's domestic and international activities and hence opened more doors to suspicions of conspiracy than it closed.

The most thorough and direct study of President Kennedy's assassination was conducted in 1978–79 by the House Select Committee on Assassinations (HSCA), which examined all three of the assassinations that had rocked the country during the 1960s—those of John F. Kennedy, Martin Luther King, Jr., and Robert Kennedy. Its conclusions differed from those of the Warren Commission in several crucial respects. In particular, the HSCA questioned the "single bullet theory," the conclusion that a single bullet killed the president and wounded Governor Connally. In so doing, it questioned the Warren Commission's core assumption that Oswald had fired all three shots, thus raising questions about a second gunman and a possible conspiracy.[5]

Each of these investigations had been based on access to documents generated by the FBI, the CIA, and the Secret Service, many of which had not been reviewed by the Warren Commission, and each investigation generated its own documents. After the investigatory groups closed their doors, these documents disappeared into storage and away from public view. Ironically, although each investigation had inadvertently stimulated a host of new theories, subsequent researchers were denied access to some of the very documents that had been used and cited by the investigators. Owing to agency restrictions, less than half of the approximately five hundred thousand pages of FBI files and barely a sample of the CIA files were available to Kennedy assassination researchers. The Rockefeller Commission released only twenty-five hundred pages of the collection it had reviewed, and although the Church Committee published or summarized a large number of formerly classified documents, five thousand pages of its records remained under lock and key when it closed its doors. The HSCA, after raising disturbing questions about some of the conclusions of the Warren Report, kept under wraps over four hundred thousand pages of the records it had reviewed.[6]

Each successive investigation, each commemoration of the president's death, and each "exposé" in the growing shelf of books in turn led to the federal intelligence agencies being inundated with requests for seemingly relevant records under the Freedom of Information Act (FOIA). Documents trickled out of their vaults, page by page, often with so many lines covered with great blocks of opaque black ink that they were essentially useless. The agencies' failure to recognize the public's interest in these closely held records had the unintended consequence of breeding suspicions of a government cover-up.

Oliver Stone's film *JFK*, which apparently authoritatively describes a complicated government conspiracy to kill the president, unintentionally proved to be the final catalyst that drove Congress to enact legislation to ensure the release of overclassified agency documents. Every assassination theory included some form of accusation of government complicity in either a conspiracy or a cover-up. By the 1990s many Americans were convinced that the CIA or FBI, or both agencies, were responsible for Kennedy's death. Stone's controversial movie even added the leaders of the military services to this mix.

To many in the public the movie was both entertaining and persuasive. A decade of suspicion about the events in Dealey Plaza, followed by revelations of 1973–75 about White House abuses of power, notably Watergate and the questionable and illegal activities of the CIA and the FBI revealed by the Church Committee, combined with the false assurances of success in Vietnam by Presidents Johnson and Nixon delivered body blows to government credibility. Stone's *JFK* accordingly struck a responsive chord and convinced young and old alike that the CIA, the FBI, and/or President Johnson were somehow responsible for the death of their young and dynamic president.

Growing tired of these suspicions about the integrity of the government they served, a bipartisan group in Congress decided to change course. Instead of initiating one more congressional investigation, these members of Congress decided to open the records.

Their immediate purpose in enacting the John F. Kennedy Assassination Records Collection Act of 1992 was to create a Kennedy Collection at the National Archives. To ensure "expeditious public transmission to the Archivist and public disclosure of such records,"[7] each government agency was required to identify and organize all records it had pertaining to the Kennedy assassination and send them to the National Archives along with an electronic finding aid to ensure easier public access. The entire process, including each agency's review of its records, was to take no more than three hundred days. The members of Congress purposefully established this precise timetable to guarantee the "expeditious" collection and transfer of records. For example, sixty days after the enactment of the statute, the National Archives had to establish the Kennedy Collection. Thirty days after their transmission, these records were to be made available to the public with the proper finding aids.

The authors of the act also concluded that the agencies should not be allowed to determine on their own the extent and availability of their assassination records. This would be akin to sending the fox to watch the chickens and would not likely assuage the very suspicions of a "cover-up." To achieve this purpose, an independent Assassination Records Review Board (ARRB) was established with extraordinary powers of oversight. The board and its staff could have access to any and all records in every federal agency, including those the agencies deemed irrelevant to the assassination. Furthermore, the board was granted broad powers to overturn agency record-withholding decisions—only the president could countermand its rulings to release records.

Although the ARRB was to be appointed by the president and approved by the Senate, the statute recommended that each of the five-member group be selected from lists of names prepared by the

American Historical Association (AHA), the Organization of American Historians (OAH), the Society of American Archivists (SAA), and the American Bar Association (ABA). The president could appoint the fifth member at will. Given that both the archivist and the presidential appointee on the board are trained historians, there currently are four historians on the ARRB: Henry Graff, William Joyce, Kermit Hall, and myself. John Tunheim, the chairman of the ARRB, is a lawyer.

The statute required that members of the ARRB be nominated within ninety days of its enactment in October 1992, but President Bush neglected to complete the process before leaving office, and the incoming Clinton administration put the nominations on the back burner as it struggled to fill more critical cabinet and subcabinet positions. It was not until the summer of 1993 that potential members of the board began to receive the necessary forms for gaining White House approval and security clearances. By December 1993, the board members were finally chosen and nominated. The Senate Committee on Governmental Affairs held hearings on the nominations the following February, but it took another two months before the Senate gave its perfunctory approval to the nominees. Finally, on April 11, 1994, the board members were sworn into office by Justice Ruth Bader Ginsburg—eighteen months after the passage of the JFK Assassination Records Collection Act.

With the exception of the National Archives, no federal agency met the deadlines carefully imposed by the Congress to assure prompt compliance. The eighteen-month delay in the formation of the board proved particularly egregious, since it enabled the various federal agencies to begin gathering, reviewing, and presumably complying with the act without the intended independent oversight.

The ARRB officially began business the day after its members took the oath of office, but it was an agency without a home or money and with no one interested in providing for it. Members of Congress seemingly assumed that their task was completed. Whether the White House neglect reflected disinterest or the disarray of the new administration, the ARRB was from the start on its own.

Obviously, the board's first order of business was to obtain operating money; seven months would pass before the board's 1994 budget was completed. In the interim, friendly personnel within the Executive Office of the President managed to find the necessary funds from the president's discretionary budget so that the board members could begin the task of choosing an executive director. By midsummer the recently appointed executive director, David Marwell, began to organize the new agency and assemble a staff. Finding office space proved to be unexpectedly burdensome, complicated by government cost allotments and the highly classified nature of the documents to be housed and reviewed. (All agencies holding security classified documents must have their offices and vaults officially approved by the CIA.) Since one of the principal tasks of the ARRB was to examine security classified documents, it had to find offices that would be easy to secure. Finally, although the board was authorized to appoint a staff of twenty-five, no documents could be reviewed until staff members had received the necessary security clearances. Each hurdle took time from the business at hand. It was a frustrated board that finally sat down to examine documents.[8]

The ARRB found itself faced with an overwhelming task before a large and knowledgeable audience without any script or stage directions. How do five individuals deliberately chosen for their unfamiliarity with Kennedy assassination documents, arguments, and theories carry out their legal mandate? The act set broad parameters: first, the ARRB was to determine whether a particular record could be defined as an assassination record; second, it was to determine whether the information in the record could be immediately disclosed or scheduled for postponement. Neither of these provisions was easy to implement. There was no guidance on how to proceed and no precedent to follow.

Given the scope of the events that could have some bearing on the assassination, the controversies surrounding the careers of both John and Robert Kennedy, and the various theories spun from the reports of the Warren Commission, the Church Committee, and the HSCA, just defining an assassination record turned into a lengthy process. The act gave the ARRB the right to examine any document in the possession of the federal government. In addition, the board was explicitly required to collect records from all of the public commissions and committees that had investigated the assassination, all records sought through past and pending FOIA requests, and all documents specified by government offices as relating to the Kennedy assassination.

Congress had provided only a general outline for this assigned task, placing most of the burden on the board to define the scope of "assassination" records. Should the ARRB concentrate solely on collecting records on Lee Harvey Oswald? Should it seek records that *could* (but might not) answer all the various theories about the president's death? Could the ARRB ensure a complete record of the events surrounding the president's assassination without including every document on a related subject? How was a line to be drawn that would take into account unforeseen information but at the same time not be absurdly inclusive? How could board members make an intelligent judgment on a definition until they were familiar with the nature of the records already compiled? Two public hearings were, as a result, devoted to drafting a workable definition and brought together a variety of views from nineteen witnesses. These hearings, however, produced little new information or insights on how to define assassination records precisely.[9]

Ultimately, the ARRB decided to rest its definition on the need to enrich the historical record. Thus an assassination record includes "but is not limited to" documents that "describe, report on, analyze or interpret activities; persons, or events reasonably related to the assassination of President John F. Kennedy." To guide the federal agencies, this definition was explained and expanded in additional pages. For example, the board specifically directed agencies to forward information about their records procedures that would help identify additional records. Among these were organizational charts, filing systems, storage systems, and indexing symbols. As this is written (April 1997), some agencies still have not complied with this request.[10]

Even a cursory reading of the act confirms that the board's mandate to open documents extends far beyond the provisions of the FOIA or the executive order on security classified records. As Senator Joseph Lieberman pointed out during the confirmation hearings for board members, the act "creates a strong presumption in favor of disclosure, with important but limited provisions for postponement of disclosure." The senator specifically sought assurance from the nominees that they supported this presumption of disclosure.[11]

The act provides both general and specific guidelines to the ARRB governing postponements (i.e., nonrelease of specified documents). Documents can be postponed for twenty-five years or less; no record, however, can be closed in perpetuity. Information can be postponed only if there is clear and convincing evidence that such disclosure would gravely threaten military defense, intelligence operations, or the conduct of foreign relations *and* thereby outweigh the public interest in access to this information. The board is specifically required to postpone information revealing an intelligence agent, or a source or method "currently utilized or reasonably expected to be utilized." Information can also be postponed if based on "an understanding of confidentiality" between a government agent and a foreign citizen.[12] Finally, documents can be postponed if they would reveal the procedures used by the Secret Service to protect the president or would reveal information that would harm individuals through public disclosure of a name or identity.

The names of agents currently on the payroll of the CIA are easy enough to postpone, but how does one judge currently utilized sources or methods? The FBI's past (and future) use of wiretaps is common knowledge. Are wiretaps (in some instances five or six in one location), then, a method that should be protected? Is an understanding of confidentiality always based on a written agreement, or, in the past, had such confidentiality been assumed by the FBI and its sources? Should such informal arrangements be honored in all cases? In assessing the disclosure of information that might be harmful to an individual, does embarrassment constitute harm?

Despite these exceptions, the act mandates a preference for disclosure over secrecy and directs the board when making these judgments to release the information unless "public disclosure would be so harmful that it outweighs the public interest."[13] Considering the high public interest in the events of 1963, the board chose to follow faithfully this recommendation and, as a result, new avenues of information have been opened.

Even when authorizing that portions of documents can be postponed, the act ensures that more information will be released than under the executive order governing declassification. Each time the ARRB decides to withhold a word or phrase, it must offer substitute language. If paragraphs or pages are withheld, the material removed must be summarized. Most researchers, when coming across paragraphs of deleted lines and even deleted words, view these withholdings with suspicion. Even the most reasonable researcher suspects that the withheld material is not only the most important but the very information desired. The board's substitute summary language will alert researchers to the fact that most of the deleted information either covers CIA crypts, FBI file numbers, or names of living individuals who will be harmed by disclosure. Sometimes, when the deletion is substantive, the board struggles to draft substitute language in an effort to accurately reflect the withdrawn material. Some postponements, particularly those describing methods still in use, cannot support substitute language, since any substitution would mislead rather than inform.

Under the provisions of the act, the ARRB must ensure that government agencies carry out their responsibilities; the board therefore was given unusual powers, including the subpoena power. It can direct the federal agencies to comply with provisions of the act, including those concerning the search for records, the establishment of a database, and ensuring the board's complete access to all the records it requests. The ARRB has not yet used the subpoena power against a federal agency but it has, for example, subpoenaed sworn testimony from the doctors who performed President Kennedy's autopsy and has subpoenaed the records accumulated in New Orleans by former District Attorney Jim Garrison (the hero of Stone's *JFK*).

The act contains one unprecedented provision that promotes disclosure while challenging the culture of secrecy that has enveloped the intelligence community. Agencies no longer retain the exclusive power to withhold "classified" information. Instead, the ARRB can order the release of information. Should agency officials dissent from that disclosure ruling, their only recourse is an appeal to the president (who alone can decide to withhold the information but must then specify each nondisclosure decision). This unique provision contrasts with provisions of both the FOIA and executive classification orders. Under provisions of the FOIA and the executive order, once agencies decide to remove information, only then can requesters challenge this decision either by bringing suit in court or appealing to executive classification review boards. Under the provisions of the Kennedy Assassination Records Collection Act, agencies have lost their absolute power to control their information. To date, only one agency, the FBI, has appealed the board's rulings to the White House. Its appeals were rebuffed.

No one expected the five board members, all of them fully employed, to read every document in every file. Some system had to be devised to give the staff guidance while the board members educated themselves on the nature of the documents. The system that was developed involved a three-part process.

First, the board members and staff spent countless hours over several months slowly becoming familiar with representative documents and the excisions these documents shared. Through these rather tedious sessions, the staff gained insight into the views of the board members and guidance for their future reviewing. The logistics of document review furthermore proved to be a challenge that was finally conquered by the inventiveness of the staff. The statute required the tracking of every document and the publication in the *Federal Register* of the number of every document released. During the first two years, the staff, with the help of a computer consultant, turned document review from a paper-driven, labor-intensive system into a document-based computerized system that automatically tracks each document throughout the entire review process.

Agencies supplied the board with only one copy of the original security classified document and did not allow for further copying, thereby causing another logistical problem. The solution to this problem was a Rube Goldberg arrangement of two television monitors connected to a relative of the overhead projector called an "Elmo." Thus the five board members were able to examine simultaneously each document.

Second, the board received a number of "briefings" from the CIA and FBI officials who were responsible for the declassification of their agencies' documents. For the most part, these officials sought to convince the board members of the importance of maintaining the redactions affixed by their agencies' reviewers.[14] Thus, in these sessions CIA representatives insisted that intelligence gathering would be seriously compromised (if not fatally injured) were redacted information to be released. FBI representatives were equally adamant, warning about the potential loss of "sources" and the "chilling" effect should information about these individuals be released, including those deceased. Some months later, Secret Service officials tried to convince the ARRB that techniques to protect the president had to be completely closed, even though the identical information had been presented to the Warren Commission and had been available to the public for thirty years.

Finally, the board began to review and open the first group of assassination-related records, sixteen CIA documents concerning Lee Harvey Oswald's trip to Mexico a few weeks before Kennedy's death. Only some of these records had previously been released, and even these had many redactions. The board voted to release all the information in the documents, including the names of intelligence agents, sources, and methods. The board's decision to release these documents served as a "wake-up call."

The Kennedy Assassination Records Collection Act firmly supported the board's decision to open the documents, and the ARRB as an independent agency with unique authority had thereby signaled its intention to carry out this mandate. This unprecedented decision was followed by similar decisions at every subsequent board meeting as board members ordered the release of more and more previously deleted information. At least one agency official vocally expressed his dismay over the board's decisions by noting his new and painful ulcer. One can imagine the meetings, gnashing of teeth, and wringing of hands as agency officials reread the statute.

CIA officials decided not to appeal the board's disclosure rulings to the president for redress. Instead, officials of that agency either sought to compromise with the ARRB or agreed to accept its decisions. Over the course of a year, upper-echelon officials argued their case for the redactions, and board members replied by pointing to the statutory provisions and the weight of the public interest.

Although CIA and FBI records differ in their content and method, the board's experience with the FBI was similar. Neither intelligence agency believed that the information it had collected was time-sensitive; that is, information that was thirty years old might not be as sensitive as information gathered only three days ago. Both agencies also wanted to protect all their sources of information, whether those sources were dead or alive, high-level spies or individuals volunteering information. Furthermore, even when their methods (the use of wiretaps, stationing agents in foreign capitals) were generally known, agency officials often refused to confirm these practices. Finally, both agencies, particularly the FBI, expected the board to accept without question the rather generic explanations they offered in defense of closure.

The board's meetings with agency officials occurred with some frequency in the first year as the board began the process of releasing documents. These meetings consumed an inordinate amount of time but provided a useful education to all concerned. The agencies learned that, in general, board members were not willing to accept generic or inadequately documented explanations. Yet the board's actions were not irresponsible. When CIA officials supplied credible proof in support of their withholding requests, board members withheld information that could jeopardize individuals or their families. The board also agreed to withhold the names of former U.S. double agents who operated in unfriendly foreign embassies, as well as names of FBI informants involved in sensitive counterintelligence and organized crime investigations. But board members remain unpersuaded by the argument that information must be protected because it has always been protected.[15]

With the full support of his colleagues, one board member in particular insisted that agency officials establish a relation between current and past practices before the board would vote to postpone the disclosure of information. Although each board member had received the proper security clearances and sat in a secure conference room behind doors opened only by key cards and number codes, high-level agency officials were reluctant to share any information about current activities. They acquiesced only when faced with the alternative—release of the information. Throughout John Deutch's tenure as director of Central Intelligence, agency officials chose to convince, compromise, and ultimately accept the ARRB's decisions for disclosure. As of April 1997, the agency has never appealed an ARRB disclosure decision to the White House.

The FBI, on the other hand, after unsuccessful efforts to influence the board through briefings by its upper-echelon officials, requested the president to overrule the decisions of the board on a broad range of documents. These records were clearly of high public interest as defined by the statute. Several concerned the FBI's efforts to reconstruct Lee Harvey Oswald's movements when he was in the Soviet Union, including Oswald's abortive effort to enter the Albert

Schweitzer college in Switzerland; others involved information the FBI had compiled on the critics of the Warren Commission, on New Orleans District Attorney Jim Garrison (Stone's hero), and on the trial of alleged conspirator Clay Shaw in New Orleans. To FBI officials, release of these and similar documents would compromise the agency's sources and methods. To the ARRB, on the other hand, this information in its entirety was a central part of the "assassination story," and for that reason the public interest outweighed the FBI's insistence on confidentiality. Although it took eight months for the White House to respond (an election intervened), the decisions of the board prevailed in every instance.

A comparison of previously released records with the board's final decisions illustrates the recurring issues and problems that have marked the board's decisions. The first involved the pervasive problem of the alleged need to safeguard agency "sources and methods." Intelligence agencies have long proclaimed their willingness to release information but not the sources or methods by which it had been obtained. Historians acquainted with research and lawyers with discovery understand that information is only as valid as its source. It matters whether information on Jack Ruby comes from a former "dancer" in his bar, an FBI wiretap, or a member of the Mafia. Similarly, knowing that information concerning Oswald's letter to the Schweitzer college had been obtained from Swiss police gives that information greater weight.

The methods employed by intelligence agencies also have particular research relevance. Information that is gained from human sources differs from that gained from listening devices. The latter is inherently more accurate. A human source may have a selective memory or may even be a double agent handing out misinformation. The methods of surveillance that the CIA used in Mexico City, for example, are important to an understanding of the agency's ability to follow Oswald's trail. The agency did have double agents in the Soviet and Cuban embassies and a half dozen wiretaps on embassy telephones, but only intermittent photographic surveillance of the embassies. (This may account for the CIA's failure to have photographed Oswald, an issue that has caused much speculation among assassination researchers.)

Some of the agencies' sources cannot be revealed under the provisions of the statute, since their disclosure would demonstrably harm U.S. foreign relations. When deciding whether to disclose or postpone information, board actions are rarely clear-cut. More often the ARRB faces a gray area that causes tension between the agencies' insistence on closure and the board's commitment to ensure maximum disclosure. In part, the board's differences with the intelligence agencies derive from the differing perceptions of time-sensitive material. As one example, both CIA and FBI officials insist on protecting the identity of their sources throughout their lifetimes and those of their descendants. But the Assassination Records Collection Act clearly states that the name of an individual "who provided confidential information" to the United States was to be protected only if release "would pose a substantial risk of harm to that person."[16] Hence, to preclude disclosure of the name of a source, the agencies must provide the board with evidence of a "risk of harm."

The original assumption of the ARRB was that neither the FBI nor the CIA would expend time and energy to prove a "risk of harm." This assumption proved to be incorrect. Eventually, both sides agreed on certain criteria. The board agreed to respect the need to withhold the identity of sources who were still alive and resided in the same cities. The agencies reluctantly agreed not to extend closure beyond the death of an individual. Even so, valuable board time was spent weighing the risk of harm versus the public interest in the identity of sources.[17]

This standoff over sources between the ARRB and the agencies reflected an underlying fundamental divergence between the commitment to openness on the one hand and the tradition of secrecy on the other. Both the CIA and the FBI regarded the recruitment and protection of sources as essential to their ability to function. Their ability to recruit sources is based upon confidentiality, they argue, and this requires closure in perpetuity. Because of its mandate to promote the public interest, the board regards the release of source names as an essential component of the information in a document. The representatives of the agencies who consistently emphasized their generous release of information never seemed to understand the importance of sources to a researcher. And in their efforts to prove "harm," FBI officials were willing to spend countless man-hours attempting to track down the bureau's former informants. Board members, meanwhile, were appalled at the agencies' seemingly irrational obsession to protect individuals whom they could no longer even locate.[18]

Unlike the CIA, the FBI rarely protects the identity of its own agents and quite freely discloses the identity of those individuals whom it investigates. The board has confronted another difficult policy issue beyond that involving protecting sources, given the privacy issues raised in light of past FBI investigations. Are the subjects of the FBI's intrusive investigations entitled to privacy? Resolving this question is further complicated by the fact that the release of "personal" information would, in turn, often be as embarrassing to the FBI as to the individuals involved. For example, deleting information to protect the privacy of a critic of the Warren Commission Report would also protect information documenting that the FBI was harassing this individual and even considering blackmail. The ARRB finally decided to release this document with minor deletions to protect the individual.

Releasing information that identifies sources in CIA documents presents a greater variety of problems. Unlike the FBI, CIA officials are as interested in protecting the agency's covert agents as well as its sources. CIA agents are never sent abroad with identifying badges. They spend their careers under cover of fictional employment status and maintain this fiction after retirement. Often their closest friends and family members never know of their employment as intelligence agents instead of foreign service officers, freelance journalists, or successful businessmen. As a result, agency officials are just as concerned to delete information that would identify their own agents as they would about the agency's "assets" or sources.[19]

The board encountered a further problem with the CIA owing to the fact that the agency never officially acknowledges that it maintains foreign stations and therefore cannot acknowledge the presence of chiefs of stations or their staff. Books, articles, and newspaper stories about the CIA, and even agency-sponsored conferences, freely discuss the location of CIA stations. Nonetheless, agency officials refuse to officially confirm their presence. Documents that stations send to Washington often contain references to personnel assigned to the specific station and usually bear the signature of the chief of station. However, because of this refusal to acknowledge publicly such stations, the CIA never releases these names. Given the published allegations about CIA activities relating to the Kennedy assassination, the names of these individuals are especially important to researchers.

From the beginning of the review process, the board decided to ignore the fiction that stations do not exist. This decision brought a new delegation from the CIA who sought to convince board members that merely the mention that a CIA station was located in identified countries would be extremely harmful to American foreign relations. Agency officials agreed that no one was fooled by the fiction and that deleting all information relating to stations inevitably bred conspiracy theories. They regarded this as a small price to pay. They argued that governments would fall, allies would be lost, and cooperation with other intelligence organizations would come to an end. Their argument of dire consequences was a familiar one. Other countries, they further insisted, could not admit to a CIA presence because doing so would provide grist for their political opposition. In addition, the United States could not admit to maintaining stations in foreign countries: for if CIA agents were to be effective, their intelligence activities (which included spying) would generally be illegal in the host countries. Citing their mandated responsibilities under provisions of its authorization statute, the ARRB informed the CIA that this or any other "fiction" could not be sustained. In a landmark concession, CIA officials agreed to a board recommendation that a "window" of four years, 1960–64, should be opened to acknowledge the existence of CIA stations. (The agency suggested one year; the board insisted on four.) Within that window, all stations could be identified in released records. On reconsideration, the CIA asked that the identities of a few stations should remain closed because of important ongoing activities. The board compromised, but only after agency officials shared with it the nature of these ongoing activities. Once the CIA did so, albeit with profound unease on the part of agency officials, the board concluded that the crucial ongoing activity would, in fact, collapse if the information identifying the station were to be released. This episode had twofold lessons: CIA officials could not retreat behind generalized statements with no supporting evidence; and the ARRB, when given credible evidence, acted responsibly to withhold legitimate secrets.

ARRB efforts have focused primarily on the voluminous files of the CIA and the FBI. Nonetheless, the Secret Service is also a central player in the history of the assassination. The agency that protects the president (and other government officials) turned out to be as jealous of its secrets as the CIA, the National Security Agency, and the FBI. Secret Service officials were slow to recognize either the mandate that the Kennedy Assassination Records Collection Act had given the ARRB or its comprehensive definition of what constituted releasable assassination records. The situation was not improved by the Secret Service's mysterious destruction, in direct violation of provisions of the statute, of a box of its records pertaining to presidential trips prior to President Kennedy's trip to Dallas. These records could have been useful in comparing the actions of the Secret Service agents in Dallas with those on previous presidential trips.

Secret Service representatives, when responding to board inquiries, were not well versed in previously opened or publicly acknowledged information involving their agency records. In one case, they requested the withdrawal of information that was already publicly available in the National Archives, and that had been cited in articles and books, including memoirs. Mindful of the statute's provision exempting from disclosure information that could threaten the lives of government officials, the board nevertheless decided against the Secret Service's demand to withdraw any document describing the agency's methods or procedures of protection that were already well known to the millions of Americans who participate in political rallies or presidential visits. Three years after the board began work, Secret Service officials finally began to share documents. The tenaciousness of the staff and the determination of board members were partly responsible for this change of heart; the negative results of FBI appeals to the White House also undoubtedly convinced the Secret Service of the futility of its efforts to avoid disclosure.

In the autumn of 1996, the ARRB staff turned its attention to the records of the National Security Agency (NSA) and the Department of Defense. Neither organization had by then turned over a complete body of its records relating to the Kennedy assassination to the board, and the documents that have been provided hardly constitute their entire collections. By its very nature as an agency that intercepts the electronic messages of foreign governments and their military, the NSA presents the board with a unique, and particularly difficult, set of issues. Undeniably, disclosure of such messages can harm legitimate security interests. At the same time, the content of such intercepted messages can be of crucial importance to assassination researchers.

NSA officials prepared the way for an informed evaluation of their records, and the related issue of nondisclosure, by carefully briefing the board on its special assignment within the intelligence community. Although the most secretive of all government agencies, the NSA has cooperated with the board and, after mutually acceptable compromises, has begun to forward a few records to the Kennedy Collection at the National Archives—with the board beginning, in the summer of 1997, to review NSA postponement requests. The procedures adopted to minimize compromising the NSA's highly sensitive records, however, have currently stymied the board staff's search for any unidentified but relevant assassination records that might be included among the NSA's vast records. Board members must also walk a tightrope as they weigh the public interest in disclosure against the risk that disclosure might harm the national security. At the time of the writing of this essay, the NSA remains an unfinished project.

One long-standing issue that the ARRB successfully resolved in April 1997 involved the fate of the Zapruder film. Although the board is willing to take copies of paper records, the evidentiary attributes of this film as well as its information place it in a very special category. The home movie that Abraham Zapruder made of the presidential motorcade on November 23, 1963, has remained the definitive visual record of Kennedy's assassination. This film had been deposited in the National Archives in 1978, but the Zapruder family retained ownership of and therefore control over the film's dissemination. All five board members strongly believed that the original film belonged to the American people, but also recognized that to achieve that end would likely require a substantial sum of money to compensate Zapruder's family for this "taking." Before coming to a decision, the ARRB addressed many questions. For example, three copies of the film were made the day of the assassination; one went to Mr. Zapruder, the other two went to the Secret Service. Why not settle for one of the copies that is already in possession of the government? Is it necessary to pay for the original film when it can no longer be shown in currently available cameras? What are the ramifications of the government's taking of what is private property? Board members posed these questions to witnesses during a public hearing held on April 24, 1997.

This hearing produced useful information on the process of "taking" private property. A film expert assured the board that in addition to the digitalization of the current film, which would preserve its images regardless of its present state, the volatile nature of new technology might completely restore the film in the near future. But restoration can be done only on originals, not copies. Two witnesses also argued for keeping the film, and while the last witness did not think the film had much evidentiary value, he emphasized its value as a symbol. (He referred to the film as a "secular relic.")

The board finally decided to "take" the film in spite of the price, leaving a cushion of time for any adverse congressional reaction to this potentially costly decision. To do otherwise would exclude from the assassination collection the visual image carried in the minds of Americans of that tragic scene in Dallas.

The board also had to confront the problem of ensuring public access to another set of documents that were of critical importance to the historical record on the assassination but that were not yet available to the public. The John F. Kennedy Presidential Library, in addition to retaining the presidential papers, holds the records of Robert Kennedy and other officials who held high-level appointments during the Kennedy administration. Ownership of Robert Kennedy's papers is still held by his family, in spite of the fact that the library has stored them for almost thirty years. Some manuscript collections of other Kennedy officials are also closed or require family permission to be opened.

The board staff reviewed the pertinent presidential records, joined by a team from the CIA and the State and Defense Departments to facilitate declassification. As a result of the ARRB's review, twenty thousand pages from the Kennedy administration's National Security files were opened, most of which concerned U.S.-Cuban relations. But for most of the first three years of the board's existence, the library has stonewalled on requests for other records, in particular those that are stored in the library without clear government ownership. The library finally became more cooperative in early 1997. Fortunately, the Kennedy Library now recognizes the importance of cooperating with the board to ensure a complete historical record of the assassination.

The documents eventually collected and released under the JFK statute may fail to resolve definitively the many questions surrounding President Kennedy's assassination, but their availability greatly enriches the historical record of that tragic event. The release of these formerly withheld or redacted documents will allow present and future historians to make intelligent judgments about the difficult questions involving the Kennedy assassination and finally provide Americans with the facts and not imagined (or suspected) evidence. Neither the authors of the statute nor those who originally wrote or testified in its behalf could have predicted the extent of the relevant assassination documentation that was maintained by various government agencies or the amount of time required to establish the board, which was, in effect, a new government agency. As the ARRB entered its third year, it became clear that the original plan for a three-year effort was unrealistic. Board efforts had begun with the staff working long hours to learn all the names, facts, and theories necessary for reviewing records and educating the board members. Federal agencies next began the laborious task of reviewing their records before turning them over to the board. This task will end only when the door to the ARRB finally closes. As this is written, board members themselves, with few exceptions, have met for two long days every three weeks to review records, meet with agency officials, and discuss new issues. Conference calls are scheduled between meetings.

In spite of this prodigious effort, the ARRB could not complete its work by the 1992 act's termination date of October 1997. Recognizing this reality in July 1997, Congress has approved funding for an additional year.

The accomplishments of the ARRB are already impressive even though there remain many months of work ahead. Assassination aficionados seeking the "smoking gun" document(s) will be disappointed. Like most puzzles, resolving the Kennedy assassination will require extensive research in the more than 3,900,000 pages that will comprise the Kennedy Collection at the National Archives. Some may regard the board's battles with the agencies as mere "nit-picking," but those well versed in the culture of secrecy will readily recognize the successes (and failures) of the board.

The tenacity of board members plus the unique disclosure provisions of the statute served to open many areas of documentation in the CIA. Some records from the Directorate of Operations, for example, that were declared off-limits to FOIA requests, were opened with minimal deletions involving some numbers and names. As noted earlier, under the terms of the act, even these deletions will be identified so that researchers can learn that the deleted phrase refers to countries, individuals, and so on. A document that has two deletions marked "source" and "northern European country" might not be perfect, but it is more useful than one having no explanation of the character of the withheld information.

For the first time, the CIA has revealed some of its "sources and methods" and has formally admitted the existence and location of CIA stations, albeit for a limited period. Contrary to CIA officials' original alarmist predictions intelligence gathering has not been curtailed as a result, and no one has been killed. Indeed, the most notable effect of opening these documents has been demands from researchers for more "windows" and more information.

The sheer volume of the FBI's records relating to the Kennedy assassination is mind-boggling. John F. Kennedy had many enemies: Cuban-Americans disappointed over the Bay of Pigs; the Mafia, angry over Attorney General Robert Kennedy's continued efforts to fight organized crime; southern segregationists angry with Kennedy's support of civil rights. The FBI investigated members and meetings of all of these groups, using informers, wiretaps, and other methods of surveillance.[20] The resultant massive files on these individuals and organizations contain documents that bear upon the assassination, and these extensive holdings must be reviewed by the agency before relevant records are transferred to either the archives or the board.

Unfortunately, the ARRB has failed to convince agency officials to change their secrecy procedures and mind-set. In spite of all the evidence to the contrary, agency officials continue to argue that the accidental release of one word or phrase will not only kill countless people but also send the country to its knees. Thus, the intelligence and counterintelligence agencies still perform line-by-line review of every page of each document. While methods at each agency vary, generally at least two people read every line; in the case of difficult decisions, the document is examined by a third person at a higher level. Under these conditions the FBI, for example, will not finish reviewing its documents to be forwarded to the Kennedy Assassination Collection until after the turn of the century.

There *are* secrets that should be protected. Each time the board members review records before ordering their disclosure, they must separate the truly secret records from those which were automatically withheld based on customary secrecy assumptions. Indeed, the ARRB's major contribution might very well be simply that its review and disclosure actions may in the future require federal intelligence and counterintelligence agencies to make that distinction. Are some decisions to withhold records just the effect of a culture of secrecy or complacency? Must the secrets of 1963 remain the vital secrets of 1997? For the first time in fifty years, CIA, NSA, FBI, and Secret Service officials have been forced (because of an independent review mandated by Congress) to peel away the layers of time and custom to reach the core question: What indeed are real secrets?

NOTES

1. Public Law 102-526, 102d Congress.
2. Members of the bipartisan commission were Chief Justice Earl Warren; Senators Richard B. Russell and John Sherman Cooper; Congressmen Hale Boggs and Gerald R. Ford; former CIA Director, Allen W. Dulles; and investment banker and former Assistant Secretary of War, John J. McCloy. Russell initially refused to serve, since he would not sit in the same room with Earl Warren. See information contained in the tape recordings at the Lyndon B. Johnson Library (LBJ L) in ARRB files.
3. *Report of the President's Commission on the Assassination of President John F. Kennedy* (Washington, D.C.: Government Printing Office, 1964), 18–25.
4. Among the first books to question the commission's report were Edward Jay Epstein, *The Warren Commission and the Establishment of the Truth* (New York: Bantam, 1966); and Mark Lane, *Rush to Judgement* (New York: Holt, Rinehart and Winston, 1966). Poll numbers from Dialog through Westlaw.
5. U.S. Senate, Select Committee to Study Governmental Operations with Respect to Intelligence Activities, *Final Reports*, 94th Cong. 2d sess., 1976 (6 books); Commission on CIA Activities Within the United States, *Report to the President by the Commission on CIA Activities Within the United States* (Washington, D.C.: Government Printing Office, 1975); U.S. House of Representatives, Select Committee on Assassinations, *Report* 95th Cong. 2d sess., 1979.
6. U.S. House of Representatives, Committee on the Judiciary, Hearing, *Assassination Materials Disclosure Act of 1992,* 102d Cong., 2d sess., May 20, 1992, pp. 80–81 (hereafter, JFK Act, 1992); Harold Relyea and Suzanne Cavanagh, *President John F. Kennedy Assassination Records Disclosure: An Overview,* Congressional Research Service (CRS), Library of Congress, March 3, 1993; 4–9, ARRB Files.
7. 106 Stat. 3443, October 26, 1992.

8. General references to the board also include the executive director and staff. All were essential to the work at hand.

9. Transcripts of Public Hearings, October 11, 1994, and March 7, 1995, ARRB Records.

10. *Federal Register* 60, no. 124; 33345–51; quotation on p. 33349.

11. Senator Joseph Lieberman, U.S. Senate Committee on Governmental Affairs, *Hearings on Nominations of Graff, Tunheim, Nelson, Joyce and Hall,* 103d Cong., 2d sess., February 1, 1994, p. 1.

12. JFK Act, Sec. 6 (1) and (4).

13. JFK Act, Sec. 6. The phrase occurs four times in the five general postponements. To be postponed, information on military defense, intelligence, or foreign relations must "demonstrably impair the national security of the United States." That is the only sentence in the statute's list of postponements that refers to the national security.

14. "Redact" is the word currently used by declassifiers, indicating they are doing nothing more than editing the document. The CIA has a redaction machine. The machine can "read" a special marking pencil and while copying the document automatically removes the words that lie beneath the marker.

15. On one memorable occasion, a board member asked an agency official why his agency always withheld a particular piece of information that appeared to be completely harmless. The official thought for a few minutes before replying that he could not remember the reason, but since the information had never been released he was sure there was a good reason.

16. JFK Act, Sec. 6 (2).

17. It is ironic that the FBI, despite its expressed concern about the protection of individual informers, maintains no record of their activities or location.

18. Two years would pass before board members came to fully understand that the FBI had turned over to their senior reviewers the search for long-forgotten sources. This led to even longer delays in important document review.

19. CIA assets or sources are rarely identified in CIA records by name, which tempers the agency's concern over their release.

20. The FBI also had informers in Communist Party meetings. In one meeting where Kennedy's death was discussed (and blamed by those in attendance on the American right), there were three FBI informers among the seven attendees.

CONTRIBUTORS

MATTHEW M. AID is a senior manager of a Washington, D.C., financial research and investigative firm and formly served as a Russian linguist and intelligence analyst for the Department of Defense. He is currently writing a history of the National Security Agency (and its predecessor agencies) covering the period 1917 to the present.

SCOTT ARMSTRONG is executive director of the Information Trust, a nonprofit organization that promotes freedom of information and print journalism. He had earlier founded the National Security Archive, served as executive director of Taxpayers Against Fraud, was a senior investigator for the Senate Special Committee on Watergate, and was a staff writer for the *Washington Post*. He is the coauthor of *The Brethren*, a researcher-writer of *The Final Days*, is currently completing a history of U.S. national security policy, and has served as a consultant or reporter for ABC News, CBS News, CNN, and the PBS *Frontline* special "Crimes and Misdemeanors" (for which he won the DuPont Silver Medal). He has received numerous other honors, including an Emmy, the James Madison Award, and election to the Freedom Foundation Hall of Fame.

ALEXANDER CHARNS is an attorney and partner in a Durham, North Carolina, law firm and a freelance journalist. He is the author of *Cloak and Gavel: FBI Wiretaps, Bugs, Informers, and the Supreme Court,* and editor of a microfilm edition of FBI files on the U.S. Supreme Court and federal judges. Charns has published articles on the FBI's surveillance of the federal judiciary in the *New York Times, Washington Post, San Francisco Examiner, Durham (N.C.) Herald, In These Times,* and *Southern Exposure.*

JAMES X. DEMPSEY is staff counsel for the Center for Democracy and Technology. He formerly served as deputy director for the Center for National Security Studies and legal counsel for the National Security Archive (representing the Archive in FOIA litigation), and from 1985 to 1994 was assistant counsel to the House Judiciary Committee's Subcommittee on Civil and Constitutional Rights. Dempsey's legislative and lobbying activities have focused on the intersection of national security and consitutional rights (terrorism, electronic surveillance, counterintelligence, and privacy). He has published articles in *Rights* and *Legal Times.*

PAUL M. GREEN is a Durham, North Carolina, attorney and is the recipient of a "special commendation" from the North Carolina Conference on Public Defenders for his role in *Simeon v. Hardin.*

JOAN HOFF is a professor of history at Ohio University and formerly served as executive secretary first of the Organization of American Historians and then of the Center for the Study of the Presidency. She is the author or editor of *American Business and Foreign Policy, 1920–1933; Ideology and Economics; Herbert Hoover; Nixon Reconsidered; Law, Gender, and Injustice; Rights of Passage; Without Precedent; For Adult Users Only;* and the forthcoming *Whither U.S. Foreign Policy.*

PAGE PUTNAM MILLER is director of the National Coordinating Committee for the Promotion of History. She is the author or editor of *Developing a Premier National Institution; Reclaiming the Past; A Claim to New Roles; Directory of Historical Consultants;* and *Resource Guide: Strengthening the Teaching of History in Secondary Schools.* Miller writes a regular column on legislative issues for the newsletters of the American Historical Association, Organization of American Historians, Society of American Archivists, Society for History in the Federal Government, and National Council on Public History. She is the recipient of numerous awards for "distinguished service," including those given by the Federation of Genealogical Societies, California Committee for the Promotion of History, and Society of American Archivists.

ANNA KASTEN NELSON, distinguished adjunct professor of history at American University, is currently a member of the Kennedy Assassination Records Review Board. She formerly served as a research associate for the National Study Commission on Records and Documents of Federal Officials, a consultant to the Library of Congress's Congressional Research Service, project director of the Committee on Records of Government, and member of the Department of State Advisory Committee on Historical Diplomatic Documentation. She is the author of *Secret Agents* and editor of *State Department Policy Planning Staff Papers, 1947–1949*, and has published articles in the *Journal of American History, Political Science Quarterly, Diplomatic History,* and *Eisenhower: A Centenary Assessment.*

ATHAN G. THEOHARIS is a professor of history at Marquette University. He is the author or editor of *The Boss; From the Secret Files of J. Edgar Hoover; J. Edgar Hoover, Sex, and Crime; Beyond the Hiss Case; Spying on Americans; Seeds of Repression; The Yalta Myths; The Specter; The Truman Presidency; Anatomy of Anti-Communism;* and *The FBI: An Annotated Bibliography and Research Guide;* and is currently writing a history of the FBI covering the period 1939–56. He has received numerous research grants and awards, including a Gavel Award from the American Bar Association and the Binkley-Stephenson Award from the Organization of American Historians.

JON WIENER is a professor of history at the University of California–Irvine. He is the author of *Come Together: John Lennon in His Time* and *Professors, Politics, and Pop,* and has published articles in the *American Historical Review, Journal of American History,* and *Past and Present.* Wiener is also a contributing editor of *The Nation,* writing a column about controversies in academic life and university politics.

INDEX

and Federal Bureau of Investigation, 8
and John Lennon, 84
and Oval Office tapes case, 8–9, 11–12, 115–39
and Pentagon Papers, 126–27
Nixon-Sampson agreement, 12, 116, 117, 134n2
Norman, Lloyd, 3
North, Oliver L., 10, 65, 142, 143–44, 145, 146
and records destruction, 10, 147, 174nn10,11, 175n15
NSC 4A, 4, 9
NSC 10/2, 4, 9
NSC 68, 2
NSC 5412, 9

Oberdorfer, Louis, 185n91
Odom, William E., 65
Office of Naval Intelligence (ONI), 17, 19
Office of Management and Budget (OMB), and secrecy policy, 180n56
O'Keeffe, Georgia, 3
O'Leary, Hazel, 165–68
Operation MINARET, 7
Operation MONGOOSE, 54
Operations Crossroads, 167
Operation Solo, 26–27, 33
O'Reilly, Kenneth, 17–18, 26, 34n2
Organization of American Historians (OAH), 32, 158n, 191, 192, 194, 198, 199
Oswald, Lee Harvey, 33, 211, 212, 213, 215, 216, 220, 221
Oval Office tapes case, 8–9, 115–39
Owens, David, 17n

Pandya, Amit A., 197
Parker, Barrington D., 149–50, 158
Paterson, Robert F., 89–90
Patterson, Eleanor, 3, 8
Patterson, Joseph, 8
Pearson, Drew, 3, 8, 17n
Pell, Claiborne, 195, 196, 197, 199
Pelley, William Dudley, 17, 18
Pelton, Ronald W., 64, 70
Penkovsky, Oleg, 50, 51, 53–54, 58n21
Pentagon Papers, 40, 126
Perkins, Bradford, 192
Peters, Joseph, 21, 21n
Petersen, Joseph S., 70
Peterson, Trudy H., 122–23
Phillippi, Harriet, 46
Podesta, John, 177n34
Poindexter, John, 9, 10, 142, 143, 146, 178n44

and records destruction, 174n10
Powers, Gary, 39
Presidential Recordings and Materials Preservation Act (PRMPA), 117, 118, 119, 123, 124, 133
Presidential Records Act, 118, 148, 154, 156, 157, 158
Presidents
and Central Intelligence Agency, 3, 37
and classification policy, 2, 3–4, 50–51, 74–75, 89, 162–63, 170, 183n81, 191, 201, 206, 207
and Federal Bureau of Investigation, 3, 8
and intelligence agencies, 4
and National Security Agency, 3, 4
and secrecy, 10
and wiretapping, 3
Prichard, Edward, 28
Privacy channel cables, 11
PROFS case, 9, 11, 122, 136n14, 142–60
Progressive, The, and Moreland article case, 72–73
Public Citizen
and Health Research Group, 42
and Litigation Group, 121, 122, 140, 151, 173n1
Public Law 86-36, 4, 69, 70–71, 72, 73
Public Law 102-138, 13, 187, 200–201, 203, 204, 206, 207
Pugh, Elizabeth A., 137n21
Purvis, Joseph, 103–4

Reagan, Ronald, 17n
and CIA records, 40, 48
and Executive Order 12356, 45, 50, 73, 191, 201, 206
and *Foreign Relations* series, 191
and Freedom of Information Act, 86, 93, 108
and Iran-contra, 143–44
and National Security Agency, 79n17
and NSC records destruction, 147
and PROFS records, 142
and secrecy, 141, 174n5
Reger, Brenda S., 175n16
Reno, Janet, 58n17
and Freedom of Information Act guidelines, 29, 92–93, 163
Reuther, Walter, 3, 17
Ribuffo, Leo, 18, 34n2
Richardson, Elliott, 115
and FBI records, 24
Richelson, Jeffrey T., 66
Richey, Charles, 150, 151–54, 159
Rockefeller, John D. III, 16n
Rockefeller Commission, 212, 213